P9-DWW-671

THE
BURNING
SHORE

THE BURNING SHORE

HOW HITLER'S U-BOATS BROUGHT WORLD WAR II TO AMERICA

ED OFFLEY

BASIC BOOKS

New York • A Member of the Perseus Books Group

Designed by Pauline Brown
Typeset in 12.25 point Goudy Old Style

Library of Congress Cataloging-in-Publication Data

Offley, Edward.

 The burning shore : how Hitler's U-boats brought World War II to America / Ed Offley.

    pages cm

  Includes bibliographical references and index.

  ISBN 978-0-465-02961-7 (hardback)—ISBN 978-0-465-08069-4 (e-book)
1. World War, 1939–1945—Naval operations, German. 2. World War, 1939–1945—Naval operations—Submarine. 3. World War, 1939–1945—Atlantic Coast (U.S.) 4. World War, 1939–1945—Campaigns—Atlantic Ocean. 5. Submarines (Ships)—Germany—History—20th century.
6. Submarines (Ships)—Atlantic Coast (U.S.)—History—20th century.
7. Atlantic Coast (U.S.)—History, Naval—20th century. I. Title.

  D781.O44   2014

  940.54'51—dc23

                              2013038412

10 9 8 7 6 5 4 3 2 1

This book is dedicated to

John Shearer Tuck
Staff Sergeant USAAF

October 13, 1917–November 14, 2012

A member of the Greatest Generation,
a loving father, and a cherished friend

CONTENTS

Contents

INTRODUCTION: THE BATTLE OFFSHORE

VIEWED FROM THE AIR, THE NORTH CAROLINA COAST WOULD not have resembled a major battlefield. Yet, as the sun climbed above the eastern horizon, bathing the pine scrub forests and inland waterways in a brilliant orange light, a brutal and desperate struggle was raging just offshore. On Tuesday, July 9, 1942, the area was a critical combat theater of World War II, as it had been for the past six months.

A confluence of factors had made this intersection of land and ocean the fulcrum of the ongoing naval confrontation between Nazi Germany and the Western Allies, a vicious maritime clash now known as the Battle of the Atlantic. By July 1942, the combatants had expanded beyond the British Empire and Nazi Germany. America's entry into the war against Germany on December 11, 1941, had thrown the US military into the fray. In turn, Hitler's *Ubootwaffe*, or U-boat Force, initiated an all-out war against American merchant shipping. *Vizeadmiral* (Vice Admiral) Karl Dönitz, commander-in-chief of the U-boat Force, aimed to win a *guerre de course* against the Western Allies, sinking their merchant ships at a rate faster than new construction could replace them. Aware that American supplies were the lifeline keeping Britain in the war, his strategic imperative was to starve the import-dependent United Kingdom out of the fight, thereby depriving the Allies of a launching pad for an invasion of Nazi-occupied Europe.*

Beginning in early 1942, Germany's U-boat forces had shifted their operations from the mid-Atlantic to the American coastline, where Allied merchant vessels steamed as they took on supplies in East Coast ports or proceeded from the Caribbean with cargos for England. Each day, scores of merchantmen traveled independently through those unprotected waters. Between the Newfoundland Grand Banks and the shallow waters off Florida, the richest hunting ground for the U-boats was the expanse of Atlantic Ocean off the North Carolina coast.

In the waters off Cape Hatteras, climate, geography, and ocean currents combined to create a bottleneck through which merchant ships had to pass as they steamed along the coast. Several dozen miles out from the string of barrier islands known as the Outer Banks, the Gulf Stream constantly flows north from warmer latitudes. Driven by prevailing westerlies and fed by saltwater currents emerging from the Caribbean and West Indies, this river of warmer water, usually about sixty miles wide and 4,000 feet deep, powers along the eastern seaboard at an average speed of five nautical miles per hour. When it reaches Cape Hatteras, about halfway down the Outer Banks, the Gulf Stream collides with the colder waters of the southerly Labrador Current, producing fog, extreme waves, and frequent storms.

---

* For a comparison of naval officer ranks in the American, British, and German navies of World War II, see Appendix on page 267.

To avoid these offshore hazards and the treacherous conditions closer inshore, merchant ships were forced to thread a thirty- to fifty-mile-wide needle between the Outer Banks and the Gulf Stream. The German U-boat sailors stalking those cargo-laden targets favored this area as a lucrative target area.[1]

U-boat commanders loved Cape Hatteras for a second reason. The underwater topography along the North Carolina coast provided protection that greatly offset the World War II–era U-boat's one serious weakness. Powered by diesel engines on the surface and battery-driven electric motors while submerged, the U-boats in 1942 were extremely vulnerable to detection by aircraft and sonar-equipped warships when operating in shallow waters. While the continental shelf is over a hundred miles wide off the mid-Atlantic states and Florida, making it difficult for U-boats to operate there with any degree of secrecy, off Cape Hatteras the seabed quickly drops to several hundred feet in just a couple dozen miles to the east, creating a readily accessible hiding spot during the dangerous daylight hours. The deep-water haven served the U-boats well. By July 7, U-boats operating off the Outer Banks had sunk forty-five merchant ships totaling 262,137 gross registered tons.[2]

In the first half of 1942, the Allies had suffered a devastating and prolonged defeat in the western Atlantic. Plagued by shortages of aircraft and warships and hobbled by poor training and inferior weaponry, the US Navy and US Army Air Forces (US-AAF) achieved scant results in their effort to halt U-boat attacks on merchant ships. Thus far in the Battle of the Atlantic, Germany had lost only four U-boats and 161 submariners in North American coastal waters. In a desperate move, the US Navy and

USAAF, over the months leading up to July, had rushed patrol squadrons to bases up and down the East Coast to provide an air umbrella over the coastal shipping routes. It was an uphill fight. The aircrews were inexperienced, their search-and-attack doctrine had serious flaws, and their aircraft sensors and weapons were insufficient to thwart the U-boat threat. Thus far, Admiral Dönitz appeared on track to achieve his strategic goal.[3]

IN RESPONSE TO THE U-BOATS LURKING OFFSHORE, US military planners had selected the new Marine Corps Air Station Cherry Point in eastern North Carolina as a temporary base for antisubmarine patrols. Although the base was still a construction site, the crisis in the Atlantic necessitated an ad hoc response. Cherry Point's location between Hampton Roads, Virginia, to the north and Charleston, South Carolina, farther down the coast, meant that aircraft from the base could cover the entire Outer Banks region. Initially, the navy and USAAF sent a number of observation and scouting squadrons to Cherry Point on temporary patrol duty, but their unarmed, short-range SOC-3 Seagull amphibian biplanes and O-52 Owl observation aircraft posed no threat to the U-boats. However, in mid-May, the Army Air Forces dispatched the first of a series of light bomber units to North Carolina that flew A-20 Havoc, B-18 Bolo, or A-29 Hudson bombers. With this new combat capability, planners devised a daily cycle of three antisubmarine patrols, each conducted by two bombers. The flights followed the same pattern. After reaching a separation point twenty-five miles offshore, one aircraft flew parallel to the shoreline up to Hampton Roads,

The twin-engine Lockheed A-29 Hudson proved to be an effective patrol bomber against U-boats during the war. Flown by the US Army Air Forces, US Navy, Royal Canadian Air Force, and Royal Air Force, Hudsons during the first twenty-eight months of the war were credited with sinking twelve out of forty-six U-boats destroyed by aircraft and forcing the surrender of a thirteenth, the Type VIIC U-570. USAAF Photo.

while the second proceeded southwest parallel to the coastline until reaching Charleston. Each mission lasted five hours, with the three patrols overlapping to ensure no gap in coverage.

On July 7, the patrols went off as scheduled. By mid-morning, the first pair of bombers was nearing the halfway point of the patrol, and a second group of airmen was preparing for takeoff. Taxiing to the head of one of Cherry Point's four runways, the pilots radioed readiness for departure. It was 10:15 A.M. The air traffic controller granted permission to take off, and the two A-29 Lockheed Hudsons raced down the runway and lifted into the air. At the twenty-five-mile point, one pilot turned onto the southwest leg toward South Carolina. The second Hudson turned to the left and headed north toward Hampton Roads.[4]

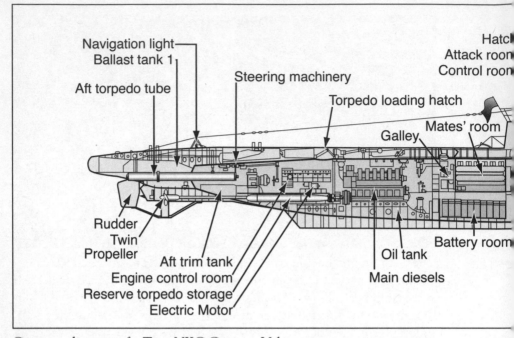

Cutaway diagram of a Type VIIC German U-boat. ILLUSTRATION BY ROBERT
E. PRATT.

ABOUT 120 MILES EAST-NORTHEAST of Cherry Point that morning, beneath a featureless spot on the surface of the Atlantic,
forty-six German sailors were suffering in almost unbearable
agony as they waited out the dangerous daylight hours submerged
near the seabed. Their Type VIIC U-boat was in its fifty-eighth
day at sea since leaving its base in France on May 19. The air inside the 220-foot-long submersible was fouler than usual because
the primitive scrubbing units that stripped the air of dangerous
carbon dioxide were failing. Worse, the ambient water temperature rose above seventy-five degrees Fahrenheit each day. Without cooler water outside the boat to offset the heat from the
U-boat's batteries and electric motors, the machinery pushed
the interior temperature to well over one hundred degrees. The

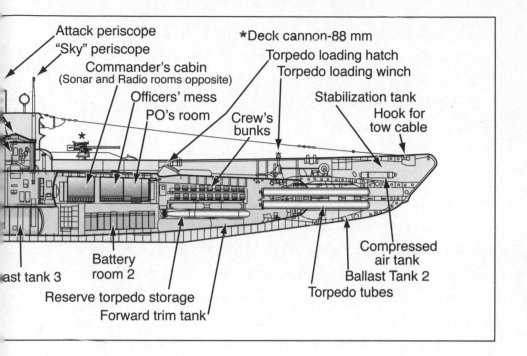

Attack periscope
"Sky" periscope
Commander's cabin
(Sonar and Radio rooms opposite)
Officers' mess
PO's room
Crew's bunks
*Deck cannon-88 mm
Torpedo loading hatch
Torpedo loading winch
Stabilization tank
Hook for tow cable
ast tank 3
Battery room 2
Reserve torpedo storage
Forward trim tank
Compressed air tank
Ballast Tank 2
Torpedo tubes

sailors suffered splitting headaches and fits of vomiting from the foul stench of diesel fumes, unwashed bodies, and human waste.

The only good news for the crew was that the boat had used up all but two of its torpedoes, so the crewmen were no longer cramped by the extra torpedoes kept in storage racks above the deck plates in the bow compartment, where most of them slept. Just aft of the bow compartment was the officer's berthing space, the commander's cubbyhole, and two tiny spaces where the duty radiomen stood watch. In the small hydrophone room, one of the two radiomen wore a headset listening for sounds of approaching enemy warships. The second radio watch-stander sat in the cramped radio room, waiting to pick up signals from U-boat Force Headquarters in Lorient, France. But most activity took place in the center of the boat in the larger *Zentrale* (control room).

Throughout the morning of July 7, the U-boat loitered in a restless state of suspended animation several hundred feet down. In quieter sea conditions, the U-boat could rest on the seabed. However, the flow of the Gulf Stream was strong enough to drag the boat against the sand and rocks, increasing the chance of damage or, even worse, detection by enemy sonar. Under the supervision of the first watch officer (1WO), a half dozen crewmen in the U-boat's control room worked to maintain a careful hover just a few feet above the seabed. The helmsman and another control plane operator oriented the submerged U-boat head-on into the Gulf Stream current, while a machinist's mate operated the trim tanks to maintain the boat's neutral buoyancy by shifting ballast water from forward to aft, or vice versa, as the situation dictated. Farther aft in the stern compartment, sailors monitored the two electric motors that drove the boat's twin propellers at just enough speed to neutralize the current. It was tedious, never-ending work to keep the five-hundred-ton U-boat properly suspended.[5]

Despite the atrocious atmosphere inside the U-boat, the crew's morale was good. They endured these hellish conditions with stoic indifference. Both the commander and his men were proud of their accomplishments thus far in their third war patrol. Their record to date was four Allied ships sunk totaling 21,789 gross registered tons, including two naval patrol vessels, and four damaged merchantmen for another 37,093 gross tons. With a fuel state approaching the minimum required for the 3,000-mile return trip to France, the U-boat commander told his men he planned to hunt for only "a day or two more" before breaking off patrol.[6]

The bow compartment of a U-boat is crammed with perishable foods and spare torpedoes at the outset of a patrol. CLAY BLAIR COLLECTION, AMERICAN HERITAGE CENTER, UNIVERSITY OF WYOMING.

At about 2:00 P.M. local time, the commander decided to cleanse the submersible of its foul air. He had taken this step on previous days to bring some much-needed relief to his crew. Blowing the ballast tanks, the crew brought the U-boat to periscope depth. Up in the conning tower, the commander raised the thin search periscope above the surface and made a quick circle. The ocean and sky appeared empty. The hydrophone operator reported no underwater sounds that would indicate the presence of an enemy patrol vessel. The commander ordered the U-boat farther up until its slender bridge structure was barely out of the water, its main deck awash.

"Blow all tanks! Diesels full speed ahead," the commander called. He popped the circular hatch open, quickly climbing up onto the U-boat's narrow, exposed bridge with three lookouts. As he and the others began scanning the sky, the boat's chief engineer ordered the two Germaniawerft six-cylinder M6V 40/46 diesel motors lit off. However, instead of opening the bridge-mounted air intakes that fed air directly to the two engines, the crew left them shut. As the two engines thundered to life, they sucked sweet sea air into the boat through the open bridge hatch in a welcome, man-made gale. The longer the diesel engines ran, the cleaner the atmosphere inside the ship would be—and with the U-boat some thirty to thirty-five miles away from the Outer Banks, it had ample room to maneuver before it would arrive in the dangerous waters above the continental shelf. The U-boat slowly headed on a course of 320 degrees toward the distant shore.

THE FIRST OF THE TWO LOCKHEED HUDSONS on midday patrol was into its fifth hour of flight and on the reciprocal leg of its southwesterly patrol route when it arrived in the vicinity of Cape Hatteras, flying parallel with the coastline about thirty miles offshore. The squadron's tactical doctrine at that time, reflecting the USAAF's inexperience in hunting U-boats, dictated that the aircraft fly at an altitude of just one hundred feet above sea level. However, the bomber's pilot opted to exploit the current weather conditions on this patrol, particularly a cloud layer at 1,200 feet. He was flying just above the broken canopy of clouds on the assumption that he and his crew could see much farther than at the lower altitude and that the clouds would cloak the aircraft from any U-boat lookouts.

It was 2:12 P.M. when the pilot spotted a tiny, feather-like line on the water about ten miles from his left-hand window. He instinctively lifted the aircraft higher up into the cloud layer, turned left to a heading of due west, and pulled back on the throttles to reduce engine noise that U-boat lookouts might detect, while alerting his four crewmen over the intercom. After a minute, the pilot quickly dropped the aircraft's nose below the layer for several seconds as everyone peered out of the aircraft. The line in the ocean was still there and becoming clearer. The Hudson remained concealed in the clouds as it approached the potential target, the pilot and crew tense with apprehension. No Army Air Forces warplane had ever sunk a U-boat in American waters. If all went well in the next few minutes, that distinction would be theirs.[7]

1

PREPARING TO FIGHT

A LINE OF ARMY TRUCKS DROVE SLOWLY UP TO THE MAIN GATE of Florida's Drane Army Airfield, where uniformed military policemen waved them through. The trucks halted in front of the airfield's induction center, and several dozen men in civilian clothes climbed down, each lugging a small suitcase. It was a weekday in early March 1941, and the latest crop of army aviation cadets was reporting for active duty at the busy airfield outside of the town of Lakeland.

One of the cadets who stepped down from the truck at Drane was a stocky, twenty-two-year-old New Yorker named Harry Joseph Kane Jr. The day before, he had boarded the southbound *Tamiami Champion* at Penn Station in New York for the overnight trip to central Florida and a chance at winning a commission—and his pilot's wings—in the US Army Air Corps.[1]

Over the course of 1940, Kane—like many of his contemporaries—had deemed it prudent to prepare himself for war. While the United States officially remained neutral as the global conflict raged in Europe, the violence was metastasizing worldwide like a runaway cancer. Germany's invasion of Poland in September 1939 had finally prompted Hitler's European foes to declare war on the Nazi regime, but the subsequent fifteen months had brought nothing but more German conquests. The Wehrmacht had invaded and occupied seven more European states and launched a prolonged air war and U-boat campaign against Great Britain. Adolf Hitler's reach now extended from the Arctic Circle to the Pyrenees and from the English Channel deep into Eastern Europe. Germany's Italian and Japanese allies were also on the move from China and the western Pacific to North Africa and the Middle East.

In Washington, DC, President Franklin D. Roosevelt pursued a two-track response to events overseas throughout 1940. He staunchly reaffirmed neutrality while arming America to the teeth. The US Navy grew from 193 to 337 warships during that period, with another 119 under construction at the end of 1940. The navy's ranks doubled from 106,000 to 210,000 men by year's end. The army also expanded—from 190,000 men in the fall of 1939 to nearly 2 million in early 1941. The US military would expand at an even greater rate during the next four years. Production of military equipment such as aircraft, artillery, tanks, and trucks was soaring. Still, during his campaign for a third term in the White House in the fall of 1940, FDR remained adamant about keeping America out of the war. He stated in a Boston speech on October 31, "I have said this before, but I shall say it again, your boys are not going to be sent into any foreign wars." He also defended his ongoing expansion of the US military, saying his objective was to create "a force so strong that, by its very existence, it will keep the threat of war far away from our shores."[2]

Despite Roosevelt's reassurances, Kane and many others of his generation were aware that American neutrality could quickly become a casualty of the spreading global conflict. In a way, the United States had already taken sides in the fight. FDR was steadily bolstering the British in their struggle against Hitler. On September 2, 1940, the United States and Great Britain concluded the Destroyers for Bases Agreement. The British agreed to provide ninety-nine-year land grants for American naval or air bases in eight British possessions in the Western Hemisphere. In turn, the United States provided the Royal Navy and Royal Canadian Navy with fifty World War I–era flush-deck destroyers. Two weeks after that, the possibility of personal military involvement became obvious for everyone in Harry Kane's age group. On September 16, Roosevelt signed the Selective Training and Service Act of 1940, which imposed military conscription on American males between the ages of twenty-one and thirty-five (the range would expand after Pearl Harbor to between eighteen and forty-five). The winds of war were clearly rising. With no desire to become a common foot soldier, Kane recalled years later that he needed "to get into something so that I wouldn't have to go into the infantry." The Brooklyn native decided to become a military aviator.[3]

For Harry Kane, this was not an impetuous decision. Rather, it was an act of cool calculation typical of the young New Yorker. Although born into a family of wealth and prestige, Kane had been forced to learn self-reliance at an early age. Kane's maternal grandfather was the co-owner of a prosperous cotton-exporting firm in Brooklyn. When his son, Henry J. Kane Sr., married Gertrude Rose Heaney at the imposing Church of Saint Francis

Lieutenant Harry J. Kane joined the
US Army Air Forces in March 1941,
receiving his commission five days after the Japanese attack on Pearl Harbor on December 7, 1941. COURTESY
OF MARGUERITE KANE JAMESON.

Xavier in Manhattan on October 28, 1916, more than nine
hundred family members, friends, and business acquaintances
attended, making it the city's largest wedding of the year. Kane's
parents bought a stately home at 306 Garfield Place in the Park
Slope section of Brooklyn, where Harry, the first of three sons,
was born on June 24, 1918.

Kane grew up immersed in the Irish Catholic community of
Brooklyn, attending private Catholic schools from kindergarten
through high school. The family's wealth provided for a com-
fortable life insulated from the Great Depression, but Kane's
childhood did not pass without trauma. His mother gave birth

to two more sons, Frank and Richard, and the family grieved when Richard died at the age of four from a sudden illness. Then, when Harry and Frank Kane were still young, their father abandoned the family, forcing the boys' mother to raise them alone. Somewhere along the way, Kane realized that if he were to accomplish his goals in life, he alone would identify them and make them come true.

After graduating from Brooklyn Prep in 1937, Kane spent three years working at various jobs, but he began paying close attention to the darkening world headlines. Choosing to join the military service before he was conscripted, Kane enrolled in a private flight school sometime in 1940, earning his private pilot's license as he mulled over whether to join the Army Air Corps or the navy's aviation branch. In early 1941, Kane opted for army aviation. His educational record and private pilot's license won him quick acceptance. At Drane Army Airfield, he would take a three-month primary flight training course. Barring academic failure, an unexpected physiological problem, or aerial mishap, Kane anticipated finishing the other two phases of flight training—a ten-week basic flight school at Gunter Field in Montgomery, Alabama, followed by a ten-week advanced flight school at Barksdale Field in Louisiana—sometime in December 1941.[4]

SEVERAL WEEKS AFTER KANE ARRIVED IN FLORIDA, in early April 1941, newly promoted *Kapitänleutnant* (Lieutenant Commander) Horst Degen took a train from northern Germany through occupied France to the Atlantic port of Saint-Nazaire. While the twenty-seven-year-old was no newcomer to military service or the ongoing European war, this particular journey marked a major milestone in his seven-year naval career. A surface navy officer since receiving his commission in 1936, Degen had transferred into the elite U-boat branch the previous July. Now, having recently finished five months of U-boat training and a three-month U-boat commander's course, Degen was about to experience an actual wartime U-boat patrol. It was a heady time for a man who had dreamed of a life at sea ever since he was a young boy.

Degen was born on July 19, 1913, in the town of Hemer in the state of North Rhine-Westphalia. His parents, Carl and Josephine Degen, were a respected couple in the town, where Carl Degen was a longtime civil servant and mayor. Horst Degen later recalled that he enjoyed "a happy, carefree time" as a boy, despite the harsh living conditions in Germany after the end of World War I. But tragedy found Degen all the same: both of his parents died before he reached the age of sixteen, leaving him and his ten-year-old sister, Ilse, to be raised by their twenty-three-year-old sister, Hanna, and her husband.

Upon finishing his last year in grammar school (the German equivalent of high school), Degen, then eighteen, traveled to the Reichsmarine Naval Barracks outside Kiel as an applicant to the German Naval Academy. There, he and other candidates were organized into groups of eight and given a battery of academic, physical fitness, and psychological tests to gauge their mental, athletic, and psychological prowess. In one test, instructors placed Degen alone in a room with one-way mirrors through which they monitored him. They told him to lift a heavy metal bar, which, as he did so, was charged with increasing levels of electricity. The candidates who resisted the shock and pain from the electrical current the longest received the highest marks. Degen himself never mentioned his score on that particular test, but his subsequent naval record indicates that he passed. Another challenge entailed following a complicated set of instructions for delivering a message to a navy officer. A classmate of Degen's, Reinhard Hardegen, later recounted his experience: an instructor dictated, "Carry this piece of paper over that obstacle, cross the ditch, turn left, run until you arrive at a tall tree," adding, "turn right, walk until you come to a man in a green coat, and say to him, 'I have been ordered to deliver this paper to you.'" The candidate's grade would depend on his ability to carry out the instructions accurately.

Horst Degen joined the navy at a time of profound change for Germany and its people. On April 1, 1933, the Reichsmarine formally admitted him as an *Offiziersanwärter* (officer candidate). Just one week earlier, Adolf Hitler—who had been serving as German chancellor in a coalition government since January 30—had persuaded the German Reichstag to pass a law formally consolidating his hold on power by granting the Nazis full legislative authority for a four-year period. Like many young members of the navy, Degen kept whatever opinions he had of the Nazi Party to himself, even as the regime tightened its grip on German society. He would later tell a navy colleague that while he himself had enjoyed a blithe upbringing as a boy, "This was no longer possible in the present days of the Hitler Youth," which had supplanted all other children's organizations and in which participation was mandatory for all.[5]

After passing the entry tests, Degen and his classmates reported to the Naval Academy at Flensburg-Mürwik. Overlooking the Flensburg Fjord, which links the ancient German city with the Baltic Sea, the academy was founded in 1910 by Kaiser Wilhelm II. At the time that Degen and the other members of the Class of 1933 entered, the academy curriculum included three months of basic infantry training on the island of Dänholm in the Baltic, followed by sailing instruction. Upon completion of that phase in the late summer, the ninety-four members of the Class of 1933 embarked on the four-year-old light cruiser *Karlsruhe* for a nine-month, around-the-world cruise.[6]

Leaving Kiel on October 4, 1933, the 8,130-ton warship carried a crew of 1,550 officers and enlisted crewmen, plus the Class of 1933 naval cadets. *Karlsruhe* skipper *Kapitän zur See* (Captain) Baron Harsdorf von Enderndorf ordered the cruiser south to Gibraltar and the Mediterranean for port visits in Sicily and Egypt, then transited the Suez Canal for the Indian Ocean and stops in Yemen, Ceylon, and India before a Christmas stopover in Indonesia. Degen would later recall enjoying a sumptuous Christmas Eve dinner with the owners of the Oranje Hotel in Padang before the *Karlsruhe* once again got underway for Australia and the long Pacific crossing to American Samoa and Hawaii.

Reaching the US West Coast in early March 1934, the cruiser docked at Tacoma, Washington, for a week before heading south to the massive US Navy base at San Diego. There, Hamilton and Elsa Marston, owners of a prominent San Diego department store, invited Degen and a fellow naval cadet to dinner, beginning a lifelong friendship between Degen and the American family. During both stops, the naval cadets also enjoyed extended land excursions to Seattle, Los Angeles, and San Francisco.

In early April, the *Karlsruhe* left San Diego for Central America and a transit of the Panama Canal, followed by port visits in British Honduras and Santo Domingo in the Dominican Republic. The ship then made a lengthy trek up the US East Coast and arrived in Boston, its final stopover, on May 12.

Whereas the German communities in Asia had welcomed the warship and its men with open arms, their arrival in America sparked anti-Nazi protests that tarnished the formal welcoming ceremonies. In Seattle and Los Angeles, the hosts of the *Karlsruhe* were forced to shepherd the cadets past boisterous protest rallies, and in Boston a small riot—quickly quelled by police—broke out near the ship at the Boston Naval Shipyard. For Degen and the other cadets, these incidents were a minor distraction. They faced another, more troublesome challenge.

By the time the *Karlsruhe* reached the United States, it resembled Noah's Ark. The training warship was carrying a variety of large mammals, thanks to several German societies that had hosted the ship at stops along its voyage. In Ceylon, the local German community presented the ship's crew with "Trinco," a baby leopard. In Calcutta, the crew took aboard "Calco," a tiny Himalayan bear cub. During a port call in Brisbane, Australia, a local German society gave the ship a baby kangaroo.

It fell to the Class of 1933 cadets to care for and feed this growing menagerie. By the time the *Karlsruhe* reached Boston, Calco the bear had grown quite large and become aggressive toward his captors. Several days after arriving, Captain von Enderndorf hosted the German consul general, Kurt Wilhelm

Viktor von Tippelskirch, his wife, and their young daughter on board the ship. While the two older men conferred, Degen escorted mother and daughter around the main deck. They came upon several large cages containing the donated animals, and the girl bent over to play with the kangaroo. "This made the bear jealous," Degen later noted. "He reached out of his cage and with one swipe of his claw, ripped her dress from top to bottom." Both the terrified daughter and the mortified naval cadet's career survived the encounter. Alas, Calco did not survive the voyage. He was seriously injured during a storm while the cruiser crossed the North Atlantic on its return and had to be shot.[7]

Now, nearly seven years later, Horst Degen was anticipating a much stiffer challenge than tending to the needs of a captive bear cub. The war that Hitler had instigated nineteen months earlier was spreading across the Atlantic Ocean, and U-boat commanders and crews were in high demand—so much so that Degen had felt compelled to volunteer for eight more months of training in order to join the U-boat Force. He was still a newcomer to U-boats when, on April 7, 1941, he boarded the Type VIIC U-552 for a thirty-day combat patrol in the North Atlantic. Since Degen had not previously served as a watch officer on a U-boat before entering U-boat commander's training, his curriculum included this "at-sea training" as a *Kommandantenschüler* (commander pupil) on an actual wartime patrol. Commanding the four-month old U-552 was twenty-six-year-old *Oberleutnant zur See* (Lieutenant) Erich Topp. Topp had graduated from the Naval Academy a year after Degen but joined the U-boat Force in October 1937, well ahead of Degen. After serving on two other U-boats, Topp commissioned the Type VIIC U-552 on

As U-552 returns to Saint-Nazaire on May 6, 1941, Horst Degen (right) said U-boat ace Erich Topp (left), "taught me all I know" about U-boat tactics during a war patrol in the spring of 1941. COURTESY OF GÜNTHER DEGEN.

December 4, 1940. In its first patrol, U-552 had sunk two ships, totaling 12,749 gross registered tons, before reaching its new port at Saint-Nazaire.[8]

By the early spring of 1941, the German U-boat Force was firmly established in France. When the German army roared through the Low Countries and northwestern France in May 1940, Vice Admiral Karl Dönitz and his staff at U-boat Force Headquarters (*Befehlshaber der Unterseeboote*, or BdU) seized the opportunity to stage U-boat operations from the Brittany ports, which offered the U-boats direct access to the North Atlantic. This both increased the length of patrols and dramatically improved what Dönitz described as Germany's "strategically un-favorable geographical position vis-à-vis Great Britain." Prior to the fall of France, the U-boats had no choice but to sail from ports on the North Sea or in the Baltic and pass through heavily defended waters north of the British Isles to reach the open Atlantic. In the months that followed the French surrender on June 22, 1940, nearly three dozen U-boats transferred from Germany to operate out of the active bases at Lorient, Saint-Nazaire, La Pallice, Brest, and Bordeaux. Anticipating British aerial attacks on the new U-boat bases, Dönitz secured the help of a major German construction company to create impregnable bunkers for the boats.

The famed German engineering firm Organisation Todt, which had developed Germany's autobahn system and other massive public works projects in the prewar years, began build-ing what would become a massive U-boat bunker along the Saint-Nazaire waterfront. Design plans called for a reinforced concrete-and-steel structure running 980 feet along the water-front and containing fourteen separate U-boat pens—eight that could hold a solitary U-boat and another six wide enough to fit two boats. The roof itself would consist of twenty-eight feet of concrete and steel reinforcements to ward off enemy air attacks. Construction was barely underway on the first three pens—which would comprise the center of the finished bunker—when U-552 tied up to the quay on March 16, 1941.[9]

The armored bunkers at Saint-Nazaire and the other French ports were an integral part of newly promoted four-star admiral Dönitz's ongoing plan for a major expansion of the U-boat Force. The forty-nine-year-old admiral was adamant that Germany could only defeat Great Britain by severing the maritime trade routes that brought food, fuel, and other critical supplies to the island nation from overseas. Thus far, however, recurring delays in new construction, bureaucratic struggles with the army and Luftwaffe for steel and aluminum, and occasional personnel shortages in the German shipbuilding industry had hamstrung Dönitz's efforts to knock Britain out of the fight. Dönitz had won Adolf Hitler's tentative approval in January 1941 for a significant acceleration of U-boat construction. Barring further snags, he anticipated that within the next eighteen months, another 205 U-boats would join the 77 then in service. As Horst Degen prepared for his first combat cruise aboard the U-552 at the beginning of April, the Battle of the Atlantic was poised to enter a new and even more vicious phase.[10]

HARRY KANE WAS A VERY BUSY BUT SATISFIED MAN in the summer of 1941. Having earned his private pilot's license prior to enlisting in the US Army Air Corps, he breezed through primary flight training at Drane Field. During the ten-week course, he flew with an instructor pilot in an open-cockpit Boeing Stearman PT-13 trainer, learning and rehearsing basic flight maneuvers. The PT-13 was designed for ruggedness, and both its cruising speed (a giddy 106 mph) and service ceiling (11,200 feet) were quite modest. Nevertheless, this biplane served the aim of the instructor cadre well, permitting novice pilots to glean the basics of flight in a reliable and sturdy aircraft.

Once Kane satisfied his instructors as to his abilities in basic tasks like takeoff, level flight, landing, and response to various

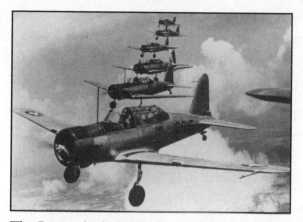

The Boeing-built PT-13 Stearman was the ubiquitous primary training aircraft for both USAAF
and navy aviation cadets during World War II.
USAAF PHOTOGRAPH.

in-flight emergencies such as stall and spin recovery, he began
learning more complex flying patterns. These included the "lazy
8," where the pilot learns confidence in making constantly
changing adjustments to the flight controls as he puts the aircraft
through a series of climbing, turning, and diving maneuvers. Another task was the "Immelmann," a climbing exercise where the
pilot pulls his aircraft up into a climbing half loop, then rolls
out in level flight on an opposite course. The daily schedule was
quite rigorous, with several flights per day to meet the US Army
Air Forces' (the command's new title had been announced in
June) requirement that every primary student make 175 successful landings during the ten weeks of training. In addition to basic
military instruction and daily physical fitness training, Kane and
the other cadets also had ninety-six hours of ground school instruction on aircraft equipment, navigation, principles of flight,
aircraft recognition, and radio codes.[11]

After Lakeland, Kane and other successful cadets proceeded to Montgomery, Alabama, where they would hone their flying skills at basic flight school. The facility was located at Gunter Army Airfield, an auxiliary facility attached to nearby Maxwell Field. In the early 1930s, Maxwell was home to the Air Corps Tactical School, whose 200 officers and 1,000 enlisted personnel made it the largest air corps installation in the southeast. Then, in 1940, the training command at Maxwell had landed another major mission, serving as the Southeast Air Corps Training Center, instructing pilots both at the base itself and at dozens of airfields across the eastern United States.

Kane and the other basic flight students assigned to Gunter Field learned to fly the Vultee BT-13 Valiant trainer, a much higher-performing aircraft than the PT-13 biplane. A low-wing monoplane with a closed canopy for the instructor pilot and student sitting in fore and aft cockpit seats, the Valiant was much more powerful than the Stearman. Its Pratt & Whitney R-985 engine enabled the Valiant to sprint through the air at 180 mph and climb up to 21,650 feet. In the basic flying course, the cadets had to master the intricacies of this more powerful airplane—and under increasingly challenging circumstances.

At Gunter Field, the unspoken motto was "Bigger, faster, trickier." During their ten weeks there, Kane and the others were introduced to more than mere accuracy maneuvers and acrobatics. After practice in ground-based trainers, they flew the Valiant relying solely on their cockpit instruments to take off, navigate through the air, and land. They relied on the rate-of-turn indicator, the bank indicator, and the airspeed indicator to fly the aircraft. Then came their initial exposure to long-range navigation, formation flying, and night flying. Ground school courses were also tougher, with the cadets studying principles of instrument flight, radio communications, and advanced aircraft and ship recognition.[12]

By late September 1941, Harry Kane was in his final phase of flight instruction at the Advanced Pilot Training School at Barksdale Field, near Shreveport, Louisiana. Built on a former cotton plantation near Bossier City, the base originally was home to a pursuit group (as early-model fighters were called) that was training in all facets of fighter operations. However, it too became an air corps flying school in late 1940. Its instructors not only processed individual cadets through the final phase of their training but also prepared entire bombardment groups in unit tactics.

Kane spent the ten weeks at Barksdale mastering the new skills required to operate a twin-engine aircraft. When he began this final phase of instruction, USAAF officials informed him that, upon graduation, he would be assigned to fly this type of plane. They did not reveal which particular model he would fly, however, which left him still uncertain as to what his specific assignment might be. In late 1941, the Army Air Forces had ten separate twin-engine aircraft in its inventory and another five new models under preliminary design. These included five light or medium bombers: the old B-18 Bolo, the new B-25 Mitchell, the new B-26 Marauder, the A-20 Havoc, and the A-29 Hudson. The service was also developing an advanced, high-performance fighter, the P-38 Lightning, as well as five types of twin-engine transports, of which the C-46 Commando and C-47 Skytrain would appear in the largest numbers. During 1940–1941, the army procured 20,914 new aircraft, of which 3,702—about 18 percent—were twin-engine models.

Regardless of which of these models Kane ended up in, he would need the same basic skills. Single- and twin-engine aircraft had different mission profiles: single-engine craft, being smaller and more maneuverable but with small fuel tanks, were used for air defense, escorting bombers, and short-range patrol missions; larger twin-engine warplanes included light bombers, medium transport planes, and—in the case of the P-38 Lightning— advanced fighter operations. To prepare him for flying aircraft of this type, Kane's final course load de-emphasized acrobatics and concentrated more on the study of aircraft systems, long-range flight planning, and meteorology.[13]

Nine months after stepping off the train at Lakeland, Florida, Harry Kane, along with his fellow flight school graduates, raised his right hand and took the oath commissioning him as a second lieutenant in the US Army Air Forces; then, for the first time, he proudly pinned his pilot's wings on his uniform. The ceremony, however, was somewhat subdued. It took place on December 12—five days after the Japanese attack on Pearl Harbor and the day after Germany's declaration of war on the United States and America's declaration of war on Germany and Italy. The global conflagration that Kane and others in his class had seen brewing for so long was finally at hand.[14]

IN THE EARLY EVENING TWILIGHT OF DECEMBER 27, 1941, a German U-boat followed an escort icebreaker through the frigid waters of the Kiel Canal. The Type VIIC U-701 edged up to the quay at the small German seaport of Brunsbüttel, where a large U-boat tender was moored just inside the lock gates leading to the lower Elbe River. As the duty watch shut down the diesel engines, Kapitänleutnant Horst Degen and his forty-five-man crew were feeling both tired and full of nervous anticipation. After his combat patrol aboard U-552 earlier in the year, Degen had been assigned to his very own U-boat—and now he was leading it out on its first patrol of the war.

Final preparations for sea had consumed the past three days. With their craft tied up to the mammoth "Tirpitz Mole" pier at the Kriegsmarine base in Kiel, Degen's crew had worked around the clock filling their U-boat with 113 tons of diesel fuel, fourteen torpedoes, 220 rounds of ammunition for the 88-mm deck gun, and enough food and fresh water for six weeks at sea. The crew did not have the luxury of celebrating Christmas in town, so Degen found accommodations for them in a naval barracks. The men spent December 25 at an impromptu party where Degen, an accomplished amateur musician, played Christmas carols on a piano as his men sang along.[15]

The brief passage through the canal on December 27 brought them from the Baltic Sea to the small town of Brunsbüttel along the lower channel of the Elbe River. The next morning, they would cast off for the short trip through the canal lock and down the mouth of the river to the North Sea and the beginning of their first combat patrol against Great Britain and the United States. The German submersibles were a common sight on the sixty-mile man-made waterway across northern Germany. Of eighteen shipyards building U-boats at the time, half were located in cities whose river or harbor access led directly to the

North Sea, and the other nine building yards were located on the Baltic. Yet all U-boats preparing for combat spent at least six months in Kiel, and those leaving for the North Atlantic had to cross back to Brunsbüttel to avoid the dangerous passage around Denmark. U-701 had made the Kiel Canal transit three previous times before arriving at the pier on the southern side of the harbor near the lock gates that last Saturday in December.[16]

For Horst Degen, the final departure from Kiel was a particularly satisfying moment in his naval career. It was the culmination of eight months of seemingly endless hard work, as well as excitement, danger, and frustration. Since his *Kommandantenschüler* patrol on U-552, he had progressed from commander's pupil to commander of a newly constructed U-boat with a crew of his own; he had also endured an agonizing six-week overstay in the shipyard while workers repaired construction errors in the boat. He and his crew had then sweated through three months of relentless combat training in the Baltic Sea under the stern eye of a training flotilla.[17]

Degen's four-week patrol on U-552 had provided an invaluable lesson on how an aggressive U-boat commander could succeed against the enemy. Initially directed by BdU to patrol some 450 nautical miles southwest of Reykjavik, Iceland, U-552 spent the first four days after leaving Saint-Nazaire conducting rigorous crash-dive exercises and other combat drills to ready the crew for any combat scenario that might occur. During the first three weeks, the lookouts saw nothing but the empty storm-tossed North Atlantic, but Topp knew that their luck could change at any moment—and it did. On April 27, while aligned in a patrol screen with three other U-boats,

U-552 sighted a solitary patrol vessel. After missing with a G7a torpedo, Topp ordered his gun crews to the deck and fired nearly two hundred rounds from his 88-mm deck gun and 20-mm flak gun into the hapless British fishing trawler *Commander Horton*, which sank with the loss of its fourteen-man crew. Like many U-boat commanders, Topp did not hesitate to go after even smaller vessels like this, particularly since the Royal Navy had commandeered scores of them to operate as antisubmarine trawlers. This boat proved to be the first in a target-rich environment for U-552.[18]

Nine hours after sinking the British trawler, Topp carried out a textbook daylight submerged attack against the independently steaming 10,119-ton British freighter *Beacon Grange*, holing it with a spread of three G7e electric torpedoes and finishing it off with a fourth. Then more riches appeared: seven hours after the *Beacon Grange* sank, Topp's radio operator intercepted a contact report of a convoy from another U-boat, which had sighted eastbound Convoy HX121. The formation of forty-nine merchant ships totaling 324,311 gross registered tons included seventeen oil tankers, which carried the highest priority for attack by U-boats. Despite the presence of fourteen escort warships, Topp fearlessly ran U-552 directly under the convoy, surfaced between two columns of ships, and struck the 8,190-ton British tanker *Capulet* with a single torpedo. The convoy's escorts subjected U-552 to an agonizing five-hour depth charge attack, but Topp told Degen that such risks were worth it: only aggressive actions by a U-boat commander guaranteed success against the enemy. "Either you are lucky or you aren't," Topp explained, "and it is no good being overcautious if you want to be successful." Degen took that lesson to heart when he got his own U-boat. And he said of Topp, "He taught me all I know."[19]

U-552 returned to Saint-Nazaire on May 6, 1941, with Lieutenant Topp and his crew having sunk a total of three ships totaling 15,929 tons and damaging the 10,119-ton *Capulet*, which was abandoned by its crew and finished off four days later by U-201. For the U-boat's crew, the in-port period meant a nineteen-day respite of liberty and relaxation while technicians repaired battle damage to the boat and prepared it for its next patrol. For Degen, however, it signaled the beginning of actual U-boat command. On U-552, he had not taken part in operating the U-boat or attacking enemy shipping, serving instead as an observer and carefully watching how Topp and his crew carried out their duties.

Now it was time to take command himself. Degen hastened to Hamburg, where at the H. C. Stülcken Sohn shipyard on the Elbe River, shipwrights had been constructing the Type VIIC U-701 over the past twelve months. It was now time to meet his forty-four-man crew and begin *Baubelehrung* (familiarization training), which had become standard practice in the U-boat Force. As the shipyard workers finished installing a myriad of equipment and components of every conceivable design—cables, power units, gyrocompass, torpedo-aiming gear, steering controls, tip-up bunks, echo sounder, signaling lamp, radio set, cook's electric range, to name a few—teams of Degen's crew watched closely and learned how to operate and maintain the U-boat's systems. As one U-boat commander put it, "We all grew up, as it were, with the boat." In a brief ceremony attended by several hundred shipyard workers on July 16, 1941, Degen ordered the German naval ensign raised on a small jack staff mounted on the rear of the U-boat's bridge and saluted as his crew stood in formation on the main deck. U-701 had finally joined the U-boat Force. Five days later, U-boat and crew headed into the Baltic for a backbreaking training program to prepare them for combat at sea.[20]

In its six years of operational existence, the U-boat Force had honed its strategy and tactics for attacking enemy merchant convoys, solitary merchant vessels, and even warships. The curriculum was tough, complex, and thorough for everyone on a U-boat, from the commander to the most junior *Matrose* (seaman apprentice). As former U-boat commander Peter Cremer later described it, the training began with forty-five to fifty-one men learning how to survive and function in a very inhospitable place: "One's whole existence had to be adapted to the U-boat—eating, sleeping, going on watch, all in the narrowest space, in close physical contact, in closest relationship with the steel hull," he wrote. "There can hardly be a branch of the services in which a man must rely so much on others, tolerate their habits and subordinate himself to the team." During their tours of duty, the men in U-701 would be living cheek by jowl in extreme conditions for weeks on end; their initial training run aboard the ship was meant to prepare them to work efficiently and in unison despite the stresses of such confinement.

Degen and his crew had only got a brief taste of life aboard their new U-boat before trouble developed. As part of the formal process of joining the U-boat Force, the U-boat Acceptance Commission in Kiel carefully inspected each newly constructed boat. When checked after returning from its initial training run, U-701 flunked. The U-boat was full of mechanical glitches, electrical wiring errors, and faulty air and oil line installations. The chief issue, Degen later said, was that U-701 was the first U-boat the Hamburg shipyard had ever built, and its workers had relied on faulty blueprints from two other shipyards. After technicians spent several weeks trying to fix the problems in a Danzig shipyard, Degen had to take the boat back to Hamburg for six frustrating weeks of remedial repairs at H. C. Stülcken Sohn. The U-boat did not return to Kiel for a second Acceptance Commission inspection until October 9, after which the crew was cleared to resume combat exercises.[21]

And exercise the crew did. Admiral Dönitz and his flotilla instructors were adamant that no U-boat crew would leave Kiel without being totally prepared. "The U-boats had to be trained as far as possible for war conditions," the admiral later wrote. "I wanted to confront my U-boat crews . . . with every situation with which they might be confronted in war, and to do it so thoroughly that when these situations arose in war my crews would be well able to cope with them." Training goals included complete acclimatization of the men to life aboard ship, familiarity with the sea under all conditions, and absolute precision in navigation, particularly astronomical navigation. In torpedo firing alone, each U-boat had to successfully fire sixty-six surface shots and carry out another sixty-six submerged torpedo firings before instructors would certify it ready for combat. Name an aspect of submarine warfare, and the U-boat crew practiced it repeatedly: remaining unseen and undetected in enemy waters, deciding whether to crash-dive or remain on the surface after detecting an unknown aircraft, conducting night surface attacks and daylight periscope-depth attacks, mastering astronomical navigation, maintaining control of the U-boat while submerged under combat conditions, carrying out defensive gunfire while operating surfaced. The instructors had detailed, muscle-straining, and mind-numbing exercises for those and scores of other combat scenarios. For eleven weeks, Degen and his crew worked nonstop with the Third U-boat Flotilla based in Kiel. Each day, U-701 and eight other newly commissioned U-boats would leave port in the predawn darkness for the exercise area, returning at sunset to give the exhausted sailors a few hours of rest in barracks ashore. They gradually mastered the complex set of skills that would make them effective in combat and embraced the philosophy of their commander-in-chief: "I wanted to imbue my crews," Dönitz explained, "with enthusiasm and a complete faith in their [U-boat Force] and to instill in them a spirit of selfless readiness to serve in it."

Now, as this eventful year drew to a close, Degen and his crew were finally ready. At 0800 on Sunday, December 28, 1941, one of the lock gates at Brunsbüttel slowly opened, and Degen eased U-701 through and into the Elbe River for the short trip to the North Sea. U-701 was on its way to fight.[22]

2

THE
GATHERING STORM

O<small>N NEW YEAR'S EVE 1941, IF ONE AMERICAN NAVY OFFICER</small> fully comprehended the potential threat that the German U-boat Force posed to Allied merchant shipping along the US East Coast, it was Admiral Ernest J. King. King had yielded command of the US Atlantic Fleet to his successor just two days earlier as he assumed duties as commander-in-chief of the United States Fleet (COMINCH). From his shabby office on the third deck of the massive Main Navy Headquarters building on Constitution Avenue in Washington, DC, King now held supreme command of a two-ocean fleet that constituted the American military vanguard against Nazi Germany and imperial Japan. King's time commanding the Atlantic Fleet had convinced him of the vital importance of that theater, and he knew just how strained the East Coast warships and their crews were. The men had suffered through two years of prolonged "Neutrality Patrols" that, for the past six months, had resembled war missions more than peacetime cruises. Yet, although their job was intensifying, they increasingly found themselves competing for resources with the navy's other commands.

The threat to merchant shipping in the Atlantic littoral was but one of a multitude of crises confronting the US Navy, most of them in the Pacific. Simultaneous attacks by Japan against the Philippines, Hong Kong, Malaya, Indochina, Wake Island, and Guam threatened to cut Australia and New Zealand off from the United States; if successful, Japan's efforts would likely doom any Allied counterattack. A major portion of the Pacific Fleet, meanwhile, lay burned and blackened in the mud at Pearl Harbor. The tiny US Asiatic Fleet, consisting of two cruisers, twenty-eight elderly destroyers, and twenty-eight submarines, could not hope to survive an imminent clash with the Japanese navy.

The dire situation in the Pacific meant that the Atlantic theater and the defense of the US eastern seaboard were relatively low on the navy's list of priorities. The Atlantic Fleet had grown significantly in 1941, but in the aftermath of Pearl Harbor, emergency plans were in place to transfer a number of aircraft carriers, battleships, and destroyers to the Pacific to offset the losses of December 7. By the end of January 1942, the Atlantic Fleet would count only five battleships, two aircraft carriers, and fourteen cruisers to operate against the Germans, who, in addition to the U-boat Force, still had a powerful surface fleet of battleships and cruisers that could threaten the Atlantic sea lanes. The fleet's workhorse destroyer force also faced severe shortages with dozens of warships idled for overdue repairs.

King now commanded a United States Navy that appeared to be coming apart at the seams. On paper, King had assumed command with executive powers unmatched in the 166-year history of his service. An executive order hastily drafted and signed by President Roosevelt two weeks earlier established that King, as COMINCH, would have "supreme command of the operating forces comprising the several fleets of the United States Navy and the operating forces of the naval coastal frontier commands, and [would] be directly responsible, under the general direction of the Secretary of the Navy, to the President of the United States." In reality, however, the sixty-three-year-old Ohio native was still struggling to assemble a headquarters staff, and most officers assigned to Main Navy remained shell-shocked by the stunning Japanese strike on Oahu. "Nothing was ready," King later said of his first days in supreme command. "I had to start with nothing."[1]

The previous year had been a wild roller-coaster ride for Ernie King. At the end of 1940, King was serving in a dead-end job on the navy's General Board in his permanent rank of rear admiral, with few prospects for promotion or major command in his future. It was quite a comedown after a stellar career spanning four decades of active service.

Since graduating from the Naval Academy in 1901, King had supervised the conversion of American warships from coal to oil propulsion. Appointed to a three-man board to study the navy's training and promotion of officers in 1919, King personally wrote a report recommending an overhaul of the officer personnel system that the navy formally implemented; it is essentially still in use more than ninety years later. Under the glare of worldwide media attention, King successfully directed the salvage of the submarine S-51 after it sank in a collision with a civilian steamer in September 1925. Three years later, he repeated the feat by raising the sunken submarine S-4. His military service reached new heights in 1937, when as a vice admiral King assumed command of the fleet's aircraft carriers.

Then, suddenly, King's career hit a brick wall. In the spring of 1939, his hopes for promotion to four stars and assignment to one of the navy's top two posts—commander-in-chief, US Fleet, which would have made him responsible for the navy's day-to-day operations, or chief of naval operations (CNO), which would have put him in charge of the service's broader strategic planning and budget—were dashed when Roosevelt filled the one current vacancy by appointing Admiral Harold R. "Betty" Stark as CNO. Assignment to the navy's General Board brought a reduction in rank to rear admiral and a cubbyhole at Main Navy. King began calling himself "a has-been" to friends and colleagues.

Soon, however, King discovered that he had one more chance for high command. In the spring of 1940, Acting Navy Secretary Charles Edison assigned King to increase the antiaircraft firepower on all navy warships. With Edison's support, King slashed through the bureaucratic tentacles that paralyzed most major reforms and got the complicated rearming program underway in just three months. The bureaucrats howled, but the program proceeded on a fast track. Secretary Edison took careful note. When he resigned to run as the Democratic candidate for governor of New Jersey in the summer of 1940, Edison wrote, in a final memorandum to FDR, "I take the liberty of bringing to your attention the need for shaking the service out of a peacetime psychology." He urged the president to consider King for appointment as commander-in-chief of the US Fleet. Instead,

Stark assigned King to command the US Atlantic Squadron (re-named the Patrol Force several months later). In many respects, this was a major comedown: a two-star billet commanding the na-vy's oldest and most ramshackle warships. Nevertheless, the job took King back to sea and resurrected his career. Three weeks after King assumed command on his flagship *USS Texas* on December 17, 1940, FDR announced that he was renaming the command the US Atlantic Fleet. With that shift, King found himself jumped two ranks to four-star admiral.

During his first months in command in the Atlantic, King struggled to secure funds to bring the fleet up to standard and to carry out badly needed repairs after long months of Neutrality Patrol operations. But while the Atlantic Fleet was still prepar-ing for war, the Royal Navy and the U-boat Force were already engaged in a fierce struggle on the high seas. The North Atlantic was not big enough to keep the peacetime US Navy out of the fight, and a series of incidents would soon lead the Americans to overtly join the battle alongside their British allies.[2]

American public opinion in the spring of 1941 was deeply opposed to US entry into the war, so Roosevelt and his admirals were forced to operate in secret when military planning or di-rect action at sea was required. Behind closed and guarded doors in Washington, DC, beginning in late January 1941, senior American and British military commanders huddled for nearly eight weeks hammering out what became known as the ABC-1 Agreement (for American, British, and Canadian military plan-ning), which enumerated basic strategic priorities in the event the United States entered the war on the side of the British. Nevertheless, FDR often kept Stark and King in the dark about what specific actions he might want them to take. Even though

ABC-1 spelled out the roles and responsibilities of the Atlantic Fleet, King was denied a copy of the report. In desperation, he set up his own fleet operation plan, which would soon be carried out by a new Atlantic Fleet unit that would directly aid Allied convoys and, by default, find itself in combat with the U-boats.[3]

On March 1, 1941, the navy established a new command called the Atlantic Fleet Support Force whose mission would be "to operate from bases overseas in connection with the protection of shipping." Under Rear Admiral Arthur L. Bristol, the command quickly selected Argentia, a protected harbor on Newfoundland's southeast coastline, as an advance base where warships and seaplanes could operate to protect the western leg of the convoy routes between North America and Great Britain. By the summer of 1941, three destroyer squadrons with twenty-seven destroyers were operating with the Support Force. Still, King knew that if Germany's battleships joined the U-boats' ongoing war against Allied shipping, the threat in the Atlantic would require even more US warships to cover an even greater area. King stationed a large group of his battleships, cruisers, and destroyers at Casco Bay, Maine, as a backup force should Germany's surface warships threaten to steam out of port to operate in the North Atlantic. While the main threat remained the U-boat Force, the German navy in 1941 still had a substantial force of major surface warships, including four battleships, six smaller "pocket" battleships and battle cruisers, six light cruisers, and several dozen destroyers. Although the Kriegsmarine leadership largely kept these warships in German waters or Scandinavian ports after 1940, the surface fleet still posed a major potential threat in the North Atlantic.

Events unfolded at an accelerating pace during the middle of 1941. Reacting to aggressive German naval movements in the

By early 1942, the Allies had organized merchant convoys for the transatlantic passage, but the US Navy failed
to organize similar defensive formations along the East
Coast, resulting in soaring losses at the hands of the
U-boats. OFFICE OF WAR INFORMATION.

Atlantic, including the breakout of the battleship *Bismarck* on
May 24, Roosevelt proclaimed an "unlimited national emergency"
that, in part, publicly committed the navy to protect Allied merchant shipping. Three weeks later, King carried out FDR's order
to occupy Iceland with a US Marine Corps brigade. King formed
Task Force 19, which consisted of most of his heavy warships—two
battleships, two light cruisers, and thirteen destroyers—to escort
three cargo ships carrying the Marine Corps brigade to Reykjavik.

Then, on August 2, King executed a task that President Roosevelt had personally set for him, one so secret that even Admiral Stark did not learn of it until the last minute: he ferried
FDR, his senior civilian advisers, and US military commanders
to a top-secret rendezvous with British prime minister Winston
Churchill and his advisers at Placentia Bay, Newfoundland. The
Atlantic Conference, as it was later called, lasted four days and

marked the beginning of a formal partnership between the two countries against Nazi Germany. For Admiral King and the Atlantic Fleet, the conference produced an operations order for the fleet to begin escorting convoys between North America and Iceland, effective September 16. When five Atlantic Fleet destroyers met eastbound Convoy HX150 on September 17 about 150 miles south of Argentia, the rendezvous marked the beginning of an undeclared war between the US Atlantic Fleet and the German U-boat Force.[4]

The first serious encounter between US and German warships occurred on September 4, a month after FDR and Churchill met at Argentia. Proceeding to Iceland with a load of mail, the American destroyer USS Greer observed a British Hudson patrol plane whose pilot signaled that he had sighted a U-boat. The Greer stood by as the aircraft dropped four depth charges. In return, the German vessel, the Type VIIC U-652, came up to periscope depth and fired a torpedo at the Greer, missing the destroyer. The encounter lasted six hours before the Greer broke off and resumed its trip to Iceland.

While the incident had little effect on any of its participants, Roosevelt used it as a pretext to escalate the Atlantic Fleet's activities. In a fireside chat, FDR announced a "shoot-on-sight order" authorizing all American warships to attack Axis U-boats and surface ships without provocation. Six weeks later, on October 15, the first American sailors died in combat in the Atlantic when the Type VIIC U-568 torpedoed the destroyer USS Kearny as it escorted eastbound Convoy SC48, seriously damaging the destroyer and killing eleven crewmen.[5]

Any lingering doubts that the US Navy was now in a shooting war with the U-boat Force vanished on October 31. On that day,

U-552, commanded by Kapitänleutnant Erich Topp—who had taken Horst Degen along on patrol as a *Kommandantenschüler* back in early April—was one of eight U-boats that attacked eastbound Convoy HX156. A single torpedo from U-552 struck the destroyer USS *Reuben James*'s port side, setting off its forward ammunition magazine and blowing the ship in half. The sinking killed 115 of its 160-man crew, including all of its officers.

Unlike the *Greer* incident eight weeks earlier, the sinking of the *Reuben James* elicited a muted reaction in Washington. While Navy Secretary Frank Knox called the attack "worse than piracy," President Roosevelt told a press conference that the incident had not materially changed the United States' position of neutrality. Having already denounced the U-boat Force as a gang of pirates and issued shoot-on-sight orders to the Atlantic Fleet, Roosevelt avoided the next logical step on the escalation ladder: a formal declaration of war. But out on the mid-ocean shipping routes, the sailors knew better. Formalities aside, the US Navy was now fully engaged as a combatant in the Battle of the Atlantic.[6]

UNTIL THE VERY END OF 1941, the United States and Germany had managed to avoid declaring outright war against each other—an eventuality that both governments wanted to avoid if possible. Japan's attack on Pearl Harbor, however, instantly transformed both countries' calculations. The attack immediately thrust the United States into the war against its new Asian enemy and soon propelled it into the fight against Hitler as well.

America's entry into the war against Germany came after a series of events unanticipated by either side that occurred over just a seven-day period before and after December 7. The Japanese attack came as a bolt from the blue to everyone in the American high command; while CNO Admiral Stark had issued an explicit war warning to the Pacific Fleet on November 27, he and most of his intelligence analysts believed that Japan would strike first in the Philippines or Malaya. Pacific Fleet commander Admiral Husband Kimmel also thought the first blow would fall in the Far East. So did Roosevelt. The Japanese fooled not just their American enemies, however; they also deceived their German ally.

Night had fallen in the Masurian woods outside the East Prussian town of Rastenberg that pivotal Sunday when an urgent telegram arrived at Hitler's command bunker at Wolfsschanze, the Wolf's Lair headquarters complex. Transmitted by the German Funkbeobachtungsdienst (Navy Cryptologic Service, or B-Dienst) the message was hand-delivered to the Führer:

JAPAN BEGAN HOSTILITIES AGAINST THE UNITED STATES ON 7 DECEMBER, AT 1930 HOURS CENTRAL EUROPEAN TIME—STRONG AIR FORMATIONS ATTACKED PEARL HARBOR (HONOLULU).

Adolf Hitler was stunned. Although Japanese ambassador Hiroshi Oshima had told the Führer just days earlier, "War may come quicker than anyone dreams," the German dictator fully expected to be informed in advance. Initially angry and embarrassed that Tokyo had left him in the dark, he now had to make one of the more profound wartime decisions since ordering the invasion of Poland twenty-seven months earlier: whether to preserve the fraying neutrality between Germany and the United

States or go to war with Great Britain's staunch ally. Although the German and Japanese regimes had been discussing a military partnership over the past ten months, they had yet to sign a supplemental accord to the 1940 Axis Treaty to coordinate their military campaigns. On the other hand, the military and political factors that had prompted the Führer throughout 1941 to avoid an overt clash with the United States—particularly with the Atlantic Fleet—were still very much in play as he read and reread the B-Dienst telegram. The biggest factor was Germany's invasion of the Soviet Union, now nearing the six-month milestone. Just five days previously, on Tuesday, December 2, a unit of the German 258th Division had reached a town north of Moscow, from which its soldiers could see the spires of the Kremlin in the distance a dozen miles away. More than 4.3 million German soldiers were battling in the subfreezing Russian winter against 3.3 million Soviet troops. This, the largest military operation in world history, on a scale almost impossible to measure, was placing a serious strain on the German armed forces in the field and the Third Reich's economy back home.[7]

But while it was unclear whether Germany could afford to open a new front against the United States, that possibility had slowly been becoming a reality over the course of 1941. For months, Hitler's naval commanders had pressed him to declare war against the United States. Roosevelt's actions at sea, they argued, had created a de facto state of hostilities. After the *Greer* incident on September 4, *Grossadmiral* (Fleet Admiral) Erich Raeder, commander-in-chief of the Kriegsmarine, and Admiral Dönitz had pleaded with Hitler to relax the stringent rules of engagement that were hampering their operations and to allow the U-boat Force to wage unrestricted submarine warfare within twenty miles of the North American coast. Still hoping to avoid formal conflict with the United States, Hitler refused, leaving in place a complex set of regulations limiting the steps his U-boat commanders could take in an encounter with American warships. And the decision was Hitler's to make. In 1941, he reigned supreme over the German state and its armed forces through the *Führerprinzip* (leader principle), whereby, under Nazi law, he—and only he—exercised supreme political and military authority.[8]

For several days after the Pearl Harbor attack, Hitler seemed to lean against going to war with the United States, telling General Alfred Jodl that he wanted "a strong new ally [Japan] without a strong new enemy [America]." The Führer's restraint was quite remarkable, especially considering what he knew about FDR's attitudes toward Germany. In addition to confronting the suddenly changed strategic situation in the Pacific, Hitler was now fully aware that the Americans and British had created formal military plans to wage war together against Germany. Three days before the Pearl Harbor attack, the *Washington Times-Herald* and the *Chicago Tribune*, both owned by the Chicago isolationist media tycoon Robert R. McCormick, appeared with a huge headline emblazoned across the top of the front page: "F.D.R.'s WAR PLANS!" Reporter Chesly Manly had gotten hold of a copy of the top-secret Rainbow Five war plan and printed its explosive contents in minute detail. The plan called for the creation of a 10-million-man US Army, including an expeditionary force of 5 million soldiers that would invade Europe alongside the British to defeat Germany. In the United States, the Rainbow Five revelation sparked relatively little controversy. The reaction in Germany was more profound.

Within twenty-four hours of the article's publication, the entire transcript of the Rainbow Five plan was under scrutiny in Berlin. On Friday night, December 5, Field Marshal Wilhelm Keitel, chief of the Supreme Command of the Wehrmacht, huddled with Grand Admiral Raeder and Luftwaffe commander-in-chief Hermann Göring to study the war plan line by line. The three senior commanders—famous for squabbling with each other over issues great and small—made a heart-stopping discovery and instantly came to a unanimous decision. According to Rainbow Five, the United States would be unable to mount a military offensive against Germany until July 1943 at the earliest. American planners also assumed that the Soviet Union would likely collapse militarily before then. This left Germany with an eighteen-month window of opportunity. By shifting its military priority from the Soviet invasion to mounting a knockout punch against Great Britain before the United States became strong enough to intervene, Germany could forestall an Allied invasion of the continent and refocus its efforts on beating the Soviets. The Third Reich would, in effect, become impregnable.[9]

Hitler returned to Berlin on Tuesday, December 9, and convened two days of meetings with his military commanders to assess the torrent of events worldwide. His commanders urged the Führer to pull the three army groups on Soviet territory back into defensive positions to regroup and rearm, while organizing a massive new offensive to take over the entire Mediterranean basin. The generals told Hitler this move would allow them to deploy over one hundred army divisions for the capture of key targets in the Mediterranean and North Africa, effectively severing Great Britain's maritime lifeline to its colonies—which, like the United States, were a primary source of its sustenance.

Keitel, Raeder, and Göring were delighted when Hitler agreed. On December 16, after a week of intense planning, the German army headquarters staff issued a formal directive calling for a halt in offensive operations against the Red Army and a withdrawal to defensive lines. The redeployment order came just in time, for Germany and the United States suddenly found themselves formally at war.

In his "Day of Infamy" address to a joint session of Congress on December 8, Roosevelt did not mention Germany once. Instead, he focused his eloquent wrath on the Empire of Japan. The next day, however, the president gave a blistering radio address to the nation in which he lumped all three Axis nations together as a collection of "crafty and powerful bandits" led by Hitler and hell-bent on world domination. He even stretched the truth about the degree of their complicity:

> Your Government knows that for weeks Germany has been telling Japan that if Japan did not attack the United States, Japan would not share in dividing the spoils with Germany when peace came. She was promised by Germany that if she came in she would receive the complete and perpetual control of the whole of the Pacific area and that means not only the Far East, not only all of the islands in the Pacific, but also a stranglehold on the west coast of North, Central, and South America. We also know that Germany and Japan are conducting their military and naval operations in accordance with a joint plan.

If Roosevelt intended his jab at Hitler to goad the German dictator into declaring war, he succeeded brilliantly. In a rambling, eighty-eight-minute address to the Reichstag on Thursday,

December 11, Hitler thanked Providence for making him the Leader in the present "historic conflict . . . decisive in determining the next five hundred or one thousand years" of European history. He essentially blamed the twelve Nazi-occupied countries in Europe for getting themselves invaded by the Wehrmacht and held Franklin Roosevelt "primarily responsible" for the entire war. After a series of boorish and nearly obscene taunts about Roosevelt's background and personal life, Hitler recounted the US Atlantic Fleet's aggressive movements in the North Atlantic and concluded by announcing that Germany and Italy were in a state of war with the United States. Within hours, the United States reciprocated.

Keitel, Raeder, and Göring's shared elation over Hitler's agreement to radically shift Germany's offensive military priorities did not last long. Upon returning to Wolfsschanze, Hitler became furious when he learned that the Soviets had counterattacked outside Moscow, pushing German forces back in retreat. When Keitel transmitted the formal directive on December 19 that Hitler had verbally approved reposturing German army groups in the Soviet Union into defensive positions, the Führer threw a screaming fit and fired army commander-in-chief Field Marshal Walther von Brauchitsch. Hitler then took personal command of the German army and ordered it to continue offensive operations against the Soviets. As the year ended, he was still bogged down in the east and had created what he himself had long feared—in Jodl's words, "a strong new enemy." In fact, the Americans and British at that time were preparing to cement the very alliance that Hitler's generals had long dreaded.[10]

THREE DAYS AFTER HITLER SACKED VON BRAUCHITSCH and ordered the Wehrmacht to carry on its bloody offensive against the Red Army, the stately silhouette of a British battleship appeared at the mouth of the Chesapeake Bay. The 37,000-ton *HMS Duke of York* had left the Firth of Clyde outside Glasgow, Scotland, on December 12 on its shakedown cruise, just five weeks after a formal commissioning ceremony at the John Brown & Company shipyard in Clydebank. Escorted by a half dozen destroyers, the 745-foot battleship proceeded south through the Bristol Channel into the Bay of Biscay to avoid a massive winter storm in the North Atlantic. In doing so, the formation passed through U-boat-infested waters but avoided the threat with the help of British intelligence. The formation then turned west to cross the Atlantic at a lower latitude than the shorter Great Circle route, which would have brought the warships on a more northerly passage in the storm-tossed waters south of Iceland and Greenland.

In addition to its crew of 1,556 officers and enlisted men, the *Duke of York* carried Prime Minister Winston Churchill, his senior military commanders and political advisers, and a delegation of more than eighty officials heading to a critical conference in Washington with President Roosevelt and his military commanders. After the warship docked at the Norfolk Naval Station at 4:15 P.M., Churchill and his delegation flew to Washington, DC, where the president himself met them at the airport. The summit, known formally as the First Washington Conference and informally by the British as Arcadia, began the next morning.[11]

Roosevelt and Churchill were well acquainted by the time the two leaders shook hands at the Washington-area airport, although they had previously met in person only twice. In July 1918, Roosevelt, then assistant secretary of the navy, traveled to Great Britain on official wartime business. At a dinner organized by his British hosts, the thirty-six-year-old Roosevelt met Churchill, who at forty-three had already served (and been forced to resign in 1915) as Britain's first lord of the Admiralty. Churchill was at that time serving as minister of munitions. It was an inauspicious start to what would become one of the most important friendships of the twentieth century. Churchill later said he did not remember the encounter at all, while FDR left the evening with an active "dislike" for Churchill's brusqueness.

Twenty-one years later, however, in the fall of 1939, circumstances and events prompted Roosevelt to reach out to Churchill. On learning that his onetime British acquaintance had become first lord of the Admiralty for the second time, FDR wrote Churchill to tell him "how glad I am that you are back here in the Admiralty." He and Churchill began a secret correspondence in which they exchanged news and opinions on the deteriorating political landscape in Europe. This relationship blossomed and deepened even as the war news went from bad to worse for the British and French. It became a truly personal friendship, even though each man had obvious political interest in the other. FDR wanted to maintain a link to the Englishman who, he correctly foresaw, would be the United Kingdom's next prime minister, and Churchill was keen on keeping Roosevelt interested in British affairs and supportive of its wartime goals.

Behind closed and guarded doors at the Washington Conference, the American and British military commanders discussed the proper course of action for their alliance in the months and years ahead. The British goal was simple: ensure that the goals of the ABC-1 war planners remain intact, with top priority given to defeating Germany first. Nevertheless, Roosevelt, Churchill, and the military leaders could not ignore the rapidly deteriorating situation in the Far East. They spent many hours debating how to organize an effective defense against the advancing Japanese. The British had suffered their own major defeat three days after Pearl Harbor when land-based Japanese aircraft sank the battleship HMS *Prince of Wales* and the battle cruiser HMS *Repulse* off the Malay coast, with heavy loss of life. At the same time, Roosevelt and Churchill alike believed it imperative for American and British soldiers to go on the offensive against Germany as early as possible in 1942, both to bolster morale on their respective home fronts and to reassure Soviet dictator Joseph Stalin that he was not fighting the Germans alone.[12]

By Sunday, January 11, the Arcadia Conference participants had hammered out a priority list of actions to be taken during the upcoming year. The measures ranged from rushing reinforcements to the newly formed American-British-Dutch-Australian (ABDA) Command in the Far East, to continuing the flow of Lend-Lease war supplies to the Soviet Union, to deploying US marines to Iceland to enable British troops there to transfer to the Middle East. The leaders also discussed two possible Allied offensives, including an Anglo-American invasion of North Africa and a possible emergency operation to land Allied troops in France in late 1942 to relieve the pressure placed by the German army on the Soviet Union.

At this juncture, the Allied leaders collided with a very hard reality: there were neither enough combat-ready army units nor enough merchant ships available to carry out those high-priority missions on the schedule that the leaders wanted. Most of the initiatives would be delayed for months because of the United States' general unpreparedness. Both American and British leaders bitterly lamented the shipping shortage. Churchill himself wrote, "Shipping was at once the stranglehold and sole foundation of our war strategy."

To address the shortfall in merchant shipping, Roosevelt pledged a massive expansion of new construction in American shipyards, doubling the objective that his administration had just announced in early December. FDR now told his administration that he wanted to increase the merchant shipbuilding goal from 12 million deadweight tons (5 million in 1942 and 7 million in 1943) to 24 million tons (9 million in 1942 and 15 million in 1943). That translated to a crash program to build 2,250 new tankers, freighters, and bulk carriers within a twenty-two-month period.

FDR and Churchill most strongly advocated the Arcadia Conference recommendation to reinforce Northern Ireland with American soldiers. While third on the final priority list, the deployment of American soldiers to Iceland and Northern Ireland would constitute a very public demonstration of the Anglo-American military partnership; it would also serve as a boon to British civilian morale and confirmation to Stalin that the Allies were on the move.

When US Army Chief of Staff George C. Marshall told the conference that 4,100 soldiers comprising an advance guard of the 34th Infantry Division would sail from New York for Belfast on January 15, Churchill exclaimed, "It is of the greatest importance that these troops get to their destination at the earliest possible moment." He would soon have reason to regret his enthusiasm.[13]

U-BOAT FORCE HEADQUARTERS IN LORIENT, FRANCE, was a beehive of activity during the last three weeks of December 1941. Working out of a crowded operations center in a handsome four-story château near the Lorient waterfront, Admiral Dönitz and his staff kept close watch on the U-boats assigned to Lorient and the four other Biscay ports. The same Sunday night that the B-Dienst message announcing the attack on Pearl Harbor arrived at Hitler's command bunker in East Prussia, a similar text came clattering out of a teleprinter at BdU's communications center.

While Dönitz's superiors in the German Naval Staff and senior officers in the other armed services were stunned by the news, at Kernével the admiral and his operations officers regarded the entry of the United States into the war with "relief," as one senior staff officer later described it. Dönitz and his U-boat commanders had endured a very frustrating year. In addition to heeding Hitler's insistence that they adhere to strict rules of engagement so as not to exacerbate relations with Washington, both Grand Admiral Raeder and his Naval Staff—as well as the Führer himself—were constantly diverting U-boats to secondary missions, thus depleting the number of boats available for attacks on Allied merchant shipping in the North Atlantic. Thirty-two-year-old *Fregattenkapitän* (Junior Captain) Günter Hessler, who had just joined the headquarters as senior staff officer under Dönitz (and who was also the admiral's son-in-law), described the sense of frustration at BdU: "No senior officer of the German Navy was more emphatic than Dönitz that the issue of the war depended on sinking as much enemy shipping as possible. . . . The Naval Staff [under Grand Admiral Raeder] made every effort to weigh the advantages and disadvantages of the auxiliary tasks requested of the U-boats, but too often circumstances such as the Führer's orders, requests from the Supreme Command, crises in the various theaters of war . . . forced them to act." Between July and early December 1941, U-boats were deployed as weather stations to aid the Luftwaffe's aerial attacks against Great Britain. They were ordered to serve as escorts for German surface raiders and blockade-runners. Eight training U-boats at Kiel were reassigned to protect the maritime flank of Army Group North as it swept through the Baltic States. Six U-boats were transferred to Norway to attack Soviet shipping. Nor was that the worst: the deteriorating position of the Afrika Korps in North Africa in late November 1941 prompted Raeder's staff to order BdU to station no fewer than twenty-five U-boats in the eastern Mediterranean and approaches to the Strait of Gibraltar. By December 10, of eighty-six operational U-boats, fifty were either operating in the Mediterranean or on standby to relieve others on patrol. Most of the remaining thirty-six U-boats were either unavailable for North Atlantic service due to repairs or operating in other theaters, such as the Arctic or South Atlantic. Hitler's fixation on the Mediterranean, Hessler later recalled, "had brought our Atlantic operations almost to a standstill."

The Pearl Harbor attack completely changed Hitler's outlook. Dönitz must have breathed a sigh of relief as he wrote the BdU War Diary entry for December 9, 1941: "The lifting of all restrictions regarding U.S.A. ships and the so-called Pan-American safety zone has been ordered by the Führer," the admiral wrote. "Therefore, the whole area of the American coasts will become open for operations by U-boats. . . . There is an opportunity here, therefore, of intercepting enemy merchant ships under conditions which have ceased almost completely for some time." Whereas the U-boats had to contend with enormous distances and dedicated escorts out in the open ocean, along the American shore ships plied predictable routes, and the American defenses were almost nonexistent. Dönitz, his operations chief Fregattenkapitän Eberhard Godt, and Hessler began plotting a massive strike against Allied merchant ships along the US East Coast, which, Hessler noted, was suddenly the richest target area in the Atlantic. And the U-boats were ready: "After two and one-half years' war experience our crews were at the peak of efficiency, while the American [antisubmarine warfare defenses] and air forces would lack experience," Hessler added.[14]

The sense of reprieve at BdU did not last long. Almost immediately, Dönitz realized that executing his new plan would be much more complex than he had thought. Godt and Hessler quickly calculated that only the long-range Type IX boats could reach the US East Coast, patrol for several weeks, and then return safely. The smaller Type VIIC boats could just barely reach Canadian waters off Newfoundland and Nova Scotia by proceeding at slow speed using one diesel engine to save fuel. BdU sent a message to Raeder's office requesting the release of twelve IXB or IXC U-boats for what was being called Operation Paukenschlag (Drumbeat). The following day, Raeder's staff informed Dönitz that he could only have six, so he decided to increase the westbound force by adding seven (later expanded to twelve) Type VIIB and VIIC "medium" U-boats to patrol off northeastern Canada. If they could not join the hunt along the eastern seaboard of the United States, at least they could prowl the waters at the western end of the transatlantic convoy routes for any ships that managed to evade the Type IX boats.

During the next three weeks, U-boat flotilla commanders in France and Germany worked around the clock preparing the six Type IX boats assigned to Operation Drumbeat and twelve Type VII U-boats that would hunt in the Newfoundland–Nova Scotia area. Dönitz ordered the six Type IX boats to leave first. Beginning with U-502 and U-125 on December 18, the long-range boats set out across the Bay of Biscay. U-123 and U-130 departed five days later on December 23, with U-66 following on Christmas Day and the last IX boat, U-109, leaving port on December 27. The medium Type VII boats departed during a ten-day period between December 21 and 31. Included in that mix were five Type VII boats scheduled to leave Kiel on their initial combat patrols between December 24 and 30. One of them was Horst Degen's U-701.[15]

3

FIRST MOVES

THE FOUR LOOKOUTS PERCHED ON THE U-BOAT'S CRAMPED bridge scanned the horizon for the first sign of the enemy. High above a thin cloud layer, the waxing moon, three days from full, transformed the surface of the sea into bright liquid mercury. Wrapped in thick clothing against the subfreezing Arctic temperature, the men savored a rare calm.

On the bridge with the three other lookouts, Kapitänleutnant Horst Degen hunched over and spoke firmly into the voice tube connecting him with the radio room. "Send by short signal: 'Have passed 60:50N. U-701.'" Down below in the small compartment, the two radiomen on watch began encrypting the message that would inform U-boat Force Headquarters in Lorient that as of midnight on New Year's Eve 1941, the U-boat was nearly finished threading the hazardous, 110-nautical-mile-wide passage between the western coast of Norway and the Scottish Shetland Islands.

Degen and his crewmen were at battle stations. Standing lookout atop the bridge in addition to Degen were thirty-one-year-old Oberleutnant zur See Erwin Batzies, a naval reservist serving as the second watch officer (2WO), twenty-eight-year-old *Obersteuermann* (Chief Quartermaster) Günter Kunert, the boat's navigator, and an enlisted crewman. Even though not a commissioned officer, Kunert was an experienced seaman who had spent years in the German merchant marine. Degen had grown to respect his abilities as a navigator and later referred to him as "my best friend" on the boat. On the bridge, Degen and the other three kept their eyes peeled behind powerful Zeiss binoculars as each swept a ninety-degree arc. They had left the German port of Brunsbüttel three days before and were transiting an area of maximum danger. Several hours earlier, the boat had passed within thirty nautical miles of the Royal Navy Fleet anchorage at Scapa Flow, home to scores of British warships. Nor was that all. For the next five days, U-701 would steam on the surface within range of land-based British antisubmarine aircraft operating from Scotland, the Hebrides, and Northern Ireland. U-boat commanders such as Degen were very aware that nine U-boats crossing the North Sea and the east-west passage between Scotland and the Faroes had been lost thus far in the war.[1]

Down below in the crowded, cramped U-boat, the other forty-two crewmen were also performing their battle station tasks, edging around the spare torpedoes, stacks of canned food, and other supplies as they quietly moved about. Despite the severe congestion, the young men were acclimated to their environment and well versed in their assignments after the months of combat drills in the Baltic.

In their nearly seven months together, Degen and his men had forged a tight bond. "Our lieutenant commander was a very correct and friendly officer despite his high command responsibility,"

Kapitänleutnant Horst Degen (with white U-boat commander's hat) musters the crew of U-701 on the U-boat's main deck prior to getting underway on patrol. COURTESY OF HORST DEGEN.

Gerhard Schwendel recalled of Degen many years later. "He was never authoritarian, but he always tried to maintain a good relationship with his team. He was thoroughly human." Other crewmen would also describe Degen as a warm and caring man. But he was far from a pushover, as *Oberfunkmaat* (Radioman 2nd Class) Herbert Grotheer had found out four days earlier.

When U-701 docked at Brunsbüttel for an overnight stopover before heading to sea on December 27, Degen had released two-thirds of the crew to go ashore for dinner. Grotheer and other sailors decided to visit the Hamburger Hof, a restaurant and pub popular with U-boat crewmen. The husband and wife

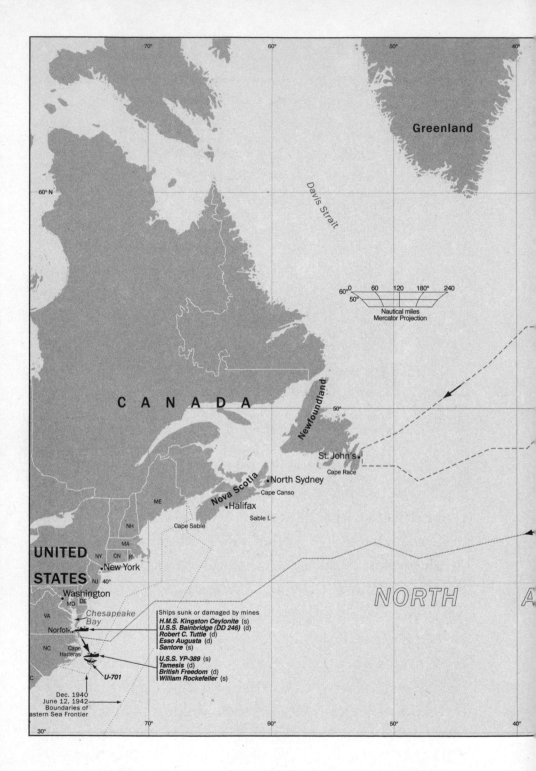

Greenland

Davis Strait

60° N

CANADA

Newfoundland

50°

St. John's

Cape Race

North Sydney

Cape Canso

Nova Scotia

Halifax

Sable I.

ME

Cape Sable

NH

MA

UNITED

NY   CN   RI

STATES

New York

NJ   40°

Washington

MD   DE

VA

Chesapeake
Bay

Norfolk

Ships sunk or damaged by mines
H.M.S. Kingston Ceylonite (s)
U.S.S. Bainbridge (DD 246) (d)
Robert C. Tuttle (d)
Esso Augusta (d)
Santore (s)

NC

Cape
Hatteras

U.S.S. YP-389 (s)
Tamesis (d)
British Freedom (d)
William Rockefeller (s)

C

U-701

Dec. 1940
June 12, 1942
Boundaries of
Eastern Sea Frontier

NORTH   A

60°   0   60   120   180°   240
50°

Nautical miles
Mercator Projection

30°

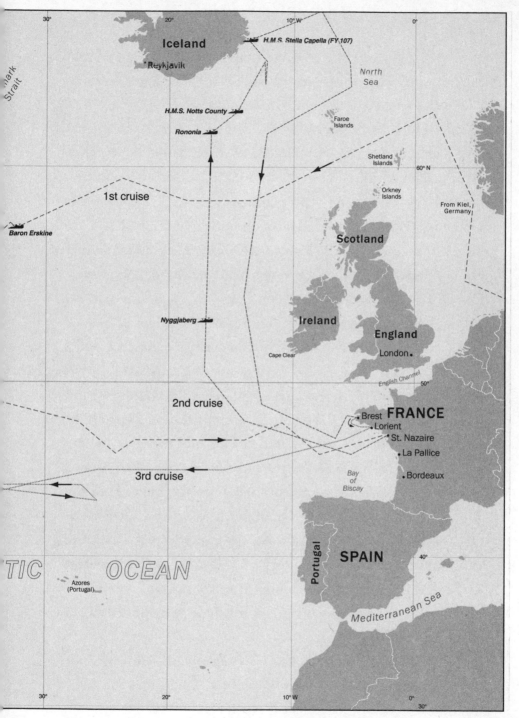

During its three war patrols, U-701 operated throughout the North Atlantic hunting for Allied merchant ships. ILLUSTRATION BY ROBERT E. PRATT.

proprietors ushered the sailors to a table and took their orders, then returned with a large guest book for them to sign. Grotheer turned the pages of the book and found the signatures of several of Germany's highest U-boat aces, including Kapitänleutnant Joachim Schepke. A recipient of the *Ritterkreuz* (Knight's Cross), Schepke was credited with sinking thirty-seven Allied merchant ships totaling 155,882 gross registered tons between September 1939 and his death the previous March. "U-100 expresses its gratitude for the lovely farewell evening at Hamburger Hof and looks forward to meet again during the next passage," he had written. "For the time being, we have great plans, and want to fight out there and win. Heil Hitler—Schepke."

As a trained radioman with a high security clearance, Grotheer had found the roster of U-boat visits to Brunsbüttel worrisome. He excused himself and returned to U-701 where he found Degen and told him of the potential security threat. Degen himself then went ashore and visited the Hamburger Hof, where the pub owners showed him the guest book and asked him to sign. He took a pen and signed his name but also blotted out the "U-701" that a crewman had added to the other U-701 crewmen's signatures. Degen then wrote an urgent report about the guest book and had it transmitted to U-boat Force Headquarters by wireless from the U-boat tender tied up nearby. Degen later said he learned that "the entire establishment had been taken apart" by security officials.

At 0400 hours on December 31, Degen went below and ordered a slight course change from 332 to 320 degrees as U-701 began the northwest leg of its trip, which would take it between the northern tip of Scotland and the Faroes. After napping for several hours, he then sat at the small dining table with several off-duty officers, including *Leutnant zur See* (Lieutenant j.g.) Bernfried Weinitschke. At 0745, the twenty-two-year-old Weinitschke, U-701's first watch officer (1WO), stood up to put on his foul-weather gear and ascended the conning tower ladder with three enlisted men to stand the 0800–1200 lookout watch. Degen was still relaxing over coffee when a loud cry suddenly came down from the bridge: "Man overboard! The 1WO has fallen overboard!"[2]

IN EARLY JANUARY 1942, 2ND LIEUTENANT HARRY KANE was not a happy man. While many U-boat men like Degen and his crew had already gone through basic training and were embarking on combat missions, the majority of American servicemen—land, sea, and air—were much less prepared for battle. The US armed forces as a whole, in fact, were ill equipped for the task before them—something that Harry Kane was finding out the hard way.

Kane found himself assigned to a medium bomber squadron stationed at a backwater base, flying what he called a "simply awful" aircraft and preparing to defend against a Japanese enemy that few pilots genuinely believed would reappear in the aftermath of Pearl Harbor.

The 396th Medium Bombardment Squadron was one of several hundred US Army Air Forces units (USAAF) created in early 1941 during the air service's rapid expansion program. It was originally designated the 6th Medium Reconnaissance Squadron upon its activation on January 15 at March Army Airfield outside Riverside, California, but renamed the 396th Medium Bombardment Squadron several months later. For a long time it wasn't much of a squadron. Under USAAF procedures, a parent unit—in this case, the 38th Heavy Reconnaissance Squadron—provided an initial cadre of one commissioned officer and three dozen enlisted men. Its mission for the first five months of 1941 had been to perform "garrison duties" for the parent squadron: cleanup, mess hall, and other manual labor. Meanwhile, new personnel trickled in. In early May, the unit transferred from March Field to Davis-Monthan Army Airfield in Tucson, Arizona, with a complement of five officers and sixty-eight enlisted men. The 396th didn't even get its first assigned aircraft until May 16, and it wasn't much of an aircraft: a Boeing Stearman PT-17, practically identical to the PT-13 biplane that the airmen had flown in primary flight training. Several weeks later, USAAF officials turned up a second Stearman, and that summer, the steadily growing squadron—up to eleven officers and 218 enlisted men—turned in the trainers for two patrol bombers that, to most army pilots, were just as useless as the biplanes.

By 1941, army aviators considered the Douglas Aircraft B-18 Bolo bomber to be inadequate in every respect. It was underpowered, it flew too slowly, and it carried an inadequate bomb load of just 4,400 pounds. Its defensive armament consisted of only three .30-cal. machine guns. A variant of the Douglas DC-2 airliner first flown in 1935, the Bolo was fifty-seven feet long with an eighty-nine-foot wingspan and stood fifteen feet high. Its two Wright R-1820-53 radial engines gave the aircraft a maximum speed of only 216 miles per hour, a range of just 900 miles, and a service ceiling of 23,900 feet. In contrast, the four-engine Boeing B-17 could carry up to 8,000 pounds of ordnance at 287 miles per hour and had a range of 2,000 miles and a service ceiling of 35,600 feet. Compared with the Bolo's three .30-cal.

machine guns, the Flying Fortress bristled with thirteen .50-cal. machine guns for defense against enemy fighters.

The day after Pearl Harbor, the 396th had transferred from Tucson to Muroc Bombing and Gunnery Range (today Edwards Air Force Base) in the Southern California desert, more than seventy miles inland from the coast. Then, on January 8, officials at Fourth Air Force Headquarters at March Field transferred the squadron to Sacramento Municipal Airport. The officers and enlisted men camped out in tents at the Sacramento Junior College stadium grounds. There, Kane was assigned as a junior copilot in the B-18 Bolo. Kane would later remember,

> We were known as the second line of defense. Every morning about three o'clock . . . pitch black dark, we, the crew, from the copilot on back through all the enlisted personnel, would have to be in the B-18's, have them cranked up, warmed up, ready to go. Of course, the older pilots could all stay in the operations room, keep warm, and all that business; but we had to stay in the airplane and keep the engines going and so forth. They would keep us out there usually with the engines running until daylight, and then they'd cut them off, and that was the end of that.

For someone with dreams of soaring through the skies, this daily routine quickly became a tedious, frustrating task.[3]

FOR THE MEN IN U-701 AND OTHER OPERATIONAL U-BOATS, the frustrations of training were a thing of the past—and the terrors of active duty were all too real. Degen and the crew of U-701 got their first taste in the waning hours of 1941.

Holding to a course of 320 degrees, due northwest, U-701 had been plowing through moderate seas in the predawn darkness with short, high swells occasionally breaking over the tower. Suddenly, a loud banging startled the four lookouts on the narrow bridge. Lieutenant Bernfried Weinitschke, the senior man on lookout watch, leaned over the rail and saw that a wave had knocked open the starboard ammunition hatch. A tall, muscular young man who had excelled in sports as a teenager, Weinitschke unbuckled his steel safety belt and scrambled over the rail to close the swinging hatch cover. His back turned to the sea, he failed to spot the rogue wave that suddenly fell on U-701. In an instant, he was gone.

Degen raced up the ladder, his heart pounding, ordering the helmsman to reverse course and bring the boat back to the spot on the heaving ocean where his 1WO had gone in. He ordered a portable searchlight illuminated to try to find Weinitschke amid the waves. After ten minutes, the lookouts could hear faint cries, and for an instant, the searchlight provided a glimpse of the young officer. Then, he disappeared once more amid the waves.

After a futile half hour of additional searching, Degen had to give up. He ordered his engine room to light off the second diesel motor and put U-701 back on a new course of 250 degrees to begin its west-southwest track into the open North Atlantic. One crewman later said the U-boat was too close to the British coast for them to safely linger. "We had brought ourselves into danger," Schwendel recalled.

Any sense of grief among U-701's crew over the loss of their 1WO did not last long. Pushing the boat's course track to a new, southwesterly slant, Degen and his men spent the rest of New

Enlisting in the German navy at the age of eighteen, Gerhard Schwendel was a fireman 1st class aboard U-701 throughout its wartime service. Courtesy of Gerhard Schwendel.

Year's Eve coping with a brewing North Atlantic storm whose thirty-mile-per-hour winds pushed the waves up to nearly fifteen feet. Foam and spray tore into the soaked bridge watch as 1941 ended. Down in the radio room at three minutes before midnight, an encrypted message came in from Admiral Dönitz: "Men of the U-boat Service: In the year anew we want to be like steel, harder, fiercer. Long live the Führer. BdU."[4]

On New Year's Day 1942, the German U-boat Force—on paper—appeared stronger than ever. Admiral Dönitz could count a fleet of 248 commissioned U-boats, including 162 of the workhorse Type VIIs and 50 of the larger Type IX boats. However, the number actually available for North Atlantic operations was quite small. BdU was able to send only thirty-three boats into the North Atlantic during December 1941 prior to the deployment of the six Type IX boats to Operation Drumbeat and the eight (later twelve) Type VIIs ordered to the Newfoundland area in a separate wolf pack, identified as Gruppe Ziethen. The rest were undergoing repairs, preparing for departure on patrol later in January or February, or assigned to other operational areas such as Norway and the Mediterranean.

Writing in his command war diary two days earlier, a glum Dönitz had noted, "The war in the Atlantic has been suspended for weeks now—the first objective must be to resume it with new forces as soon and thoroughly as possible." Disappointed that the Naval High Command had released only six of the larger, long-range Type IXB and IXC boats for Operation Drumbeat, Dönitz and the BdU operations staff at Lorient devised a deployment order that aimed to maximize their impact along the US East Coast. "Their object must be to intercept *single* vessels and to make use of the enemy's inexperience and the fact that [the Americans] are not used to operations by U-boats," Dönitz explained. "For this purpose, operations must not and cannot be too massed; rather the boats should spread to such an extent that good prospects of success are ensured."

Inexperience was a major handicap for US coastal defenders up and down the eastern seaboard, but BdU would have to wait for more U-boat deployments before taking full advantage of the Americans' weakness. For now, it would make most sense to focus on those parts of the coastline where ships would be gathering in the largest concentrations before heading across the Atlantic in guarded convoys. Accordingly, Dönitz decided, for the initial strike, to send three of the long-range U-boats to the area of New York and the second trio up around Halifax, Nova Scotia, to operate in proximity with the Type VII U-boats in Gruppe Ziethen. Other fruitful hunting grounds, such as the Florida coastline, the Caribbean, and the Gulf of Mexico would have to wait until more long-range U-boats became available.[5]

Like the Americans, the crew of U-701 were still inexperienced in combat, although Horst Degen and Obersteuermann Günter Kunert had previously experienced war at sea—Degen on the destroyer *Hans Lody* and his patrol with Erich Topp in U-552 and Kunert in another U-boat. Like the other four U-boat crews en route to their first combat patrol out of Kiel, the crewmen on U-701 kept up with their shipboard tasks while trying to remember all of the lessons they had taken in during their training in the Baltic. Making life even more difficult, U-701 was steaming into the teeth of a fierce winter storm. "In this confined space it was not pleasant," Gerhard Schwendel recalled. "We were all tense. We knew nothing about the hardships of the Battle of the Atlantic."

Two days after Weinitschke was lost at sea, the waiting came to an abrupt end. On Friday morning, January 2, at 0700 hours Greenwich Mean Time, U-701 was about 150 miles southwest of the Faroes. The storm was easing from a fresh gale down to a moderate breeze. Despite the light overcast, the full moon—which would not set for another two and a half hours—illuminated the heavy swells over which the boat was moving. The lookouts taking position on the bridge were as alert as the outgoing watch when, suddenly, a hail came from the bridge.

U-701 was close ahead of an eastbound Allied convoy. Degen ordered a ninety-degree turn to port to avoid running into its escorts and leaped up the ladder. "When I arrive on the bridge, I see close astern, in moonlight bright as day, about 30 medium-sized steamers," Degen wrote in his war diary. "Because the horizon behind U-701 is dark, the enemy lookouts cannot detect the U-boat as it rises and falls in the heavy swells," he added. "What an opportunity!" Degen called his crew to battle stations.

Unbeknownst to Degen, he was shadowing eastbound Convoy HX166, consisting of twenty-eight merchant ships with a total cargo capacity of 195,744 gross registered tons. The formation was twelve days out of Halifax, Nova Scotia, with a diverse cargo of military supplies, grain, meat, cotton, and wheat. Of particular value were the eleven oil tankers whose holds were awash in 93,341 tons of avgas, benzene, paraffin, and other petroleum products. Five US Navy warships had escorted HX166 to the mid-ocean meeting point south of Iceland, where on New Year's Eve they had handed it off to an American escort group of four destroyers and one *Treasury*-class coast guard cutter. On New Year's Day, a local escort formation of four British destroyers and two corvettes had relieved the US Navy escort group northwest of Scotland's Isle of Lewis for the final leg of the convoy's journey.

After a crash dive to avoid one of the escorts, Degen surfaced at 0810 to find the convoy on a course of 155 degrees and just six nautical miles away. Two hours later, he ordered Radioman 2nd Class Herbert Grotheer to flash a "convoy sighted" message to BdU Operations. When the convoy made a turn to starboard five minutes later, Degen described the situation as ideal: "The last 10 steamers, including a big tanker, appear to us as a wide, broad group before the bright horizon." With the eastern horizon steadily brightening, Degen realized he could no longer wait to close the range.

At 0910, Oberleutnant zur See Batzies, filling in for the lost Weinitschke, turned the firing lever, and four G7e electric torpedoes raced out of the forward tubes toward the merchant ships 3,800 yards away. Three minutes later, Degen reversed course and launched a G7e from his solitary stern tube. The seconds ticked by with no sign of impact and detonation. All missed. With the Scottish coast only seventy-four nautical miles to the southeast, Degen decided not to press his luck in a follow-up attack and ordered U-701 to resume its west-southwest heading.

Four days later, U-701's luck turned. The boat had traveled 718 nautical miles out into the North Atlantic and was now proceeding down the broad oceanic corridor where east- and westbound convoys moved in their journeys between North America and Great Britain. It was evening twilight when his lookouts spotted smoke and masts bearing to port. Accelerating to sixteen knots, Degen maneuvered the boat to pass ahead of the solitary merchantman and then crash-dived. Within thirty minutes, the freighter had closed to within 5,400 yards. He waited until the ship was only nine hundred yards off and then ordered a spread of two torpedoes. This time, the men of U-701 felt twin shock waves slam into their vessel's hull, and when he raised the periscope, Degen saw two towering columns of water where the two 620-pound warheads had exploded against the merchantman's hull.

After the boat surfaced, Degen, Batzies, and two lookouts scrambled onto the bridge. The ship was sinking fast by the bow, its forecastle already submerged. A distant flurry of motion told them the crew was abandoning ship. Degen slowly approached the scene and edged U-701 within earshot of the lifeboats and several life rafts. Ship's master George Sharp Cumming and thirty-three crewmen from the 3,657-ton British freighter *Baron Erskine* had been en route from Tampa, Florida, to Loch Ewe, Scotland, with a cargo of phosphates when the twin blasts rocked their ship. They were now helpless hostages to the North Atlantic in winter. Degen asked the crewmen in one boat for the name of their ship, and someone replied falsely that it was the *Baron Haig*. Degen then ordered *Matrosengefreiter* (Seaman 2nd Class) Alfred Wallaschek, the U-boat's twenty-one-year-old cook, to bring up a supply of food, liquor, and tobacco for the stranded merchant sailors. He also gave the British crewmen the best course to land: Reykjavik, Iceland, was 475 nautical miles to the north-northeast. Degen's act of generosity toward the British crew came to naught; they were never seen again, perishing in the next winter storm that blew over the North Atlantic.

Breaking off from the stricken merchantman, U-701 resumed its transit toward Newfoundland on a course of 230 degrees at seven knots, its crew pleased that they had succeeded in sinking an Allied merchant ship. But to their disappointment and frustration, the fates once more conspired against the U-boat.

Just forty-five minutes after the *Baron Erskine* slipped beneath the waves, Degen's lookouts sighted another steamer about forty-five degrees off the starboard bow steering a northeast course toward the British Isles. Despite the overcast sky and steadily deepening twilight gloom, Degen called his crew to battle stations and turned to a course of 340 degrees to intercept. When

the U-boat and its target closed to 1,000 yards, Degen fired two
G7e electrics with a running speed of thirty knots. The seconds ticked by, and then something strange occurred. Peering
through his Zeiss binoculars, Degen could see no sign of a warhead detonation; yet a loud cheering suddenly erupted down in
the U-boat's interior. Not only Herbert Grotheer manning the
passive hydrophone listening gear but all of the crew throughout
the boat had heard two loud thuds. Both torpedoes had struck
the 7,000-ton enemy merchantman, but their warheads failed
to detonate. Even more surprisingly, the ship neither changed
course nor radioed an emergency message signaling that it was
under attack. "Has he not noticed anything?" Degen later wrote
in his war diary. "Run ahead and initiate a new attack. It is completely dark. I want to shoot before the moon sets." Turning to
a new heading of 300 degrees, with the target bearing 327 degrees true, Degen ordered U-701 to close to five hundred yards
and then fired two more G7es from the other pair of bow tubes,
aiming at the freighter's port side. Both missed. Thoroughly frustrated, Degen ran off at a new course of forty degrees from the
ship and fired his last torpedo from the stern tube, again from a
nearly point-blank range. Another miss.

With four weeks remaining on his first combat patrol, Degen
now commanded a nearly unarmed U-boat. Since sighting the
convoy five days earlier on January 2, he had expended all twelve
torpedoes stored inside U-701's pressure hull, leaving only two
G7a compressed-air torpedoes in above-deck storage canisters. "I
now have no more torpedoes in the boat," Degen noted. "Hope-
fully good weather will come, in order to reload [from] the upper
deck tubes." Even that wish, however, would go unfulfilled.

For the next week, U-701 struggled into the teeth of an unrelenting winter storm. Unable to reload his boat with the two deck-stored G7as, Degen realized that the rest of his patrol would likely pass with U-701 operating as "a reconnaissance and reporting unit" directing other U-boats to any Allied ships that his lookouts might spot. His next set of orders, however, suggested that Degen might have at least one more chance to sink another merchant ship. At 1337 hours on January 13, BdU ordered Degen to proceed to a designated attack area just off the southeastern coast of Newfoundland, more than six hundred nautical miles to the west-southwest. A somber Degen recorded in his diary, "My attack area still lies far away." U-701 struggled on through the towering waves.[6]

4

WAR IN
THE ETHER

EVEN AS HORST DEGEN AND HIS MEN CONTINUED THEIR storm-tossed patrol, a wolf pack of five longer-range Type IX U-boats was headed for the North American coast (a sixth, U-502, had been forced to abort its patrol due to a serious oil leak). Other lone hunters also stalked the deep of the North Atlantic, each on its own mission, each fighting to survive long enough to carry out the orders from U-boat Force Headquarters in Lorient.

One of these lone hunters, a Type VIIC U-boat, was proceeding in a westerly heading some seven hundred miles due south of Iceland—a course not unlike those of the Gruppe Ziethen boats designated to attack Allied shipping off the Newfoundland Grand Banks. However, on Wednesday, January 7, 1942, U-653 was carrying out a radically different operation on behalf of Admiral Karl Dönitz. Like his academy classmate Horst Degen, thirty-two-year-old Kapitänleutnant Gerhard Feiler was on his first wartime patrol since U-653's formal commissioning seven months earlier. Unlike Degen, who was about two

77

hundred nautical miles to the northwest of U-653 and heading for Cape Race on the southeastern Newfoundland coast, Feiler had orders to remain in the central North Atlantic. For the past two weeks, Feiler's four radiomen, working around the clock, had transmitted fake encrypted radio messages on a variety of different frequencies. Dönitz noted in the BdU *Kriegstagebüch* (daily war diary) that Feiler's mission was "to form a radio decoy . . . which will give the impression of the presence of a large number of U-boats in the Atlantic." U-653, a single boat, was attempting to create the electromagnetic footprint of an entire wolf pack.

The false radio gambit was one small element of a second front in the Battle of the Atlantic that remained cloaked in the highest secrecy. While the U-boats, Allied escort warships and aircraft, and embattled merchant vessels conducted their overt struggle at sea, U-653's radiomen, together with a larger group of scientists, mathematicians, and code breakers, waged this invisible war across the electromagnetic spectrum, with most of its participants on both sides huddled in top-secret monitoring stations and other guarded facilities ashore.

The U-boat campaign against Allied shipping depended on Admiral Dönitz's ability to send and receive secure communications between his headquarters in Lorient and U-boats at sea. When U-boat commanders operating in the open ocean reported sightings of Allied merchant convoys, BdU Operations—aware of the location of U-boats in the area from their daily position reports—could then redeploy them to intercept the merchant ships. Similarly, the code breakers at B-Dienst in Berlin gleaned the location and future course tracks of Allied convoys by intercepting and decrypting messages between the Royal Navy's

Western Approaches Command in Liverpool and convoy escort groups at sea. The British, in turn, were running an equally ambitious cryptologic campaign against the entire German armed forces, with a particularly intense effort against encrypted U-boat communications.

In what would later be recognized as one of the great ironies of World War II, both the Germans and Allies by early 1942 had succeeded in penetrating their enemy's most carefully guarded naval communications without the other side knowing it. When U-boats suddenly swarmed around an embattled convoy, Allied flag officers attributed the incident to chance and the Germans' good luck rather than successful code breaking. So, too, when a series of convoys successfully evaded U-boats positioned athwart their line of advance, BdU more times than not blamed the weather or random chance for preventing German lookouts from sighting the distant masts and smoke plumes of several dozen merchantmen. The thought that one's own encrypted communications might be open to the enemy was too painful to consider.

When Admiral Dönitz gathered with his operations staff at the château at Kernével Harbor on that first Wednesday in January for the daily morning conference to assess U-boat operations, Kapitänleutnant Feiler's radio deception operation remained foremost in their thoughts. As he did on most mornings, Dönitz would have paused for several minutes to study the oversize copy of the "1870G Nord-Atlantischer Ozean" chart that hung on one wall of the operations center.

Unlike most nautical maps that relied on latitude and longitude marks to help pinpoint ship locations, the German naval chart featured a dense matrix of numbered squares covering

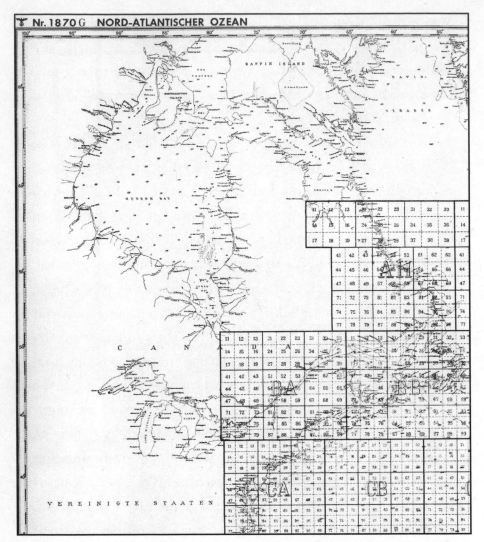

The German Naval Grid system utilized a two-letter, four-number code to indicate positions of U-boats and convoys while avoiding standard latitude-longitude references that would enable Allied code breakers to penetrate BdU communications. HER MAJESTY'S STATIONERY OFFICE, UNITED KINGDOM.

the oceanic areas on the map. From above Iceland to the South Atlantic and Indian Oceans, a series of quadrants, each identified with a two-letter code and measuring 486 nautical miles per side, marked off the trackless ocean. Inside each lettered quadrant were between sixty-eight and eighty-eight smaller squares identified by a two-digit number, measuring fifty-four miles per side. And within each of those secondary quadrants, yet another subdivision of eighty-one numbered squares marked a relatively tiny swath of ocean measuring six by six nautical miles. Ordered into effect on September 10, 1941, this was the German navy's unique way of plotting U-boat positions, enemy contacts, and convoy routes.

Rather than identifying a designated location by latitude and longitude—a recurring numerical pattern that security officials feared would facilitate enemy code-breaking efforts—the Kriegsmarine had created the German naval grid system. When a U-boat reported a convoy contact or the BdU staff issued a redeployment order to a U-boat commander, the message used the two-letter, four-number grid reference (see naval grid chart on p. 80). In an attempt to complicate enemy code breaking, radiomen would also encipher the grid square references themselves in a separate process to mask their true identity. Festooning the chart that Wednesday were twenty-eight pins depicting the U-boats on patrol in the North Atlantic, including the seventeen boats—U-701 among them—bound for North American coastal waters. Gerhard Feiler's pin was affixed to grid square AL 44, nearly five hundred nautical miles south of Iceland. All but four of the U-boats headed for North America had passed to the west or southwest of U-653.

During the course of the morning staff briefings, Korvetten-kapitän Günter Hessler, Dönitz's senior operations officer, informed the admiral that Feiler would be breaking off to return to port later that day because of a low fuel state. This marked the end of a counterintelligence ploy that BdU had intended to safeguard several distinct U-boat operations in the North Atlantic. For the previous two weeks, Dönitz and his staff had hoped that Feiler would attain two objectives with his radio transmissions: the first was to alleviate British pressure on a group of U-boats operating near the Strait of Gibraltar by enticing Allied escort ships patrolling there to chase after the phantom U-boats hundreds of miles away to the northwest. The second was to mask the ongoing movement of the five Operation Drumbeat Type IXs and the twelve VIIs toward their attack areas off the North American coast. By January 7, U-125—the leading Drumbeat boat—was only nine hundred nautical miles from its assigned operating area off Long Island, New York, and the Type VIIC U-86 was just 230 nautical miles from Cape Race, Newfoundland, with the other U-boats coming up behind. Anything that could prevent the British and Americans from detecting this attack force in time and organizing a vigorous defense was critical to success in the upcoming operation. But with Feiler's breaking off from patrol, the Germans had one less tool at their disposal.[1]

THE CRYPTOLOGIC WAR ON BOTH SIDES OF THE Battle of the Atlantic involved a range of advanced mathematics, theoretical research into the arcane technology of cryptologic machines, careful analysis of intercepted messages, and a dose of covert thievery. The German penetration of Allied convoy codes occurred in several stages beginning on July 10, 1940, when the German surface raider *Atlantis* had captured the British liner *City of Baghdad* in the Indian Ocean after its crew hastily abandoned ship. A boarding team had discovered a copy of the Allied Merchant Ships Code, a two-part code used by the British Admiralty to send messages in Morse code via radio to convoys at sea. Four months later, the *Atlantis* crew seized another British freighter and found an updated copy of the code.

Within weeks of this second seizure, B-Dienst cryptanalysts were "breaking" the encrypted transmissions and providing the U-boat Force with clear-text messages from the Western Approaches Command redirecting convoys at sea away from areas of suspected U-boat activity. By early 1942, German communications experts had thoroughly penetrated the primary Royal Navy codes as well. These included the Administrative Code, Auxiliary Code, Merchant Navy Code, and Naval Code No. 1. But the most valuable success came when B-Dienst analysts began to crack Naval Cypher No. 3, a sophisticated code that the Admiralty introduced in October 1941 for the use of Allied merchant convoys and their escorts. The contents of Naval Cypher No. 3 were critical to U-boat operations since they included information about convoy departures from port. The penetration of Naval Cypher No. 3 also provided Dönitz and the BdU operations staff with the weekly top-secret British U-boat Situation Reports that apprised escort groups of known and suspected U-boat locations. These reports allowed BdU both to remove U-boats from harm's way and to place them where least expected and thus most deadly. Dönitz later credited the B-Dienst staff with providing him 50 percent of the operational intelligence the U-boat Force employed to hunt down Allied convoys throughout the war. Nevertheless, the intelligence windfall that the B-Dienst analysts harvested paled in comparison to the success of their British counterparts, who did what the Germans thought impossible: penetrate the secrets of the Enigma encryption machine.[2]

Admiral Dönitz's confidence in the Enigma *Marine Funkschlüssel-Maschine* was understandable. The encrypted communications system was extremely complex, and its designers were convinced that enemy decryption of tactical military messages transmitted to and from the U-boats was an impossibility. Since anyone with an antenna could intercept the high-frequency radio signals broadcast from the ground transmission station in France or a U-boat's two-hundred-watt transmitter, it was mandatory that the U-boat Force have the means to encipher all messages in such a way that the enemy could not "break" the series of random Morse Code letters into clear text. First conceived as an encryption device for commercial use by German engineer Arthur Scherbius in 1927 (based on a Dutch engineer's original patent he obtained), the Enigma failed to attract commercial customers but caught the eye of German military communications experts. By 1942, all of the German military services relied on variants of the Enigma machine, which had gone through numerous modifications over the previous decade. The U-boat Force at the start of 1942 utilized the M3 naval Enigma.

The battery-operated M3 Enigma device resembled an office typewriter housed in a varnished oak box with a hinged lid. It sported several strange electrical add-ons: in addition to the twenty-six-letter keyboard, it had a flat panel on which twenty-six small circular windows were arranged in three rows, each marked with a letter of the alphabet. When the operator depressed a key, it closed an electrical circuit, and a small light bulb behind one of the windows illuminated. The letter that appeared in the lit window represented the encryption of the letter that the radio operator had just typed. The secret of Enigma lay in how the machine turned one letter—the keystroke—into a different one—the illuminated letter appearing in the circular face of one of the glow lamps—seemingly at random.

The Enigma machine used by the U-boat Force in early 1942 used three moving electromechanical rotors and a "reflector" (a nonmoving rotor) to continuously change the circuit path from keyboard to glow lamp. The Kriegsmarine provided every Enigma machine with eight different rotors, each identified with a roman numeral from I to VIII. All of the rotors identified by a particular roman numeral had identical letter-to-letter wiring designs, and the circuitry for differently numbered rotors was never the same. A U-boat officer would check a published schedule to determine which three rotors to place into the machine and the order in which to mount them on the small shaft around which they turned. The sequence of Enigma rotors installed in the machine changed every other day, adding yet another layer of complexity to the system.

Besides the rotors, designers had added two additional layers of encryption to the Enigma machine. One device was an "alphabet ring" mounted on each rotor and the reflector like a tire on a wheel. The ring displayed the rotor position indicator letters that appeared in small windows on the face of the machine.

Each rotor could thus be turned individually until the letters designated for that day's use appeared in the Enigma's faceplate windows and were then locked into a stud. This enabled the Enigma operator to change the rotor circuit for each letter prior to use. Another encryption layer came from a cable plug board on the front of the machine. The plug board had twenty-six electrical sockets corresponding to the alphabet as well. Following another preplanned schedule, the operator would connect specific pairs of letters using a series of short electrical cables with plugs on both ends.

When the Enigma operator typed his message, the electrical impulse from each keystroke traveled from the keyboard through the plug board cables, then moved through the three moving rotors to the reflector, which redirected it back through a different path in rotors and plug board. Thus, when a letter emerged from the rotor system and plug board, its identity had changed from seven to nine times since the radioman had pressed the key.

Nor was that the end of it.

The genius of the encryption system was that in addition to the external inputs, the rotors interacted with each other when the machine was in use. As the operator typed each succeeding letter in the message, the right-hand rotor advanced either one or two letter positions by a ratchet-and-pawl mechanism on its outer edge. The other two movable rotors also advanced, but only after a larger number of keystrokes. In reality, every letter of an Enigma message was encrypted by a unique circuit pathway. In effect, the same letter of the alphabet would encrypt to a different letter each time the operator pressed that key.

For additional security, the navy provided each U-boat with a *Kenngruppenbuch* (recognition group book) containing 17,576 three-letter "trigrams." The radio operator would select a trigram identifying the specific cipher in use (the German navy assigned separate ciphers to different user groups, such as the Atlantic U-boats, blockade-runners, and so on). Next, the radioman would select a second trigram at random for the message key for that specific message. This identified the starting position of each rotor—the letters appearing in the small windows at the front of the machine. He then added a null letter as the first letter in the cipher indication trigram and a null letter to the end of the three-letter message key. He next wrote both groups on a message form. Finally, he encoded the two four-letter groups using a separate bigram (two-letter) table and wrote them on the form.

The sophistication and complexity of the Enigma were nothing short of staggering. Yet, for all of its extraordinary safeguards, the British by January 1942 were regularly reading the contents of the messages between BdU and the U-boats—incredibly, often within a day of transmission.[3]

THE EFFORT BY WESTERN GOVERNMENTS to crack Enigma had begun seven years before the outbreak of the war, when Polish cryptanalyst Marian Rejewski began researching the encryption technology. A brilliant mathematician, Rejewski in 1932 managed through "permutation theory," a higher algebraic analysis, to unlock the secrets of the Enigma rotor wiring—the heart of the encryption process—for Rotors I through III. In 1938 he had also solved Rotors IV and V, though by then the German navy had distributed three more, Rotors VI to VIII, for use in naval communications. Still, Rejewski's critical knowledge enabled the Polish *Biuro Szyfrow* (Cipher Bureau) to build several replica Enigma machines. On the eve of war in July 1939, the Poles gave one of them to the British, who rushed it to a guarded estate fifty miles northwest of London called Bletchley Park, where the newly organized Government Code and Cypher School was scrambling to penetrate German military communications.

In late 1939, the British designed the prototype of what they would call a "bombe," a fast electromechanical machine duplicating the Enigma wiring design. Entering service in March 1940, the bombe solved the Enigma rotor settings mechanically, which then allowed cryptanalysts to break the messages into clear text. By August 1941, Bletchley Park was decrypting most naval Enigma traffic within thirty-six hours.

After breaking an Enigma message, the cryptanalysts transmitted the clear text via a secure teleprinter line to the British Admiralty's Operational Intelligence Centre in the underground Citadel in London. There, a small team, led by barrister–turned–Royal Navy volunteer reserve commander Rodger Winn, cross-checked the material against other intelligence for further confirmation. Winn and his staff then passed carefully sanitized intelligence reports to the Admiralty Trade Division and to Western Approaches Command in Liverpool. Using that information, Admiral Percy Noble and his operations staff guided convoys at sea in eluding the wolf packs and warships in hunting them down.[4]

By the end of 1941, the staff at Bletchley Park had grown to over 1,500 mathematicians, linguists, cryptanalysts, and clerks, all laboring around the clock. The staff targeted communications from all German bodies—ranging from the Luftwaffe and Wehrmacht to the Schutzstaffel (SS, Defense Corps)—but one of their highest priorities, given the crucial stakes at hand in the Battle of the Atlantic, remained attacking the encrypted Enigma messages between Admiral Dönitz's headquarters in Lorient and his U-boats at sea.

Despite Enigma's presumed inviolability and Kapitänleutnant Feiler's radio-deception ploy, the British knew exactly what was developing in the North Atlantic during the first eleven days of January 1942. In a "Most Secret" weekly U-boat Situation Report on January 5, Winn wrote,

> The U-boat situation has one feature of particular interest: since [December 24] until [January 3] a U-boat has been employed solely to create a fictitious impression in our minds by moving rapidly through the Northwest Approaches [between Scotland and the Faroes] and making signals at short intervals on varied frequencies so as to simulate the presence of a considerable number of U-boats in the area. . . . The object of this ruse is thought to be the concealment of one or all of three actual moves that are developing: (a) a concentration of 6 U-boats off Cape Race, St. John's and Argentia.[5]

Despite the great lengths to which BdU had gone to use U-653 to protect its other U-boat forces in the North Atlantic, the British—thanks to their extensive code-breaking efforts— had seen through the ruse easily and had pinpointed exactly where the true threat lay. Had Dönitz known of the British awareness of U-653, he would have become catatonic—because he would have realized that Enigma was not secure.

Over the next week, Winn and his team also assembled a gradually clearing picture of the westward progress of the seventeen U-boats heading for Operation Drumbeat and New-foundland. Even though the five Type IX boats kept their radio transmissions to a minimum, Degen and the other Ziethen boats engaged in regular communication with BdU. By Monday, January 12, Winn had assembled a stark picture of what was unfolding along the eastern coast of Canada and the United States:

> The general situation is somewhat clearer and the most striking feature is a heavy concentration [of U-boats] off the North American seaboard from New York to Cape Race [Newfoundland]. Two groups have so far been formed. One, of 6 U-boats, is already in position off Cape Race and St. John's, and a second, of 5 U-boats, is apparently positioning off the American coast between New York and Portland [Maine]. It is known that these 5 U-boats will reach their attacking areas by 13th January.[6]

Understanding procedures established between the British Admiralty and COMINCH Headquarters in Washington eight months earlier, Winn transmitted this information to Admiral Ernest King's headquarters at Main Navy via a secure line through the Intelligence Section (NID 18) of the Admiralty's delegation at the British embassy in Washington, DC. Unlike on December 7, when the six aircraft carriers and fourteen escort warships of the Japanese strike force attained total surprise via radio silence and deceptive movement across the northern Pacific, the British on January 12, 1942, provided the US Navy with explicit and accurate warning of an imminent and widespread attack by German U-boats against coastal shipping.

Incredibly, the Americans did nothing—inviting a naval catastrophe that would dwarf the losses at Pearl Harbor.[7]

5

OPERATION
DRUMBEAT

THE TORPEDO STRUCK WITHOUT WARNING. AT ONE MOMENT, the British freighter *Cyclops* was heading northeast parallel to the New England shore, pushing through moderate swells that moved from left to right across its bow. The next moment, a thunderous explosion went off on the freighter's starboard side. Seawater, smoke, and flames cascaded high into the gloomy overcast sky.

It was 1849 hours Eastern War Time (EWT) on Sunday, January 11, 1942, and Operation Drumbeat, Vice Admiral Karl Dönitz's U-boat assault on American coastal shipping, was underway a day earlier than he had ordered. Master Leslie Webber Kersley, his ninety-six-man crew, seven gunners, and seventy-nine passengers aboard the 9,076-ton *Cyclops* were nearing the home stretch of a 13,485-mile trip from the Far East to the British Isles when U-123, under the command of Kapitänleutnant Reinhard Hardegen, suddenly attacked. The thirty-six-year-old merchantman was carrying 6,905 tons of general cargo its crew had loaded in Hong Kong and Auckland, New Zealand, before crossing the

Pacific and entering the Caribbean through the Panama Canal en route to the British Isles via Nova Scotia. The sudden blast and gaping hole in the starboard side meant that the ship's monthlong trek from the Far East had come to a sudden and disastrous end just eighteen hours shy of its scheduled arrival in Halifax. As the ship settled quickly by the stern, Kersley ordered passengers and crew to take to the lifeboats.

U-123 had become the first ship in the Drumbeat wolf pack to bring down an Allied ship in coastal waters. Dönitz had told Hardegen and the other U-boat commanders assigned to this first strike against the United States that while they would operate independently along the Canadian and American East Coast, he wanted their attacks to begin simultaneously for maximum psychological impact. He later transmitted an encrypted Morse code message to the Drumbeat U-boats identifying the attack date as January 13 (late in the day on January 12 in the Eastern time zone). While insisting on the simultaneous attack, Dönitz had given his U-boat commanders one exception to the rule: any Allied merchant ship displacing 10,000 tons or more could be attacked no matter the date and location. Hardegen decided to take advantage of this caveat when a ripe target suddenly appeared in his lookouts' binoculars.

It was a typical move for the twenty-eight-year-old naval officer, who had found his true calling in the U-boat Force. A native of the Hanseatic city of Bremen in northern Germany, Hardegen since childhood had dreamed of a career at sea. At the age of eighteen, he entered the Kriegsmarine as a midshipman candidate. As one of ninety-one members of the Class of 1933 along with Horst Degen, Hardegen sailed on the warship

Karlsruhe for its around-the-world cruise. Upon receiving his commission, Hardegen found himself assigned to the German naval air force—an organization that, under the dictates of the 1919 Treaty of Versailles that ended World War I, did not officially exist. Hardegen spent four years as a patrol plane pilot before being unceremoniously transferred to the U-boat Force in November 1939. After serving as first watch officer (1WO) on the Type IXB U-124 for two patrols from August to December 1940, during which time the U-boat sank seven Allied merchant ships totaling 30,624 gross registered tons, Hardegen took command of the small Type IID U-147. In one patrol in early 1941, Hardegen sank the 4,811-ton Norwegian freighter *Augvald*. Then, on May 17, 1941, U-boat Force Headquarters assigned Hardegen as the Type IXB U-123's second commanding officer. Commissioned just a year earlier, *Eins Zwei Drei* (One, Two, Three), as the crew affectionately nicknamed their U-boat, had already conducted four wartime patrols under Kapitänleutnant Karl-Heinz Moehle, sinking sixteen ships totaling 80,730 gross registered tons.

Despite his success as a 1WO on U-124, Hardegen's brief command of U-147 told this new crew little of his skills as a U-boat commander. Any doubts U-123's crewmen may have had about their new skipper, however, were quickly assuaged. On his first two patrols with U-123, Hardegen sank six ships for a total of 26,318 gross registered tons.

In this latest victory, Hardegen and his men had conducted a textbook attack against the *Cyclops*. With darkness setting in, Hardegen had ordered U-123 to close within 1,600 yards of the ship. Following standard procedure for a surface torpedo attack,

Oberleutnant zur See Rudolf Hoffmann, Hardegen's 1WO, had manned the *Uboot-Zieloptik* (UZO), a set of oversized binoculars whose fourteen-inch lenses gave him an incredibly clear image of the target despite the fading evening twilight. Mounted on a swivel post on the bridge, the UZO glasses transmitted the bearing, range, and target angle to a *Vorhaltrechner*—an electro-mechanical deflection calculator—in the conning tower down below, which in turn fed the correct heading to the target into the gyroscope of the designated G7a torpedo in tube number 3. After announcing the intended depth of the torpedo run—3.5 meters—through a voice tube to the torpedo room, where a torpedo mechanic cranked in the number by hand, the twenty-four-year-old Hoffmann hit the electromagnetic launch button to fire the weapon, calling out, "Release!" Back came an instantaneous reply from the torpedo gang: "Failure!" The firing system had malfunctioned. But four seconds after that, the torpedo mechanic manually fired the torpedo and called up, "Launched!" Ninety-seven seconds later, the G7a detonated against the British merchantman's hull.

Several minutes later, *Funkmaat* (Radioman 3rd Class) Fritz Rafalski reported that the *Cyclops* was transmitting "SSS," the emergency signal for a U-boat attack, in clear Morse code. Hardegen ordered his machine-gun crew to destroy the freighter's wireless office and antenna to silence the signal. Then, as the darkness deepened, Hardegen and his lookouts saw a number of crewmen reboarding the ship. He turned U-123 around and fired a second G7a in a coup de grâce from one of his two stern tubes. The torpedo struck the *Cyclops*, and its 616-pound warhead detonated, collapsing the ship's hull and sending it under within five minutes. Following his admiral's general order not to attempt rescue of survivors, Hardegen ordered U-123 back on its base course of 220 degrees, a heading that would place the boat off Long Island, New York, the following day.

Responding to the SSS signal, the Canadian minesweeper HMCS *Red Deer* rescued Kersley, sixty-one crewmen and gunners, and thirty-three of the *Cyclops*'s passengers late on January 13, but the other eighty-seven men aboard the freighter were not so lucky. Two perished in the torpedo attacks, and the other eighty-five died of exposure in the frigid North Atlantic. The U-boat slaughter of Allied merchant ships along the American and Canadian East Coast had begun.[1]

As U-123 put down its first merchant ship some 326 nautical miles east of Boston, the other four Drumbeat U-boats were nearing their patrol areas for the designated attack launch on Tuesday, January 13. Admiral Dönitz had assigned them initial operating areas from Canada's Gulf of St. Lawrence to Cape Hatteras, spread out in such a way that each U-boat could operate freely without interference from the others. U-123 had orders to patrol near the coast off Long Island and attack shipping coming to and from New York Harbor. The southernmost U-boat—scouring the sea lanes off Cape Hatteras—was the Type IXC U-66, commanded by thirty-seven-year-old *Korvettenkapitän* (Commander) Richard Zapp. The next patrol area alongside Hardegen's went to the Type IXC U-125 under twenty-six-year-old Kapitänleutnant Ulrich Folkers, who had orders to operate to the east of the New Jersey–New York coastline. By midday on January 11, U-125 was about 420 nautical miles east of New York.

The other two U-boats in Operation Drumbeat had orders to operate off the Canadian coast in proximity to the twelve Type VII boats in Gruppe Ziethen. The new Type IXC U-130 under thirty-six-year-old Korvettenkapitän Ernst Kals was to patrol off Nova Scotia and Newfoundland. At the same time, the Type IXB U-109 commanded by thirty-two-year-old Kapitänleutnant Heinrich Bleichrodt was to enter the Gulf of St. Lawrence between Newfoundland and the Canadian mainland, searching for shipping from the St. Lawrence River. U-109's risky mission deep inside Canadian territorial waters was par for Bleichrodt's already exemplary record. During two patrols of the Type VIIB U-48 in late 1940, Bleichrodt sank fourteen Allied ships totaling 77,524 gross registered tons. Unfortunately for them, bad weather off Newfoundland would plague U-130, U-109, and the twelve Gruppe Ziethen U-boats. The initial U-boat attacks in North American waters would not go as smoothly as Admiral Dönitz had hoped.[2]

VICE ADMIRAL ADOLPHUS A. "DOLLY" ANDREWS was trapped in a naval commander's worst nightmare. Upon assuming command of the North Atlantic Naval Coastal Frontier—soon to be renamed the Eastern Sea Frontier (ESF)—ten months earlier, the sixty-two-year-old Galveston native had become responsible for the protection of harbors, anchorages, and coastal shipping in five naval districts whose operational areas ran from the US-Canadian frontier at Quoddy Head, Maine, to the command's southern boundary line at Onslow Bay, North Carolina. His area of responsibility included all the major East Coast seaports, as well as the Atlantic littoral out to two hundred nautical miles. During the first week of January 1942, the navy decided to expand the Eastern Sea Frontier to include the Sixth Naval District based in Charleston, South Carolina. This brought the rest of North Carolina and all of the South Carolina and Georgia coastlines and ports into the command. Andrews was now responsible for defending 253,400 square miles of ocean, an area approximately the size of Texas.

Coastal defense had long been a backwater function of the US Navy, but as 1942 dawned, Andrews and his staff knew well that the U-boat threat was imminent and that the US East Coast was about to become a major maritime battlefield. Looming above all else was the fact that Andrews's command lacked any significant combat capability to fight the U-boats.[3]

Peacetime direction of the Eastern Sea Frontier was not a glamorous assignment like commanding a blue-water fleet, but it still required significant leadership and management skills. It also required diplomacy, for ESF was one of the few military headquarters where the US Navy and Army Air Forces—locked elsewhere in a protracted dispute over the control of land-based maritime patrol aircraft—literally rubbed elbows on a 24/7 basis. Andrews had honed these skills during his thirty-eight-year career since receiving his commission as an ensign. Graduating the top-ranked midshipman in the Naval Academy Class of 1901, Andrews had held a series of increasingly responsible jobs both in the battleship fleet and ashore. In a previous three-star assignment between 1938 and 1941, he commanded the Battle Force, a prewar formation of the navy's aircraft carriers and battleships. He had earlier commanded the battleships USS *Massachusetts* and *USS Texas* after serving as a department head or executive officer on four others. His shore assignments included command of the navy's Navigation Bureau and a stint as assistant chief of staff to the Atlantic Fleet commander. Andrews also had a talent for ingratiating himself with presidents, politicians, and senior military officers while holding a wide range of staff assignments ashore.

Andrews's reputation among his fellow admirals was mixed. Historian Samuel Eliot Morison condescended to describe Andrews as "senatorial in port and speech," while Secretary of War Henry L. Stimson, weary of his stilted, formal way of speaking, dismissed Andrews as a "terrible old fusspocket." To the junior members of his ESF staff, Andrews was a typical admiral: formal, reserved, distant, and a bit of a brass hat. Ensign Peter Rollins found this out one day in late 1941 at the First Naval District Headquarters on the Boston waterfront. In preparation for an inspection by the admiral, the staff members had scoured the office to a state of perfection. The scheduled inspection time came and went with no sign of the great man. After two hours, Rollins leaned back against a window and lit his pipe. A moment later, Andrews and a large delegation of senior officers swept into the room. The staff snapped to attention. Rollins hastily dumped the smoldering tobacco from his pipe but missed the ashtray, and it landed on the varnished surface of his desk, creating a cloud of pungent smoke. All heads turned to the frantic young man whose desktop threatened to burst into flames. As Andrews glared at the young officer, Rollins hastily brushed the glowing embers into his waste can. The mass of paper inside the can ignited. Rollins began stamping on the blaze. His foot became wedged in the can and flames began climbing up his leg. In desperation, Rollins hopped around, banging the waste can on the floor until the flames finally went out. Foot still wedged in the can, leg blackened with soot, he finally snapped to attention. Andrews was still staring at him, his features bleak and unmoving. Then, without a word, the admiral turned on his heel and swept out of the room, the inspection abandoned. The staff gathered around the sooty ensign and congratulated him for making such a profound impression on the admiral. It was Rollins's first day on active duty.[4]

Behind his wooden façade, in the first weeks of 1942 Andrews was clearly worried about his command's shortcomings in the face of the imminent German U-boat threat. The US military's general war plan WPL-46 (Rainbow Five) charged ESF with defending the sea frontier, protecting and routing coastal shipping, supporting the Atlantic Fleet, and supporting army and other military forces within the frontier. And as Andrews well knew, the Germans would be an exceedingly dangerous enemy.

Based on prior experience, Andrews and his fellow admirals recognized the revived U-boat Force as the most likely threat they would face. American commanders had been forced to contend with a similar U-boat offensive off the US East Coast in 1918, at the tail end of World War I. That campaign had been brief, intense, and deadly. During a six-month period, just six U-boats sank ninety ships for a total loss of 166,907 gross registered tons and 435 fatalities. Faced with an even more dangerous situation, Andrews already knew that no help was available. Admiral Ernest King wrote Andrews on New Year's Day in reply to a request to transfer some destroyers to his command: "A review of the situation indicates that it would be inadvisable to detach any vessels from their present duty with the fleets, at least until additional new construction destroyers have been commissioned and have joined" the service.[5]

Andrews had taken a number of steps to bring the command to a state of maximum readiness. He ordered naval district staffs in Boston, New York, Philadelphia, and Norfolk to lay defensive minefields and deploy torpedo nets and booms, to organize inshore patrols, and to ready all available patrol craft and airplanes for possible combat.

Yet, despite the efforts of Andrews and his ESF subordinates, the navy's divided command organization in the Atlantic would thwart attempts to mobilize a defense against the U-boats. As Eastern Sea Frontier commander, Admiral Andrews was responsible for coastal defense and escort of shipping, but he had no major warships with which to carry out those vital missions. They belonged to the Atlantic Fleet commander—Admiral King between December 7 and 31, 1941, and Vice Admiral Royal E. Ingersoll, who relieved King on January 1, 1942. Between mid-December and January 11, the US Atlantic Fleet had seen a sizable reduction in its combat power as a result of Pearl Harbor, but it still remained a strong naval force. Admiral Harold Stark, succeeded on December 31 by Admiral King as Commander-in-Chief of the US Fleet (COMINCH), had ordered transferred to the Pacific Fleet the aircraft carrier USS Yorktown, battleships USS Mississippi, USS New Mexico, and USS Idaho, and eleven frontline destroyers to offset combat losses on Oahu. Even with those transfers, Admiral Ingersoll still had three aircraft carriers, five battleships, and a half dozen cruisers on his fleet roster, as well as a potent force of eighty destroyers and six *Treasury*-class coast guard cutters. Moreover, in late December—during the final days of his Atlantic Fleet command—Admiral King wrote Chief of Naval Operations (CNO) Admiral Stark to apprise him of the decline in U-boat attacks on the transatlantic convoy routes and to warn that "the imminent probability of submarine attack" along the US East Coast and "the weakness of our coastal defense force make it essential that the maximum practicable number of our destroyers be based at home bases." King himself would then turn and ignore his own clear-sighted and straightforward recommendation after his ascension to overall command of the US Navy.[6]

What remains inexplicable more than seventy years after the fact is the failure of either Admiral King or Vice Admiral Ingersoll to carry out King's own earlier advice to Admiral Stark to redeploy a sufficient number of destroyers to fight off the anticipated U-boat offensive in American coastal waters. On January 12, 1942, the Atlantic Fleet destroyer force was spread out across the Atlantic from Iceland to the coast of Brazil in the following formations: a total of thirty-nine destroyers and six *Treasury*-class coast guard cutters were assigned to five convoy escort groups operating out of Argentia, Newfoundland, and Hvaljfordur, Iceland (although a half dozen of them on that day were in East Coast naval shipyards undergoing repairs); another twelve destroyers were operating in the Gulf of Mexico and Caribbean; five destroyers were assigned to the South Atlantic Patrol; yet another five destroyers were on individual operating assignments in Bermuda and elsewhere. That left a group of nineteen frontline Atlantic Fleet destroyers at anchor or tied up to the piers at East Coast naval bases from Casco Bay, Maine, to Norfolk on January 12.[7]

Andrews had only a small, ramshackle fleet with which to take on the U-boats. It comprised two small coast guard cutters and eighteen tiny patrol boats that had to cover the entire 1,200-mile swath of the Atlantic from the Canadian border to Jacksonville, Florida. On December 22, Andrews had warned outgoing CNO Admiral Stark, "There is not a vessel available that an enemy submarine could not outdistance when operating on the surface. In most cases the guns of these vessels would be outranged by those of the submarine." His ships were too slow and outgunned—no match for the U-boats. Nor was that his only problem.

The Eastern Sea Frontier's coastal defense air arm was even more pathetic than its bathtub flotilla. In December 1941, Andrews—on paper—had a fleet of 103 aircraft. In reality, only a dozen could be described as a combat capable. Even the six PBY-5A Catalina flying boats assigned to ESF were militarily problematic. Andrews noted in his command's war diary that it would take six hours to load them with live depth charges, rendering them useless to mount quick-reaction flights in response to a U-boat sighting.[8]

Andrews did have one useful tool at his disposal: each day the British Operational Intelligence Centre in London transmitted updated U-boat positions and other vital intelligence to US Navy Headquarters in Washington, DC, which then routed them to other subordinate commands, including Eastern Sea Frontier. On Monday, January 12, ESF communications officer Lieutenant j.g. Richard H. Braue knocked on Andrews's door and entered, carrying a locked message box. Following a well-established procedure, Braue unlocked the box, removed a sheet of paper with the decrypted message, and held it out at arms length for the admiral to read. The message stated, in part,

No. O.I.C./S.I./57
U-BOAT SITUATION
Week ending [January 12, 1942]

The general situation is now somewhat clearer and the most striking feature is a heavy concentration [of U-boats] off the North American seaboard from New York to Cape Race. Two groups have so far been formed. One, of 6 U-boats, is already in position off Cape Race and St. John's [Newfoundland], and a second, of 5 U-boats, is apparently approaching the American coast between New York and Portland [Maine]. It is known that [there are] a total of 21 boats [heading west].[9]

Less than ten hours later, a second, direct message from COMINCH to all major American and Canadian naval units in the Atlantic rocketed into the ESF code room, giving the latitude-longitude locations of the U-boats:

INFO RECEIVED INDICATES LARGE [U-BOAT] CON-CENTRATION PROCEEDING TO OR ALREADY AR-RIVED ON STATION OFF CANADIAN AND NORTH-EASTERN US COASTS X 3 OR 4 BOATS NEAR 40N 65W X 5 OR 6 SOUTH [OF] CAPE RACE PROBABLY NORTH OF 43N X 8 MORE WEST OF 30W PROCEEDING WEST IN FOLLOWING APPROX POSITIONS X 56 N 32W X 55N 38W X 48N 33W 47–30N 32W X 47–30N 44W X 48N 42W X 52N 42W X 52–30N 41W.[10]

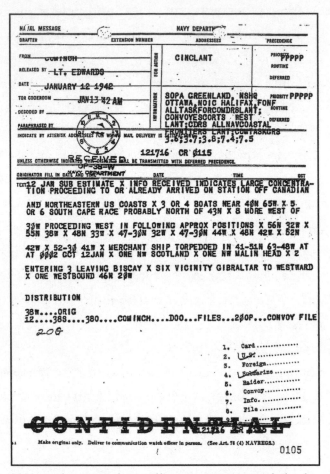

NAVAL MESSAGE — NAVY DEPARTMENT

DRAFTER — EXTENSION NUMBER — ADDRESSEES — PRECEDENCE

FROM COMINCH

RELEASED BY LT. EDWARDS

DATE JANUARY 12 1942

TOR CODEROOM JAN 13 '42 AM

DECODED BY

PARAPHRASED BY

FOR ACTION: CINCLANT — PRIORITY PPPPP / ROUTINE / DEFERRED

INFORMATION: SOPA GREENLAND NSHQ OTTAWA NOIC HALIFAX FONF ALLTASKFORCOMDRSLANT CONVOYESCORTS REST LANT CDRS ALLNAVCOASTAL FRONTIERS LANT COTASKGRS 3.6;3.7;3.8;7.4;7.5 — PRIORITY PPPPP / ROUTINE / DEFERRED

INDICATE BY ASTERISK ADDRESSEES FOR WHOM MAIL DELIVERY IS

121716 CR 0115

UNLESS OTHERWISE INDICATED THIS WILL BE TRANSMITTED WITH DEFERRED PRECEDENCE.

ORIGINATOR FILL IN DATE AND DEPARTMENT — DATE — TIME — GCT

TEXT 12 JAN SUB ESTIMATE X INFO RECEIVED INDICATES LARGE CONCENTRATION PROCEEDING TO OR ALREADY ARRIVED ON STATION OFF CANADIAN

AND NORTHEASTERN US COASTS X 3 OR 4 BOATS NEAR 40N 65W X 5 OR 6 SOUTH CAPE RACE PROBABLY NORTH OF 43N X 8 MORE WEST OF

30W PROCEEDING WEST IN FOLLOWING APPROX POSITIONS X 56N 32W X 55N 38N X 48N 33N X 47-30N 32W X 47-30N 44N X 48N 42W X 52N

42W X 52-30 41N X MERCHANT SHIP TORPEDOED IN 41-51N 63-48W AT AT 0002 GCT 12JAN X ONE NW SCOTLAND X ONE NW MALIN HEAD X 2

ENTERING 3 LEAVING BISCAY X SIX VICINITY GIBRALTAR TO WESTWARD X ONE WESTBOUND 46N 20W

DISTRIBUTION

38W....ORIG
12...38S....380....COMINCH....DOO...FILES...200P...CONVOY FILE
20G

1. Card...........
2. U.S............
3. Foreign........
4. Submarine......
5. Raider.........
6. Convoy.........
7. Info...........
8. File...........

CONFIDENTIAL

Make original only. Deliver to communication watch officer in person. (See Art. 76 (4) NAVREGS.)

0105

Hours after British intelligence pinpointed the location of a dozen U-boats heading to the American coast to attack shipping, the Operational Intelligence Centre flashed the information to US Navy Headquarters, which then, in the early hours of January 13, 1942, transmitted this message warning the US Atlantic Fleet (CINCLANT) and all other naval units on the East Coast. Despite more than twenty-four hours' advance warning of the U-boats' arrival offshore, the navy did nothing to thwart the attack. NATIONAL ARCHIVES AND RECORDS ADMINISTRATION.

For Admiral Andrews, the nightmare now loomed before him. The U-boats were just hours away from unleashing a full-scale offensive against the Eastern Sea Frontier. Unlike the hapless Admiral Husband Kimmel at Pearl Harbor, who saw his fleet half disarmed in a surprise attack that came as a genuine bolt from the blue, here was a clear and explicit tactical warning that gave the numbers, locations, and anticipated timing of Admiral Dönitz's planned Drumbeat offensive. Yet Andrews could do absolutely nothing about it.

There was, however, something that Admiral Ingersoll at Atlantic Fleet Headquarters in Norfolk or Admiral King at Main Navy in Washington could do: as the U-boats crept in toward their attack positions late in the day on January 12, the nineteen combat-ready destroyers then resting in East Coast ports were readily available to take on the advancing U-boats. It would have been a simple and straightforward mission for the Atlantic Fleet to carry out: surge the destroyers out to sea to mount a search-and-destroy operation against the advancing wolf pack. Yet, inexplicably, King and Ingersoll did nothing. They had assembled the destroyers and other warships to escort a large troop convoy mustering in New York and destined for Northern Ireland. Since the deployment of American soldiers to Iceland and the British Isles was a top priority of the Arcadia Conference still underway in Washington, DC, neither admiral was inclined to delay its departure, even in the face of the imminent U-boat threat.[11]

At 2000 hours EWT on Tuesday, January 13, 1942, the USS Gwin was at sea in the western Atlantic approximately twenty-five nautical miles south of Newport, Rhode Island. The 347-foot *Gleaves*-class destroyer, just two days shy of its first anniversary as a commissioned US Navy warship, had left Boston earlier that afternoon for an overnight passage to the naval anchorage at Staten Island, New York. *Gwin* was a heavily armed warship, with five 5-inch/.38-cal. dual-purpose guns; six 20-mm antiaircraft guns, ten 21-inch torpedo tubes, and a full complement of depth charges. Having emerged from the Cape Cod Canal at 1713 hours EWT, Commander J. M. Higgins and his crew of fifteen officers and 260 enlisted men were holding steady on a west-southwest course that would skirt the southern coastline of Long Island as they proceeded at a leisurely speed of just eleven knots. Unbeknownst to the 276 American sailors, a fierce new chapter in the Battle of the Atlantic was about to erupt very close by.

At that same hour, U-123 was forty nautical miles south of the *Gwin*. Just fifty-four hours after sinking the freighter *Cyclops*, Kapitänleutnant Reinhard Hardegen and his fifty-one-man crew were also heading for New York. U-123 still had fourteen torpedoes aboard, and by order of Vice Admiral Dönitz, Hardegen's initial attack area consisted of the coastal waters off Long Island and the approaches to New York Harbor. Though neither knew it, Commander Higgins and Kapitänleutnant Hardegen were sailing on a parallel course—the Americans heading to a brief in-port visit and the Germans on their way to battle.[12]

Shortly after midnight local time on Wednesday, January 14, one of Hardegen's lookouts spotted the moving lights of an Allied merchant ship at about 4,400 yards to port ahead of the U-boat, moving on a reciprocal course before vanishing in a fogbank. As the ship emerged from the fog, looming up to port, Hardegen ordered all four bow tubes flooded, and several minutes later Hoffmann hit the firing lever to send a pair of G7es racing off toward the target just nine hundred yards away.

The 9,577-ton Panamanian oil tanker *Norness* was carrying a cargo of 12,200 tons of fuel oil to Liverpool when Hardegen pounced. The first torpedo from U-123 missed, but the second in the salvo struck the tanker on its port side near the stern, blasting a giant hole in the hull and sending a massive shower of fuel oil that covered the tanker's main deck. Although the explosion created a 150-foot column of flames and thick smoke, and fuel covered the tanker's deck and superstructure, the ship itself did not immediately catch fire. Nevertheless, the *Norness* was doomed. As the ship began listing to one side, its masts toppling onto the main deck, Captain Harold Hansen raced up to the bridge, only to be warned by a lookout that a German U-boat was visible off to port. Fearing a second torpedo might ignite the fuel into a major conflagration, Hanson ordered his forty-man crew to abandon ship. One crewman had already perished when the torpedo detonation blew him over the side into the frigid ocean, and a second man drowned when a lifeboat capsized, throwing him into the water. Twenty-five individuals made it safely into a second lifeboat, and six more escaped on a life raft. Hansen and seven others then successfully lowered the ship's only motorboat, but when they cast off, its engine would not start. In desperation, the eight survivors hand-paddled away from the sinking *Norness*. Nine minutes later, a second torpedo crashed into the tanker directly beneath its bridge, setting off another towering smoke column.

The *Norness* had been able to transmit an emergency radio message at the beginning of Hardegen's attack, but no US Navy warships scrambled from port to hunt for the U-boat lurking offshore. Twenty-seven minutes after firing the first of four torpedoes at the tanker—two of which missed—Hardegen ordered a fifth torpedo launched, and this finished off the *Norness*, which sank rapidly by the stern as its surviving crewmen watched from a distance.

Meanwhile, the destroyer *Gwin* continued on its leisurely westward path toward Staten Island. Whether from atmospheric interference at sea or human incompetence ashore, the tanker's destruction went undetected for more than twelve hours until a navy ZNP dirigible spotted the tanker's near-perpendicular bow section jutting from the water and a lifeboat with twenty-five of the thirty-nine survivors floating nearby. The dirigible's aircrew then contacted the Newport-based destroyer *USS Ellyson*, which was underway for routine systems tests six weeks after its formal commissioning, and directed it to the site to pick up the survivors. The 165-foot-long coast guard patrol vessel *Argo* was also in the vicinity and retrieved a small number of the Norwegian crewmen, and the American fishing boat *Malvina D* later found Captain Hansen and his crewmen in the disabled motor lifeboat.

While the search-and-rescue operation proceeded southeast of Montauk Point, the US Navy on January 14 finished the final details of assembling Task Force 15 at the Brooklyn Navy Yard and its Staten Island anchorage. The task force included the battleship *USS Texas*; aircraft carrier *USS Wasp*; cruisers *USS Quincy*, *USS Wichita*, and *USS Tuscaloosa*; and eighteen front-line Atlantic Fleet destroyers, including the *Gwin*. Their mission

was to rush American soldiers to Iceland and Northern Ireland
to relieve the marines on Iceland and free up British troops in
both locations for redeployment to North Africa. Task Force 15
was to protect Convoy AT10, a cadre of four troopships carrying an army battalion to Iceland and 4,508 soldiers to Northern
Ireland.[13]

The day after the sinking of the *Norness*, on Thursday, January 15, Convoy AT10 sailed from New York and formed up at
sea inside what Admiral King would call a "curtain of steel,"
a cordon of all twenty-three Task Force 15 warships. Convoy
AT10 would make it safely to Iceland, then Londonderry, Northern Ireland. Nevertheless, the decision to sail the troop convoy
stripped the US East Coast of the last meaningful defense against
the German U-boats. It was all that Dönitz could have hoped
for—and more.[14]

6

HORRIFIC LOSSES

Shortly before dawn on Thursday, January 15, the same day that Task Force 15 was scheduled to leave New York, Kapitänleutnant Horst Degen ordered his control room watch-standers to blow the ballast tanks. U-701 breached the surface of the western Atlantic to find the weather still as stormy as it had been for the past six days. The southwesterly gale still blew, and the waves often topped thirty feet, causing the U-boat to pitch and roll severely each time it reached a crest, then plunged once more into the trough of the sea. Despite the rough weather, however, Degen frequently found it necessary to surface; he and his crew would endure the pounding just long enough to suck clean air into the boat and recharge the batteries before once more seeking shelter in the depths. Even for that short time, the seas were often so tumultuous that Degen dared not send the regular complement of watch officer and three lookouts to the bridge.

When he was able to man the bridge fully, Degen and his lookouts faced the nearly impossible task of searching visually for the silhouettes of Allied merchantmen and enemy warships;

the towering waves reduced visibility to a minimum. But their diligence finally paid off. Thirty minutes after surfacing at dawn on January 15, U-701's lookouts suddenly spotted a merchant steamer ten degrees off the port bow just five nautical miles away and heading directly toward them. Since his only two remaining torpedoes were lodged in storage canisters below the exterior deck plates, Degen ordered a crash dive to avoid detection.

With no change in the weather in sight, the U-701 crewmen gritted their teeth and continued with their arduous daily routine. But elsewhere along the North Atlantic littoral, Operation Drumbeat was getting into high gear.

Another Gruppe Ziethen U-boat had already claimed the first victim in Newfoundland waters. Oberleutnant zur See Erich Topp in U-552 had been patrolling southwest of Cape Race in the late afternoon of January 14, when his lookouts sighted a midsize merchant freighter. Because of the heavy seas, Topp closed to within nine hundred yards before launching. Even so, the turbulence caused three of five torpedoes fired to miss. Nevertheless, two torpedo impacts made quick work of the 4,113-ton British freighter *Dayrose*, breaking the ship in half. Only four crewmen out of the total complement of thirty-eight aboard survived, another testament to the peril of winter in the North Atlantic. Topp dispatched a brief message to U-boat Force Headquarters reporting the kill.

Topp's message was the first firm confirmation that the Drumbeat and Ziethen U-boats had made it to their attack areas. The BdU daily war diary noted, "It is not known whether the boats have reached their positions off the coast of USA. It is possible that they will arrive later than the estimated time because of bad weather. U-552 reports bad weather south of Newfoundland so that boats must be having difficulty taking position, to say nothing of attack." The uncertainty would quickly disappear as, within the next two weeks, thirteen of the U-boats from the two groups, plus three boats from the follow-on wave, broke radio silence to announce the destruction of Allied merchant ships in coastal waters from Newfoundland to Cape Hatteras.[1]

The next blow came from U-123, which by the early morning hours of January 15 was closing in on the Fire Island lightship off the southern coast of Long Island, roughly midway between Montauk Point and the Verrazano Narrows entrance to New York Harbor. Task Force 15 and Convoy AT10 had not yet left the safety of the harbor, and so the waters offshore were relatively empty of US Navy warships. It was, in other words, the perfect hunting ground for Kapitänleutnant Reinhard Hardegen and his men.

Standing silently on the narrow bridge, Hardegen and his lookouts had been mesmerized for the past three hours by the bright glow on the horizon coming from the lights on Long Island. Then, as they approached the Verrazano Narrows itself, the lights from the Manhattan skyscrapers cast a blurred light on the western horizon. The sight sparked deep personal emotions for Hardegen, who, along with Horst Degen and his other Class of 1933 midshipmen, had so much enjoyed their visit to New York just nine years earlier. "I cannot describe the feeling with words," he wrote in a German government-approved memoir the following year, "but it was unbelievably beautiful and great. . . . We were the first to be here, and for the first time in this war a German soldier looked out upon the coast of the

U.S.A." He would recall in detail the lights of Coney Island and its giant Ferris wheel and the eerie sight of automobiles driving along the shore on Atlantic Avenue.

At 0100 Eastern War Time (EWT), Second Watch Officer Horst von Schroeter relieved Hardegen on the bridge, and the skipper went below to rest. His respite did not last long. Forty minutes later, with U-123 heading in a generally eastbound course, the lookouts called out bright lights to starboard and astern, also moving eastbound out of the Ambrose Channel. Hardegen bounded back up the conning tower ladder. With the target backlit by the city lights and showing full illumination itself, Hardegen had no difficulty identifying it. Leaning toward the voice tube, the skipper told his crew that "a big tanker" was overtaking their U-boat.

The 6,768-ton British motor tanker *Coimbra* was traveling unescorted out of New York with a 9,000-ton cargo of lubricating oil for the British Isles when a solitary G7e electric torpedo struck it on the starboard side just aft of the superstructure. Hardegen had allowed the tanker to close within eight hundred yards before First Watch Officer Rudolf Hoffmann on the *Uboot-Zieloptik* binoculars launched the torpedo. The results were catastrophic. A violent explosion sent a fireball of burning oil hundreds of feet into the dark sky, and the fiery fluid then came cascading down onto on the bridge and main deck. Within minutes, the *Coimbra* was totally engulfed in flames except at the stern. When U-123 lookouts saw crewmen hurrying aft to man a deck gun there, Hardegen ordered a coup de grâce from one of his stern tubes. Eighteen minutes after the first hit, a second torpedo struck amidships, breaking the stricken tanker in two.

Five minutes later, the broken hull sections were resting on the seabed 175 feet down, the bow, like that of *Norness*, protruding from the waves from its foremast to the stem. In a sarcastic end-note to the attack, Hardegen concluded, "These are some pretty buoys we are leaving for the Yankees in the harbor approaches as replacement for the [absent] lightships."[2]

WITHIN DAYS OF U-123'S KICKOFF OF Operation Drumbeat, the eastern seaboard was in a state of crisis. Senior officials at the Eastern Sea Frontier in New York and Main Navy Head-quarters in Washington, DC, found themselves trapped in a dual quandary: how to cope with the intensifying onslaught without sufficient ships and aircraft in hand, and what—that is, how much—to tell the American public about the sudden battle es-calating just offshore. Neither problem offered a ready solution.

At first, the navy had been able to ignore the possible public-relations repercussions of the U-boat rampage. While the *Cyclops* and *Norness* had been relatively close to the East Coast when attacked, they were still far enough out at sea that no di-rect sign of the torpedo detonations, fires, and towering columns of smoke reached the eyes of the general population. After the loss of the *Cyclops*, naval authorities in Halifax and Washington waited two days until tersely announcing that an unidentified, 10,000-ton merchant ship had been sunk about 160 nautical miles off the coast of Nova Scotia. After U-123 torpedoed the *Norness*, no immediate alert was dispatched to American search-and-rescue units because no shore station had heard the ship's emergency distress message. As a result, the Eastern Sea Frontier did not become aware of the attack until the US Navy dirigible sighted the hull fragments and nearby survivors at midday on January 14. Still, a navy spokesman told reporters of the *Norness* sinking at 2300 EWT on January 14, just five hours after learning of the incident.

The sinking of the *Coimbra* changed everything. The destruction of the British tanker just twenty-seven nautical miles from the eastern Long Island beach town of Southampton sparked what can only be described as a panic-driven cover-up by the Eastern Sea Frontier and Admiral Ernest King's headquarters in Washington. The effort was doomed to fail from the outset. The fireball from Reinhard Hardegen's torpedoes slamming into the ship was so large and so bright that dozens of residents along the southern coast of Long Island saw the sudden plume of light offshore. They alerted local police and fire departments and the local coast guard station, and a private airplane conducting an offshore patrol found the *Coimbra's* wreckage and the ten survivors out of a crew of forty-six British merchant seamen six hours later at 0830. Nevertheless, navy officials opted to stonewall and then to deliberately misinform the news media and public about the attack. This move to conceal the shocking failure of both the Atlantic Fleet and the Eastern Sea Frontier to deal with the U-boat threat would prove futile.[3]

Following the first two sinkings along the northeastern seaboard, ESF had mounted what could best be described as a halfhearted attempt to prevent another such disaster from taking place. When the message disclosing the sinking of the *Norness* had arrived at Eastern Sea Frontier Headquarters at 1800 hours EWT on January 14, Lieutenant Commander F. W. Osburn Jr. had been serving as the command's night duty officer. After Rear Admiral Edward C. Kalbfus, president of the Naval

War College and senior officer for naval units in Narragansett Bay, briefed Vice Admiral Adolphus Andrews on the *Norness* sinking at 12:20 A.M. on January 15, Andrews ordered a search for the U-boat. At 0645 hours, Osburn called Floyd Bennett Field in southeast Brooklyn, where two PBY-5A Catalina flying boats were temporarily assigned, and ordered them to search the coastal waters off Long Island for "several unidentified vessels" reported to be steaming in that sector. An hour after they launched, at 0830, a third aircraft reported a "ship awash" offshore sixty-one nautical miles east-southeast of Ambrose Light at the mouth of New York Harbor. Just two hours and forty-five minutes later, the Eastern Sea Frontier staff reported that the ship in question was the *Coimbra*.[4]

With the four laden troopships comprising Convoy AT10 scheduled to leave New York Harbor within hours, the navy sat tight on news of the latest U-boat attack. However, local authorities on Long Island did not. The *New York Times* documented the confusion in a front-page article that appeared the next morning, on Friday, January 16:

> Breaking many hours of silence during which the Navy had refused to confirm or deny widely circulated reports of the sinking of another tanker off the South Shore of Long Island early yesterday, a spokesman for the Navy Department announced last night that a thorough check with naval and Coast Guard officials had failed to produce any confirmation of the sinking.

The details came out in any event. Chief Ross Frederico of the Quogue Police Department told a *Times* reporter that a patrol plane had sighted ten men in a life raft floating in stormy seas several dozen miles south of the Shinnecock Inlet at around 0900. A second official, Hampton Bays Police Chief John H. Sutter, confirmed that account and added that the aircrew had seen the partially submerged wreck of the merchant ship. The reporter also learned that several coast guard vessels had raced out to the site in search of survivors of the sinking.

Navy officials in New York and Washington refused to comment on the incident for the next thirty-seven hours. It wasn't until 1600 hours EWT on Friday, January 16, that a navy spokesman in Washington finally confirmed the sinking. He also moved the site of the U-boat attack another seventy-three miles further out to sea: "A tanker named Coimbra, flying the flag of a foreign ally, was observed in a sinking condition on the morning of January 15," the unnamed spokesman said in a statement. "Its position was approximately 100 miles east of New York." Even after the release of the statement, Admiral Andrews and the Eastern Sea Frontier continued to refuse to comment. Official navy records are silent on the rescue of Coimbra's ten survivors. This would not be the last example of the US Navy feigning operational security to mask its incompetence. As the U-boats steadily escalated their attacks during the last half of January, desperate navy officials would resort to outright lies and complete fabrications to cloak the disaster at sea.[5]

BY THE TIME U-701 REACHED its designated attack area east of the Avalon Peninsula on Newfoundland's southeastern coast in the twilight dawn hours of Sunday, January 18, the Battle of the

Atlantic in Canadian waters was raging with white-hot intensity. In just six days, six U-boats—the Type IXC U-130 and the Type VII U-86, U-87, U-203, U-552, and U-553—had already destroyed nine Allied merchant ships and damaged a tenth. The total losses comprised 36,172 gross registered tons, along with the deaths of 237 Allied merchant sailors out of the 333 personnel aboard the stricken ships. Compared with the Newfoundland area attacks, the Operation Drumbeat campaign along the US East Coast was initially taking a distinct second place in targets destroyed. Thus far, only two of the Type IX U-boats had drawn blood: Hardegen's U-123 with three kills for 25,421 gross registered tons and Korvettenkapitän Richard Zapp's U-66 with a solitary sinking for 6,635 tons.

The first drops of blood drawn by the U-boat campaign in North American waters quickly turned into a hemorrhage: in the first three weeks, fifteen of Vice Admiral Karl Dönitz's U-boats succeeded in destroying thirty-five Allied merchant ships and a British destroyer totaling 181,546 gross registered tons, killing 1,219 crewmen, gunners, and passengers. The toll included twelve oil tankers, twenty freighters, and the Canadian passenger liner *Lady Hawkins*, whose death toll—251 crewmen and passengers out of 306 souls aboard—was the highest for any single ship. The highest-scoring U-boats were Kapitänleutnant Reinhard Hardegen's U-123, with eight ships totaling 49,421 tons and a ninth ship of 8,206 tons damaged; Korvettenkapitän Richard Zapp's U-66, with five ships totaling 36,114 tons; and Korvettenkapitän Ernst Kals's U-130, with five ships destroyed for 31,658 tons and a sixth ship totally wrecked for 6,986 tons.

Unfortunately for Horst Degen and his crew, who spent a difficult and tedious week patrolling off the Newfoundland coast

Crewmen stand atop the narrow bridge and on the main deck as U-701 returns to port in France following a North Atlantic patrol. COURTESY OF HORST DEGEN.

from the northern tip of the Avalon Peninsula to Cape Race, U-701 did not add to its total of ships sunk. Degen had managed on January 16, during a lull in the stormy weather, to transfer his two remaining torpedoes from their topside canisters into the bow and stern torpedo rooms. However, heavy fog, snow, and ice and steady aerial reconnaissance patrols continued to thwart U-701. The boat made five attempted attacks on solitary merchant ships without success before starting the homeward transit on Saturday, January 24. The next morning, Degen sighted a westbound 5,000-ton Allied freighter that had appeared on the northern horizon at dawn, but when he fired one of his two G7a torpedoes at the merchantman, rough sea conditions caused the torpedo to run under the hull and to miss.

The return trip to the U-boat base at Saint-Nazaire passed without major incident until January 31, when BdU ordered U-701 and six other U-boats to form a search-and-rescue operation to find survivors of the 5,081-ton German blockade-runner *Spreewald*. Disguised as the Norwegian freighter *Elg*, the freighter was heading back to Bordeaux, France, when Kapitänleutnant Peter-Erich Cremer in U-333 mistakenly attacked and sank it, killing forty-eight crewmen and British merchant seamen being held on board as prisoners. U-701 and the other boats searched unsuccessfully for the next seven days for a missing lifeboat carrying twenty-four people, ultimately abandoning the effort. Passing through the lock into Saint-Nazaire's inner harbor on Monday, February 9, U-701's weary crew stepped ashore for the first time in forty-four days for a fifteen-day reprieve from the Battle of the Atlantic at a seaside hotel in La Baule, ten miles west of the port. In his final entry for the first patrol in U-701's war diary, Degen noted, "Crew and boat were strongly tested on a long voyage." And with Operation Drumbeat in full swing across the ocean, harder tests were certainly yet to come.[6]

WHILE THE CREWMEN OF U-701 were delighting in what Gerhard Schwendel later called the "pure luxury" of real beds with clean sheets, fresh food, hot showers, and evenings touring the local bars and restaurants of La Baule, the prevailing emotions at Eastern Sea Frontier Headquarters and Main Navy in Washington were the complete opposite—a mixture of frustration, anxiety, and fear. Assigned to write Vice Admiral Andrews's daily war diary at ESF Headquarters, Lieutenant j.g. Lawrance R. Thompson in late January penned a blunt assessment of the command's poor performance to date against the U-boats. Tersely summarizing the U-boats' tactics of operating alone and attacking merchant ships under cover of darkness, Thompson identified one problem that would bedevil ESF Headquarters for months: "Three of the ships sunk had been silhouetted against the lights from the shore." But that was not the only problem, Thompson added. The Eastern Sea Frontier simply did not have the warships and aircraft required to thwart the U-boats.

With most of the Atlantic Fleet's destroyer force preoccupied with mid-Atlantic escort groups or special missions like Convoy AT10, Admiral Royal Ingersoll in Norfolk had no warships to loan to the Eastern Sea Frontier. Rather than redeploying the stretched destroyer force to confront the U-boats offshore, King and other senior navy officials went public with a fusillade of lies.

A formal policy of censorship imposed by the federal government on January 15 facilitated the navy's campaign of misinformation. In the immediate aftermath of Pearl Harbor, President Franklin Roosevelt had signed an executive order creating a federal Office of Censorship and charged its director, former Associated Press executive news editor Byron Price, with drafting formal guidelines for press self-censorship in covering military operations and other sensitive topics. The seven-page "Code of Wartime Practices for the American Press" (and a similar manual for radio stations) called upon journalists to forswear publishing any information on troop movements, operations of navy and merchant ships, military aircraft, the location of military facilities, war contracts, and even weather forecasts—unless government officials had released such information. The program aimed at protecting vital operational military secrets as the armed forces geared up for a tough war. As it turned out, it also gave the US Navy an effective cloak to hide its lack of preparedness against the U-boats when the number of attacks soared in late January.[7]

Navy Secretary Frank Knox, Admiral King, and other senior admirals must have thought their attempts to suppress or delay releasing information on the U-boat attacks were becoming insufficient to allay potential civilian doubts about the sea service's performance. On January 23, just eleven days after the British warned of the U-boats approaching the East Coast, an unnamed navy spokesman issued a remarkable statement to reporters in Washington, DC:

> There are many rumors and unofficial reports about the capture or destruction of enemy submarines. Some of the recent visitors to our territorial waters will never enjoy the return portion of their voyage. Furthermore, the percentage of one-way traffic is increasing, while that of two-way traffic is satisfactorily on the decline. But there will be no information given out about the fate of the enemy submarine excursionists who don't get home, until that information is no longer of aid and comfort to the enemy.
>
> This is a phase of the game of war secrecy into which every American should enter enthusiastically. . . . The press and the radio have made a great, patriotic contribution by voluntarily disciplining themselves in the matter of reporting such incidents as may have come to their attention unofficially. All the

people can make the same contribution. Even if you have seen a submarine captured or destroyed [!], keep it to yourself. Let the enemy guess what happened. . . . By this conduct every American can make his contribution to the Navy's worldwide effort to eliminate the enemy submarine menace.

The Associated Press article containing the navy's keep-it-to-yourself policy quoted Secretary Knox reaffirming the secrecy guidelines. The article added that Knox had "relaxed his rule of silence only once," and that had been to say on November 21, 1941, that the US Navy had either sunk or damaged fourteen U-boats to date during the unofficial clash at sea in the North Atlantic. This was a total fabrication.

The navy also took a more proactive stance when it felt compelled to obscure the horrific statistics. On Wednesday, January 28, Aviation Machinists Mate 1st Class Donald F. Mason was piloting a PBY-5A Catalina seaplane on patrol off Newfoundland when he spotted a U-boat down on the surface. Throwing the ungainly aircraft into a dive, Mason dropped a spread of depth charges as the U-boat hastily submerged. Mason duly noted his attack on the enemy, but by the time his report reached Navy Headquarters, someone had penned the eloquent, inspiring— and fictional—message that within hours became a national sensation: "Sighted Sub; Sank Same." The *New York Times*, among dozens of other newspapers, trumpeted the alleged sinking and characterized the report as having a "brevity worthy of Oliver Hazard Perry, whose message after the Battle of Lake Erie was the laconic 'We have met the enemy and they are ours.'"

In fact, the US Navy had yet to sink a single U-boat.[8]

7

PARANOIA

THE SPRING OF 1942 WAS AN UNRELENTING DISASTER FOR THE Anglo-American alliance at sea. During the two-month period spanning February and March, the Allies suffered four major setbacks that caused merchant shipping losses to soar. First, on February 1, Vice Admiral Karl Dönitz changed his command's Enigma system by deploying a new encryption machine on U-boats and ashore. The new M4 *Marine Funkschlüssel-Maschine* utilized four rotors instead of three to scramble the text. As a result, the decryption bombes at Bletchley Park suddenly went silent, and British code breakers lost their detailed situational awareness of U-boat deployments in the North Atlantic and elsewhere. Second, by mid-February the German code breakers at B-Dienst had significantly broken into Naval Cypher No. 3, gleaning invaluable intelligence on Allied convoy movements. Third, on February 18, U-boat Force Headquarters opened up a second front in the Caribbean that later expanded to the Gulf of Mexico. This new U-boat campaign against North American shipping provided the U-boat commanders with a target-rich environment to rival that of the still-undefended Canadian and

American coastal waters. The fourth Allied setback was the continued failure of the US Navy to reinforce the hamstrung Eastern Sea Frontier (ESF)—and now the Caribbean Sea Frontier as well—with sufficient destroyers and long-range patrol bombers to mount an effective defense against the marauding U-boats.[1]

The loss of naval Enigma was a serious blow to the British and American antisubmarine warfare effort. It took the three-rotor bombes twenty-six times longer to find the daily settings of a four-rotor Enigma machine than it had for the older, three-rotor models, rendering obtaining timely intelligence from U-boat message traffic impossible. In fact, apart from isolated—and minor—breakthroughs, the new Triton network used by Atlantic U-boats would remain impenetrable for most of 1942. While British code breakers continued to penetrate lower-security German naval channels and reaped tactical intelligence from high-frequency direction-finding (HF/DF) radio intercepts, photographic reconnaissance, and other means, hunting U-boats at sea had become a far more difficult task.

The British Operational Intelligence Centre's (OIC) U-boat Situation Report for the week ending February 9 confirmed that the loss of German naval Enigma had rendered tracking U-boat movements nearly impossible. However, Bletchley Park was able to infer from isolated HF/DF intercepts and the pattern of ship losses that at least ten U-boats were moving westbound across the North Atlantic to form a third wave of attack off the Newfoundland and US coastlines. This time, officials at the Eastern Sea Frontier acknowledged the OIC warning, but the Americans could still do very little to protect shipping along the eastern seaboard. Vice Admiral Adolphus Andrews and his staff were still grappling with an impossible situation since neither the Atlantic Fleet nor COMINCH intended to reinforce the command's motley defenses. Admiral King sent no reinforcements. Admiral Dönitz sent several more waves of U-boats.

In February 1942, sixteen U-boats patrolling in North American waters west of 060 degrees west—a north-south line running from the eastern tip of Nova Scotia to eastern Venezuela—sank thirty-five Allied merchant vessels and one warship totaling 225,390 gross registered tons; just five long-range Type IX boats that began operations in the Caribbean on February 16 sank another fifteen ships totaling 86,507 tons and damaged five more during the last thirteen days of the month alone. Their favorite targets in the oil-producing regions of the Caribbean were, unsurprisingly, Allied oil tankers. Among the ships destroyed in the first phase of the Caribbean operation were ten tankers with a total of 57,560 gross registered tons. Their comrades operating in the chill waters of the western Atlantic did even better, sinking thirteen tankers totaling 103,059 gross registered tons.

The month of March brought two developments that seemed to promise relief to the Eastern Sea Frontier—yet both would prove illusory. First, U-boat attacks suddenly ceased at the end of February. Lieutenant Lawrance Thompson wrote in the ESF War Diary that the first week of March "was unexpectedly and pleasantly free from enemy activity." This was technically accurate: U-boats sank only five merchant ships in the western Atlantic during that time, four of them off Newfoundland and the fifth four hundred miles south of Bermuda. But attacks suddenly spiked again during the week of March 7 to 14 as no fewer than nine U-boats arrived off the eastern Canadian and US coasts.

Another eight U-boats would appear off Nova Scotia and the American Atlantic coast during the last two weeks of the month. Together, they went on to sink forty-seven merchant ships and two warships totaling 289,123 gross registered tons, damaging another four for 25,841 tons.[2]

Admiral Royal Ingersoll at Atlantic Fleet Headquarters was well aware of the deepening crisis and made what appeared to be a significant offer to Vice Admiral Andrews. In a message to all destroyers under his command on March 8, Ingersoll stated, "When such employment is practicable and does not interfere with escort fleet vessels, tasks, and fleet operations, destroyers and other suitable escort ships making passage through Sea Frontier Zones incident to scheduled movements should be utilized to fullest extent in the protection of merchant shipping." On the surface, it appeared that a sizable part of the Atlantic Fleet destroyer force—some eighty to ninety warships—would soon be available to hunt U-boats in the western Atlantic. In fact, the results were pathetic. During the last three weeks of March, only fourteen destroyers and *Treasury*-class cutters briefly paused in their higher-priority missions to help in the fight against the U-boats. The total number of days on actual patrol ranged from one to sixteen for the different warships, for a total of sixty-three ship-days; this meant that, on average, only two destroyers were operating per day along the 1,100-nautical-mile Eastern Sea Frontier. By the end of March, Admiral Andrews and his subordinates in the six naval districts were in a full-fledged panic.[3]

The U-boat rampage along the US East Coast did not just cause sharp strains within the US Navy. As the losses mounted, the British also became exasperated. They regarded the U-boats'

Naval Intelligence officials search the bodies of nine crewmen from the 2,438-ton collier *David H. Atwater*, which was sunk by gunfire from U-552 off Virginia's eastern shore on the night of April 2, 1942. Hundreds of merchant sailors perished at the hands of the U-boats during the bloody campaign along the East Coast in the first half of 1942. NATIONAL ARCHIVES AND RECORDS ADMINISTRATION.

success as a sign of American ineptitude and were frustrated by the US Navy's refusal to heed the harsh lessons the Royal Navy itself had learned between 1939 and 1941, when U-boats first began attacking British shipping in the Atlantic and Mediterranean. Winston Churchill cabled FDR aide Harry Hopkins on March 12 to decry "the immense sinking" of oil tankers along the American coast and in the Caribbean. At one point, the British Admiralty dispatched Commander Rodger Winn from the OIC Submarine Tracking Room to Washington, DC, to plead with the US Navy's leaders to begin an effective response to the U-boats. His agenda included urging them to create a submarine tracking room of their own as a fusion center for all tactical intelligence regarding the enemy and to personally press Admiral Ernest King to instigate a coastal convoy system. As the British well knew, convoying ships was the best—indeed, the only—proven way of defending shipping and even mounting successful attacks against U-boats. Hunting for submersibles in the open ocean was like looking for needles in a haystack; by massing the U-boats' targets together and surrounding them with a ring of escort warships, however, American military planners could draw in and overwhelm the hunters.

As Winn later recounted, Rear Admiral Richard S. Edwards, King's deputy chief of staff, was initially opposed to forming a submarine tracking room. Edwards told Winn that the US Navy wished to learn its own lessons and had plenty of ships with which to do so. At that point, the mild British lawyer-turned-U-boat-hunter blew his stack. "The trouble is, admiral, it's not only your bloody ships you are losing," Winn heatedly replied. "A lot of them are ours!" This was no exaggeration on the OIC official's part. Out of 216 Allied merchant ships sunk by the U-boats in North American coastal waters and the Caribbean between January and mid-April 1942, 98 were operating with the British Merchant Navy—51 flying the Union Jack and another 47 from Nazi-occupied countries that had joined the Allied cause—some 45 percent of the overall total. US-flagged losses came in a close second, with ninety ships sunk during that same period. Admiral King in a subsequent meeting agreed with Winn and told the British officer that the US Navy would create its own submarine tracking room. However, other measures—notably a coastal convoy system—would take much longer to implement.

The carnage offshore continued without letup, but Horst Degen and Harry Kane were not among the participants in this es-
calating battle. The happenstance of war had sent them on quite
different adventures elsewhere: Degen and U-701 to patrol off
Iceland, Kane and his aircrew to more training flights along the
West Coast. At this juncture, Harry Kane and his men—and not
Horst Degen and his crew—would experience one of the more
bizarre encounters of the war.[4]

THE ATTACK BEGAN SHORTLY BEFORE SUNSET on February 23,
1942. Commander Kozo Nishino brought the 2,584-ton Japanese cruiser submarine I-17 inshore west of Santa Barbara, California, then ordered his ninety-three-man crew to surface and
his gun crew to arm the 144-mm (5.5-inch) deck cannon. As
I-17 loitered less than two hundred yards from the beach, its
gunners began firing at the giant Bankline Company aviation
fuel storage farm on the bluffs overlooking the shore. During the
next twenty minutes, I-17 lobbed seventeen shells, each weighing
eighty-four pounds, at the sprawling facility. Most shots went
wild, and only one shell landed within thirty yards of one of
the storage tanks. After his last shells had either splashed into the
Santa Barbara Channel or plowed into empty land behind the fuel
farm, Nishino then ordered I-17 back out to sea.

The Japanese attack was risky and audacious but militarily
ineffective. Its psychological shock value, however, was profound: for the first time since the war began eleven weeks earlier, an Axis warship had bombarded the US mainland. This
threw the entire West Coast population into a state of near
hysteria. The next morning, a headline that could be read with

the naked eye from one hundred yards away dominated the *San Francisco Chronicle*'s front page: "SUB SHELLS CALIFOR-NIA! War Strikes California: Big Raider Fires on Oil Refinery 8 Miles North of Santa Barbara." The *Los Angeles Times* headline was equally shrill: "ARMY SAYS ALARM REAL: Roaring Guns Mark Blackout." The Fourth Army went on alert from San Luis Obispo to the Mexican border. Public fears of a possible Japanese carrier air attack or even invasion along the West Coast—concerns that had subsided slightly in the twelve weeks since Pearl Harbor—now spiked anew.

The US Army had not been idle on the West Coast since the December 7 Japanese attack. At the outbreak of war, Lieutenant General John L. DeWitt, as Fourth Army commander, had eleven infantry and five antiaircraft artillery regiments throughout the region, although most units lacked two-thirds of their allotted equipment. In the first weeks after Pearl Harbor, the army rushed reinforcements to vital parts of California, Oregon, and Washington state. By early February 1942, DeWitt commanded six infantry divisions, a cavalry brigade, and fourteen antiaircraft artillery regiments. Of nearly 250,000 army troops based in the Fourth Army area of responsibility, more than 100,000 manned antiaircraft batteries that ringed dozens of vital military bases, harbors, and defense plants. In the early evening hours of February 24, 1942, they were still on full alert some twenty-four hours after I-17 opened fire on the Bankline fuel farm. Within the next five hours, Lieutenant Harry Kane and his aircrew would inadvertently douse the fire with gasoline.[5]

It was supposed to be a routine training mission, Kane recalled years later. By now, his squadron had grown to twenty-two officers and 225 enlisted men. Many of them were newcomers and required extensive individual training in their aircrew roles. "At one time we got a whole batch of new navigators into the squadron and we had to take them all out and give them some real tough training," Kane said. Training for these new navigators often took the form of long coastal patrol flights, which—as Kane soon discovered—could quickly turn deadly, given the paranoia about enemy forces operating in the same areas.

On the evening of February 24, Kane took off from Sacramento with a full crew, including a newly assigned navigator lieutenant. The flight plan called for Kane to fly out two hundred miles due west from San Francisco, then turn to follow a southerly course for about 360 miles, which would place them out over the Pacific due west of Los Angeles. At that juncture, the navigator would have to calculate the moment at which Kane should turn the aircraft to a heading of 074 degrees to fly straight in to land at March Field, located some sixty-five miles east of Los Angeles near Riverside. The plotted course would also bring Kane's aircraft in over Los Angeles itself, flying close over the Long Beach Naval Station and Naval Shipyard and numerous defense plants, including the Douglas Aircraft factories in Santa Monica and Long Beach and the Lockheed factory near Burbank.

The first three hours of the flight passed without incident. After turning at the two-hundred-mile point west of San Francisco, Kane and his crew flew the southbound leg for just under two hours when the lieutenant announced that it was time to turn to the heading of 074 degrees and proceed toward the Southern California shoreline about four hundred miles away. At about 7:30 P.M., Kane noticed that the sky was darkening from a thick cloud bank that lay ahead of the aircraft. He decided to take radio direction-finding fixes on Los Angeles and San Diego radio stations as a backstop for the navigator's calculation. At that point, Kane discovered that all of the stations were off the air. He tried descending below the cloud layer to get a visual sighting of the coast but abandoned the effort when a crewman fearful of crashing into one of the Channel Islands started screaming for him to pull up. As they neared the coast, the cloud bank cleared up, to the aircrew's relief.

Two hours later, Kane and crew found themselves orbiting above March Field, delighted that the navigator's fix had been so accurate. Then a voice from the control tower suddenly called out in his headset, "Lieutenant Kane, you are requested to land at March Field as soon as possible. The general wants to see you." Kane turned to his navigator with a puzzled look on his face. Normal procedure was for ground control to call an aircraft by its tail number, but they had asked for him by name. Minutes after landing and taxiing the aircraft to its parking spot, Kane found himself braced at attention while a furious Major General Jacob E. Fickel chewed him out.

"You stupid blankety, blank, blank, do you realize what's happened?" Kane remembered the Fourth Air Force commanding general barking.

"No sir," Kane said.

"You were an unidentified aircraft and you have blacked out all of Los Angeles and all of San Diego and put the radios in both places off the air, and I have sent four P-38's up looking for you with instructions to shoot you down!"

Unbeknownst to Lieutenant Kane and his aircrew, US Army Air Forces officials in Sacramento had forgotten to inform their counterparts at March Field of the long-range navigational exercise that Kane and crew were conducting. Sometime between Kane's turn to 074 degrees and the aircraft's approach to the Los Angeles shoreline, an army radar set picked up what its operators concluded was an unidentified aircraft heading in from the open ocean. No doubt exhausted and stressed from the previous day's alert following I-17's bombardment of the Bankline fuel farm, the radar operators and antiaircraft gunners likely concluded that Admiral Isoroku Yamamoto's carrier fleet had returned to attack Southern California. Army gunners went to their antiaircraft batteries, and civil defense officials ordered a total blackout from San Luis Obispo to the Mexican border, including the radio stations. And then—several hours after Kane and his crew landed safely at March Field—all hell broke loose.

At 0222 hours Pacific War Time, the night skies from Santa Monica to Long Beach thirty miles away suddenly erupted with brightly illuminated searchlights and long, fiery streams of antiaircraft tracers. It was the start of a five-hour mass panic that resulted in three deaths, dozens of injuries, and widespread property damage. One news report later described the spectacle as "the first real show of the Second World War on the United States mainland." Calls from frightened residents claiming to have seen anywhere from several dozen to more than one hundred aircraft flying overhead inundated police and fire stations. Since the blackout regulations required motorists to extinguish their headlights and pull over to the side of the street, the roads and highways quickly became gridlocked, especially since tens of thousands of defense workers were heading to or from their shifts.

But the antiaircraft (AA) shells, not the public panic, did the real damage. Army officials subsequently reported that 1,430 AA

In the aftermath of a Japanese submarine's shelling of a Southern California oil farm, edgy antiaircraft gunners filled the night skies over Los Angeles with searchlights and gunfire shortly after Lieutenant Harry Kane and his aircrew made an unannounced flight over the city. The mass panic was caught by newspaper photographers. Copyright © 1942, *Los Angeles Times*, reprinted with permission.

rounds were fired during the ordeal. With no aircraft overhead to strike, the explosive shells soared high into the sky and then fell all over Los Angeles. Shrapnel slammed into the municipal airport, broke windows of the Long Beach branch of the Bank of America, and forced overnight shipyard workers in Long Beach to dive under their equipment for safety. Dr. Franklin W. Stewart and his wife were at home when a 3-inch AA shell crashed through the roof and exploded in a home office, destroying the room and the family kitchen but leaving them unharmed. City resident Victor L. Norman was not in his bedroom when a shell burst through the ceiling, which was fortunate for him. The detonation shredded everything in the room into small pieces. Two motorists died in collisions with other vehicles, and a California state guardsman driving a truck full of AA ammunition suffered a fatal heart attack.

The night of mayhem came to be called the "Battle of Los Angeles," and very few people knew then (nor do they now) that it was indirectly caused by Kane's flyover—or, more accurately, the USAAF officials who had mismanaged it. Given the widespread paranoia among many Californians about the threat of sabotage and subversion from Japanese Americans—aliens and citizens alike—many members of the public were quick to accuse the Japanese of carrying out the mysterious aircraft flights or guiding them from the ground. Since the federal government had already begun its plan to evacuate over 110,000 Japanese Americans to internment camps, local and federal authorities announced the arrests of twenty of them in connection with the incident. Nor was that the end of it. The confusion and paranoia quickly spread from Los Angeles to Washington, DC.

Garbage in, garbage out: relying on local reports from the chaotic scene, Secretary of War Henry L. Stimson announced on Thursday, February 26, that the incident had involved fifteen mysterious aircraft flying at altitudes ranging from 9,000 to 18,000 feet. "It seems reasonable to conclude that if unidentified planes were involved, they may have come from commercial services operated by enemy agents" seeking to discover the location of antiaircraft batteries, he intoned. Navy Secretary Frank Knox disagreed, flatly dismissing the whole affair as "a false alarm." General DeWitt made the best of a bad situation, publicly commending the antiaircraft gunners, pursuit squadrons, civil defense wardens, and everyone else who had played a part in the debacle.[6]

The originators of the panic, meanwhile, were long gone. When Major General Fickel—the officer who had chewed Kane out upon his landing—and his senior staff realized that the error stemmed from USAAF Headquarters in Northern California, they quietly let Kane off the hook, and he and his aircrew flew back to Sacramento the day after the incident. By the time of Stimson's announcement, Kane and his aircrew had resumed their training at Sacramento Municipal Airport, largely unaware of the chaos and excitement they had so innocently sparked.

Some 5,440 miles to the northeast, Horst Degen and the crew of U-701 were also unaware of the fiasco in Los Angeles. They had other, more pressing things on their minds. While Commander Nishino was shelling the fuel farm, BdU technicians were loading fourteen torpedoes into U-701's forward and aft torpedo rooms and its topside canisters. At the moment that Harry Kane and his aircrew were scaring the bejesus out of Southern California, Degen's crewmen were finishing the backbreaking work of loading fuel, ammunition, water, and food supplies for the boat's next patrol. And at about the time Secretaries Stimson and Knox were going public with their radically different versions of what had occurred over Los Angeles, U-701 was on its way to the waters off Iceland for its second war patrol.[7]

Vice Admiral Karl Dönitz should have been a happy man as the month of February 1942 drew to a close. For the previous six weeks, his U-boat commanders in the first wave of attacks along the US East Coast and Newfoundland had reported successes far beyond what he and his staff at BdU Operations had anticipated. After hearing Reinhard Hardegen's postpatrol report for U-123 after its return on February 9, Dönitz summarized the situation along the American littoral in practically gleeful terms: "The expectation of encountering many independently routed ships, clumsy handling of ships, slight, inexperienced sea and air patrols and defenses was so truly fulfilled that conditions had to be described as almost completely of peacetime standards." It was almost as if the Americans refused to believe that a war was on.

Dönitz and his staff were aware, however, of a number of negative incidents stemming from the Drumbeat and Ziethen patrols. At least six of the U-boat commanders, including Degen, reported torpedo failures that had prevented them from sinking Allied merchant ships even at very close range. Both Degen and Horst Uphoff in U-84 cited failures in the contact pistols of their torpedoes that resulted in their hearing the dull boom of torpedoes slamming into the hulls of merchant ships but no warhead detonation. Other U-boat skippers complained that the depth-setting gear inside their torpedoes had failed, causing the weapons to underrun their targets without going off. Winter storms off Newfoundland had also played havoc with a number of the U-boats. But these were relatively minor issues. Threatening to undermine the U-boat campaign in American waters was something else: paranoia at the highest level of the Nazi regime. The source of the problem was none other than Adolf Hitler himself.[8]

For several months, the Führer had been worrying about the security of northern Norway, a vital corridor for iron ore and nickel supplies keeping the German war machine in operation. After British commandos staged hit-and-run raids near Narvik and Ålesund the night of December 26–27, Hitler summoned Admiral Erich Raeder to his Wolf's Lair headquarters. "If the British go about things properly, they will attack northern Norway at several points," Hitler said. "This might be of decisive importance for the outcome of the war." He then demanded the immediate transfer of the Kriegsmarine's major surface warships to Norwegian waters.

To Raeder's and Dönitz's acute dismay, three weeks later Hitler had announced that Norway was now the "zone of destiny" for the war. In a meeting on January 22 with Vice Admiral Kurt Fricke, Raeder's chief of staff, the Führer—according to official minutes of the meeting—demanded "unconditional obedience to all his commands and wishes concerning the defense of this area." One of them was that twenty U-boats would permanently patrol the Iceland-Faroes gap and Norwegian coastal waters, an exorbitant reallocation that threatened to seriously undermine the Drumbeat-Newfoundland campaign just eleven days after it had begun. Well aware of Hitler's impulsive firing of Field Marshal Walther von Brauchitsch three weeks earlier, Raeder and Dönitz had no desire to challenge the dictator—although Dönitz, at least, knew full well that the U-boats were in a decisive phase of the battle against Allied merchant shipping in the Atlantic. "I believed at the time, and I still believe, that our overall war effort would have been best served had we seized the opportunity offered by the exceptionally favorable conditions in the Atlantic and concentrated every available U-boat on the war in shipping," Dönitz later recalled. However, BdU issued the orders to send eight of his U-boats designated for the western Atlantic to the Iceland-Faroes gap. One of them was U-701.

Degen's new deployment lasted thirty-five days and took him and his crew over 4,619 nautical miles of ocean between the U-boat's departure from Saint-Nazaire on February 26 and its return to France on April 1. Crewman Gerhard Schwendel recalled that after the patrol, a German news bulletin announced that U-701 had destroyed "an entire convoy bringing war materials from America to England." In actuality, during twenty-two days spent lurking off the southeast coast of Iceland, it managed to sink two small coastal steamers and two British antisubmarine warfare trawlers for a minute total of 1,610 gross registered tons—less than one-half the tonnage of the 3,657-ton freighter *Baron Erskine*, its solitary kill on its first war patrol. While the winter weather frequently disrupted their patrol patterns, the real reason for the lack of success among U-701 and the other boats was that the Führer's intuition had packed them off to an empty stretch of the North Atlantic.

On Friday, March 27, U-701 was still northwest of Scotland on its homeward course, when BdU transmitted a message directing it to return to Brest rather than Saint-Nazaire. Several hours later, Oberfunkmaat Herbert Grotheer decrypted an Enigma message alerting all U-boats at sea to "proceed at high speed" to a rendezvous point in the Bay of Biscay. Three hours later, a follow-up message reported that a British special operations force had attacked Saint-Nazaire but had been repulsed. In Operation Chariot, the British targeted the large Louis Joubert dry dock at Saint-Nazaire, the only facility on the French Atlantic coast large enough to repair major German surface warships such as the battleship *Tirpitz*. Loss of the dry dock would force the Kriegsmarine to return any major warships needing repairs to German home waters, significantly reducing that particular threat in the Atlantic. The Royal Navy converted the World War I–era destroyer *HMS Campbeltown* (formerly the *USS Buchanan*) into a floating time bomb, with a cache of 4.1 tons of high explosives concealed below decks in several steel containers. Escorted by 18 smaller torpedo and patrol boats bearing a force of 346 Royal Navy crewman and 265 British army commandos, the destroyer steamed up the Loire River at midnight on March 28 and, despite heavy German gunfire, rammed the dry dock at 0138 hours—just four minutes behind schedule. German defenders put up a fierce fight that killed 169 of the raiders and resulted in the capture of 215 others, while another 228 men safely evacuated. The Germans failed to detect the explosives onboard the destroyer, and at noon the next day, the *Campbeltown* blew up with such force that it destroyed the dry dock gate and killed around 360 German soldiers and French civilians. The mission was a total success: the dry dock remained unusable for the rest of the war and would not be repaired until 1947.

The Saint-Nazaire raid had little effect, however, on the U-boat campaign in the Atlantic. U-701 continued its homeward journey, arriving in Brest on Wednesday, April 1. While U-701 underwent repairs at its new home in a Brest U-boat bunker, Degen and his men once more savored life ashore after a frigid month inside their steel tube. Six weeks later, U-701 was ready for sea again.[9]

8

UNPREPARED DEFENDERS

As U-boats rampaged along the US East Coast in the spring of 1942, one of the Allies' newest lines of defense struggled to respond to the crisis. During World War I, the British had sent then-primitive aircraft and dirigibles offshore to hunt for the kaiser's first-generation U-boats, but they lacked effective sensors and weapons to locate and destroy the enemy. As a result, aircraft sank none of the 204 U-boats lost between 1914 and 1918, although the British continued to expand aerial patrols since they succeeded in driving the submersibles under water, thereby allowing Allied ships to escape attack.

It had been well known that aviation could be an effective tool against submarines; difficult for U-boat commanders to detect, airplanes were unusually effective at spotting and forcing the submersibles under water. Yet, although the Allies possessed several strong and growing air service branches, infighting hobbled most of them as the Battle of the Atlantic accelerated.

In the United Kingdom, the Royal Air Force's Coastal Command was struggling against its two more powerful rivals—Bomber

Command and Fighter Command—for aircraft, resources, and trained personnel. In the United States, the USAAF and the navy were gridlocked over which service should take on the fight against the U-boats with the scarce numbers of long-range bombers then available. The USAAF, under long-standing federal law, owned and controlled all land-based bombers, while the navy merely operated seaplanes and smaller land-based aircraft to patrol the nation's sea frontiers.

Nor was this interservice rivalry alone hampering the development of aircraft antisubmarine capabilities. The USAAF itself was consumed with its own ongoing expansion, as Lieutenant Harry Kane and the rest of the 396th Medium Bombardment Squadron were well aware when March ended and April blew in on a fresh spring breeze. The weather had improved, but frustration levels remained high. Still based at Sacramento Municipal Airport, the 396th aircrews continued a nonstop slog of combat crew training and administrative duties that seemed as if they might outlast the war. "Most of it was training and patrol, flying up and down the Pacific Coast," Kane later said. "There [were] other squadrons further north that [trained] up around Oregon and Washington." Four months after Pearl Harbor, the USAAF was nowhere near ready to take on the Germans and the Japanese. Aviation strategists since the 1920s had predicted that air power would someday become a primary military force for any industrial nation, and the USAAF had indeed accomplished much in the past three years. But the newest military branch still had an incredible distance to go before it could feasibly take the war into the skies over the Axis.

The Army Air Corps (as it had been called until mid-1941) was born four years after Orville Wright made the first powered flight in an airplane at Kill Devil Hills, North Carolina, in 1903. Buried within the army bureaucracy, its predecessor, the Aeronautical Division of the Signal Corps, initially had a maximum personnel strength of three men. While World War I saw a spike in its growth to 227 aircraft, during the early 1920s the air branch languished. It would take the rise of Adolf Hitler and the spectacle of German airpower wreaking havoc in the Spanish Civil War to prompt President Franklin Roosevelt and army leaders to get Congress to open the money spigot for new aircraft, airfields, training centers, and pilots. After the 1938 Munich crisis, when Hitler bullied the British and French into allowing Germany to swallow the Czech Sudetenland, FDR said he wanted to build a modern air corps of 20,000 combat aircraft and develop an aviation industry production capability of 2,000 aircraft per month.

As the specter of war drew nearer, Roosevelt had to revise his initially ambitious goal as planners' estimates of what army aviation would require rapidly expanded: in April 1940, FDR told Congress he wanted American industry to produce 50,000 aircraft per year. Nevertheless, a month after the fall of France in June 1940, air corps planners formally proposed to field a force of fifty-four combat groups and receive over 4,000 modern warplanes by April 1942. Each bomb group fielded between seventy-two and ninety-six aircraft. Just seven months later, on February 14, 1941, General George C. Marshall ordered air corps commander-in-chief Major General Henry H. "Hap" Arnold to prepare for a force of eighty-four combat groups totaling 7,800 aircraft. To man this emerging behemoth, Marshall also directed the expansion of army pilot training in 1941 to 30,000 cadets per year. This also unleashed construction crews from coast to coast building hundreds of new air corps bases, as well as pilot and aircrew training centers. The USAAF would ultimately grow to a force of 231,099 aircraft of all types, including 35,000 long-range bombers and 68,712 fighters, and a manpower of 2.1 million personnel.

In the spring of 1942, however, the USAAF was still a mere shadow of the force it would become by the end of the war. Harry Kane and his fellow fliers in the 396th were part of a fighting organization still in its infancy. Few USAAF bomber units were fully certified for combat, and none had the sensors, weapons, tactics, and aviator skills needed for the difficult mission of locating and destroying a U-boat. This was especially true on the US East Coast.[1]

On December 8, 1941, the I Bomber Command under Brigadier General Arnold N. Krogstad had begun patrol flights offshore. Krogstad had a force of fewer than fifty bombers, including nine long-range B-17s, a handful of the underperforming B-18s, and several dozen medium-range B-25 and B-26 bombers. Daily patrols of two aircraft apiece originated at Bangor, Maine; Westover Field, Massachusetts; Mitchel Field, New York; and Langley Field, Virginia. The B-17s patrolled out to six hundred miles offshore, while the medium-range bombers flew shorter circuits of up to several hundred miles. Meanwhile, single-engine utility and trainer aircraft from the I Air Support Command bolstered Vice Admiral Adolphus Andrews's ragtag air fleet of 103 similar planes in mounting short-range missions several dozen miles off the coast. These latter aircraft were unarmed, and most lacked radios, so their value—if any—was in tricking U-boat commanders into crash-diving upon sighting them, thereby safeguarding any civilian ships in the area until navy warships—if available—could rush to the scene.

While the army's B-17 aircraft enjoyed a greater range than its motley collection of utility aircraft and trainers, the bombers' aircrews were totally unprepared for hunting U-boats. They lacked aerial depth charges, the aircraft had no effective bombsights or radar, and they had received no training in hunting enemy submersibles. A typical incident occurred nine days after Pearl Harbor when one of Krogstad's B-17s sighted an unidentified vessel in Block Island Sound. It was the *Benham*-class destroyer *USS Trippe*, which was steaming independently from Norfolk Naval Station to Newport, Rhode Island. The 1,850-ton warship had reached a point fourteen miles south-southeast of Montauk Point at the eastern tip of Long Island, when at 0640 hours Eastern War Time (EWT) its lookouts sighted an unidentified multiengine aircraft flying at an altitude of 5,000 feet. As officer of the deck Lieutenant R. C. Williams tersely noted afterwards, "Plane was challenged [by blinking Aldis Lamp] but correct reply not received. Four bombs landed 200 yards on port bow at 0643 as plane circled overhead. . . . Crew was called to General Quarters when attacked, but plane was out of [antiaircraft gunfire] range before fire could be opened." Fortunately for the destroyer *USS Trippe*, the bomber aircrew's accuracy matched their vessel-recognition skills, and the bombs fell more than two hundred yards away from the two-year-old warship. Unharmed but doubtlessly energized, the *Trippe*'s crew resumed their normal duties as the warship continued on to Newport.

As if that sorry performance level weren't bad enough, Krogs-tad's command was being disassembled in front of his eyes as the U-boat campaign heated up in late January 1942. At the begin-ning of the year, he commanded four bombardment groups, three heavy (B-17s and B-18s) and one medium (B-25s and B-26s). Within three months after Pearl Harbor, all but one of these units had been detached from I Bomber Command. Arnold rushed two of them to Australia to form part of an emergency bomber force to defend that country from Japanese invasion. He shifted the third bomber group to the West Coast as part of aerial re-inforcements against a feared Japanese attack there. As the USAAF official history later described it, "Army forces were themselves seriously inadequate. In addition to the insufficient number of AAF forces available, Army units began anti-subma-rine operations under serious handicaps of organization, train-ing, and equipment. . . . Army planes [were] manned by crews who were ill-trained in naval identification or in the techniques of attacking submarine targets." The U-boats at this juncture clearly had the upper hand in the Atlantic.[2]

Even the British were still struggling to master air power against the U-boats. The Royal Air Force Coastal Command, which had managed to obtain a small number of effective LB-30 Liberator bombers (a model of the USAAF B-24), was making progress in devising new tactics and deploying new sensors and weapons to bring the fight to the U-boats at sea. Military com-manders and civilian scientists at the center of this effort were optimistic that in time the land-based patrol squadrons would prove vital in thwarting Admiral Karl Dönitz's campaign against Allied merchant shipping. But the overall effort was taking time, and the learning curve was steep: from September 1939 until the beginning of 1942, German and Italian U-boats destroyed 1,124 Allied ships totaling 5.27 million gross registered tons; until August 1941 Coastal Command patrol planes had yet to sink a single U-boat and, in the subsequent four months, had only managed to destroy five U-boats and force a sixth to surrender to Royal Navy warships.

The British effort to turn around the abysmal performance of antisubmarine patrol aircraft had begun in mid-1941, when a team of civilian scientists attached to Coastal Command employed an investigative technique, which came to be known as operations research, to pinpoint flaws in the U-boat hunters' tactics, equipment, and weapons. Led by renowned physicist Paul M. S. Blackett, the scientists pored over operational records and closely interviewed aircrews to obtain a detailed picture of what was happening at sea. They quickly came up with some easy-to-implement changes that dramatically improved the lethality of Coastal Command aircraft. When the scientists' research showed that U-boat lookouts were spotting approaching aircraft far away enough to safely crash-dive before an attack, the team recommended that the paint on the undersides of the bombers be changed from black (Coastal Command had inherited Royal Air Force night bombers) to white. The result: U-boat sightings—and sinkings—jumped 30 percent. Blackett and his team also learned that aerial depth charges were set to detonate at one hundred feet, too far down, they concluded, given the weapon's lethality radius of just twenty feet. They recommended the detonation take place at twenty feet, which again significantly increased the U-boat kill rate. And a review of squadron maintenance records led the researchers to devise a straightforward schedule of repairs and flying hours that doubled the number of Coastal Command aircraft available for patrols.

Unfortunately for General Arnold and his bomber crews, Coastal Command and the USAAF had no information-sharing program. This meant that the Americans would have to spend the same prolonged period learning the same painful lessons that the British were on the way to mastering. In the spring of 1942, Allied aerial supremacy over the North Atlantic U-boats remained a vital but elusive objective. For the time being at least, the air war against the U-boats offshore would continue to favor the Germans.[3]

DURING THE FIRST WEEK OF APRIL 1942, Vice Admiral Andrews and his staff at Eastern Sea Frontier Headquarters got seemingly excellent news from the Atlantic Fleet in Norfolk. Admiral Royal Ingersoll was assigning six destroyers to patrol off the US East Coast. Two of them had orders to steam for Cape Hatteras. The *Gleaves*-class destroyers USS *Hambleton* and USS *Emmons* were frontline warships, each armed with four 5-inch/38-cal. gun turrets, a quintuple 21-inch torpedo tube launcher amidships, as well as a half dozen .50-cal. machine guns. For attacking submerged U-boats, both destroyers had a pair of depth charge launching rails at the stern, as well as a centerline Y-gun depth charge projector that could heave charges to either side of the ship at lengths of up to fifty yards. Thanks to the new SC-series radar sets, the warships could easily track U-boats running on the surface, and their advanced QCJ sonars would easily find the enemy when submerged. With a flank speed of thirty-two knots powered by four 50,000-shaft-horsepower steam boilers, they could race through the water at twice the speed of a surfaced U-boat or patrol at twelve knots for 6,500 nautical miles without refueling. Since British Naval Intelligence reports suggested no fewer than five U-boats were operating in the Cape Hatteras area, hopes were running high at ESF Headquarters that the US Navy might finally start evening the score in the inshore battle. All hands involved would soon discover, however, that sending the warships out hunting for U-boats without the proper tactics was like swatting at hornets with a baseball bat.[4]

Arriving off the Outer Banks at 1600 EWT on Thursday, April 2, the *Hambleton* and *Emmons* quickly fell into a patrol pattern that sent them steaming up and down from Wimble Shoals to Point Lookout a dozen or so miles off the coast. Instead of sighting U-boats, however, the destroyers repeatedly spooked the merchant vessels steaming independently up and down the coast. One of them, the American freighter *Del Sud*, mistook the warships for U-boats in broad daylight and opened fire on them, fortunately with the same poor aim as the B-17 that went after the *Trippe*. Several days later, while responding after sunset to a radioed U-boat sighting report from a nearby freighter, the *Hambleton* fired off a barrage of star shells to light up the vicinity. Instantly, every merchantman within sight of the rockets immediately reported that a U-boat was shooting off illumination rounds. After three days, the destroyer lookouts had not seen a single U-boat.

At least one U-boat operating in the vicinity, however, was well aware of the destroyers' presence. Oberleutnant zur See Georg Lassen and his fifty-six-man crew in the Type IXC U-160 were ending their first week on patrol off Hatteras and had already sunk three merchant ships totaling 18,568 gross registered tons when the *Hambleton* and *Emmons* arrived in the area. Watching the warships hug the coastline as they steamed turn and turn about from Wimble Shoals to Point Lookout, Lassen regarded the *Hambleton* and *Emmons* as a minor nuisance but not a real threat—and certainly not a reason to break off his hunt.

Near midnight on Saturday, April 4, U-160 had been stalking a large oil tanker when it came close upon the two warships. Lassen calmly crash-dived to avoid the destroyers, which passed by without detecting him, and then resumed tracking his target. The next evening, Lassen's lookouts spotted the 6,837-ton American oil tanker *Bidwell* steaming independently on a northbound course. He sent a solitary G7a torpedo crashing into the tanker's port side, ripping a twenty-foot hole at the waterline and sending its cargo of 3.5 million gallons of fuel oil skyward in a towering pillar of fire. But before U-160 could do any further damage to the mangled tanker, the two destroyers inadvertently saved it. Spotting the distant smoke plume, they raced to the scene, prompting Lassen to dive deep to avoid detection. The *Bidwell*'s master and crew assessed the damage and, when the fire unexpectedly died out after a while, were able to resume course for New York. Neither destroyer ever detected U-160. Upon returning to the area several hours later, Lassen found only empty ocean and mistakenly reported to U-boat Force Headquarters that he had sunk the tanker.

The destroyers' weeklong foray off Cape Hatteras ended on Thursday, April 9, as the *Hambleton* and *Emmons* and their exhausted crews headed back to Norfolk. Their mission had been a failure: neither warship had even spotted, let alone sunk, a single U-boat, and despite the brief surge in Atlantic Fleet destroyers assigned to coastal defense, merchant ship sinkings for the first half of April in the Eastern Sea Frontier remained horrific. During the first week of the new month, eight U-boats operating within the sea frontier boundaries sank ten merchant ships totaling 66,026 gross registered tons and damaged another two vessels for 13,894 gross tons. By mid-month, U-boats operating in the ESF had sunk twenty-four ships totaling 149,695 gross tons and damaged another five for 37,298 gross tons. Of that total, eight merchantmen totaling 49,705 gross registered tons went down in the Cape Hatteras–Cape Lookout area, and another four totaling 30,058 gross tons sustained damage.

At ESF Headquarters, the mood was grim as the after-action report from the destroyer surge came in. The *Hambleton* and *Emmons* returned to Norfolk with nothing to show for their efforts but deck logs charting a weeklong, 2,830-nautical-mile trek from Wimble Shoals to Cape Lookout and back. Commander Charles Wellborn Jr., leader of Destroyer Division 19 and the senior officer aboard the two destroyers during the patrol, was blunt in his after-action report. "It will be extremely rare for patrolling destroyers to make actual contact with a submarine in which an alert submarine commander attempts to avoid contact," he wrote. "While patrolling operations of this type are of some value in combating enemy submarine activities, the submarine menace on our Atlantic coast can be defeated only through the operation of a coastal convoy system." Slowly but surely, other American commanders were coming to share Wellborn's assessment.

Vice Admiral Andrews and his counterparts in the Gulf and Caribbean sea frontiers were by now convinced that only a coastal convoy system guarded by escort warships and land-based patrol aircraft could thwart the U-boats. At a conference in Washington, DC, on March 20, they outlined a convoy system to be put in place as soon as the navy could assemble sufficient escort ships. Since, on average, thirty-five merchant ships a day departed the Gulf of Mexico or Caribbean for northern ports, the planners determined that two separate coastal convoy routes— one connecting America's northeastern ports with the Gulf of Mexico and a second linking them with the Caribbean—would be necessary. The plan called for Caribbean shipping to muster at Guantánamo Bay, Cuba, and Gulf of Mexico shipping to gather at Key West, Florida, with each northbound convoy comprising between forty and fifty merchant ships. Each convoy would proceed up the East Coast and arrive at Hampton Roads on the fourth day after getting underway. Continuing north, the formation would arrive in New York on the morning of the fifth day. Southbound convoys would follow the route in reverse. Six escort groups of five warships apiece would protect the north- and southbound convoys between Key West and New York, with four groups at sea on any given day and the other two in port for maintenance and crew rest. Another forty-eight escort warships would service the Caribbean convoys. The only problem with the plan was there was still no sign that COMINCH could make the desperately needed escort ships available. The Atlantic Fleet's cupboard remained bare. Admiral Ernest King told the conference that there wouldn't be enough escorts to begin the coastal convoy system until mid-May at the earliest—and that was the best-case scenario.

With the US Atlantic Fleet tied up in major operations from western Africa to the British Isles, coastal convoys remained relatively low on the list of naval priorities. During the month of April, the Atlantic Fleet mounted eight separate major support operations from Iceland and Scapa Flow, Scotland, to West Africa and the South Atlantic. The missions ranged from escorting troopship convoys, to ferrying fighter planes to Ghana for the Royal Air Force, to reinforcing the British Home Fleet. They tied up both Atlantic Fleet aircraft carriers, two of the fleet's five battleships, nearly half its fourteen cruisers, and more than fifty destroyers.

Admirals King, Ingersoll, and Andrews would have to improvise if they were to have any chance of halting the carnage along the US East Coast while they waited for convoy escort warships to become available. Three of the measures the admirals devised would provide modest results against the U-boats—but by the time they did, a fourth ploy initiated weeks earlier had already resulted in disaster.[5]

FRANKLIN ROOSEVELT HAD AN IDEA for countering the U-boat offensive raging offshore and summoned Admiral King to the White House to discuss it. It was Monday, January 19, 1942— just eight days after U-123 kicked off Operation Drumbeat—and both FDR and the new COMINCH were well aware of how few defenses existed in the Eastern Sea Frontier. The president recounted to King how the British during World War I had used "Q-ships"—merchant vessels with concealed cannons, depth charge launchers, and other antisubmarine weapons manned by naval personnel disguised as merchant seamen—to ambush and sink U-boats when they ventured close in to attack. By one account, between 1914 and 1918 the British had converted about 180 merchantmen into Q-ships and succeeded in sinking eleven U-boats while losing twenty-seven of the disguised merchantmen. Although the ratio of Q-ships lost to U-boats sunk was high, FDR still believed the ploy merited consideration. Why couldn't the US Navy revive that concept? FDR asked. King took Roosevelt's suggestion as an order. Within twenty-four hours of his meeting with the president, King had organized Project LQ and assembled a handpicked team to acquire, convert, arm, and secretly commission two Q-ships into fleet service.

The next day, King's staff identified two thirty-year-old A. H. Bull Steamship Company freighters, the SS *Evelyn* and SS *Carolyn*, as the best candidates for the project. Within three days of King's meeting with FDR, the admiral's staff had identified and assigned twelve officers, six apiece, to the Q-ships and were busy arranging for 135 enlisted crewmen to man each vessel. Shipwrights at the Portsmouth Naval Shipyard installed four 4-inch/50-cal. deck cannons on each vessel with painted canvas covers to conceal them until the gun crews were ready to open fire. In addition, each vessel had four .50-cal. machine guns, six Y-gun depth charge projectors, and a QCL sonar system. In all other respects, the two 318-foot-long ships would retain the innocent silhouettes of their original identities. Their cargo holds were filled with lumber to keep them afloat in case of a torpedo strike.

On Monday, March 23, the two Q-ships, renamed the USS *Atik* and USS *Asterion*, got underway for a brief shakedown cruise, then headed into the Atlantic. Two days later, disaster struck. The *Atik* was steaming south about three hundred miles

east of Norfolk when at 1700 hours lookouts aboard a German U-boat spotted the thick cloud from the merchant vessel's
smokestack. Veteran U-boat commander Kapitänleutnant Reinhard Hardegen and U-123 were back in American waters for a
second combat patrol. Hardegen closed to within seven hundred
yards and fired a single G7e electric torpedo into the freighter's
port side just ahead of its bridge. As the ship took on a list to
port, U-123 passed behind the stern, and its lookouts saw sailors
climbing down into lifeboats. Then, to his astonishment, the *Atik*
opened fire. "I continue to turn hard, when suddenly amidships
covers and tarpaulin drop down and he opens fire with at least
one gun and two . . . machine guns," Hardegen later wrote. He
ordered U-123 to flank speed and turned away from the Q-ship
as 4-inch shells splashed around them and .50-cal. machine gun
bullets hammered the bridge. A midshipman on board was fatally
wounded. Having pulled away and submerged after the gunfire,
Hardegen moved in at periscope depth and fired a second torpedo at the *Atik*, striking its engine room. This shot finished off
the Q-ship, whose surviving crewmen this time took to the lifeboats in earnest. Nearly ninety minutes later, a heavy explosion
ripped through the partially submerged hull. Hardegen resumed
his patrol. None of the *Atik*'s crewmen were ever seen again.

While the Q-ship concept was a miserable failure—on eight
patrols during 1942 and 1943, the *Atik*'s sister ship, USS *Asterion*,
never sighted, much less, attacked any U-boats—several other
makeshift initiatives by the Eastern Sea Frontier proved more
successful. Although none of these projects actually managed to
destroy any U-boats, they did manage to complicate Germany's
campaign along the East Coast in April 1942.[6]

The first venture was the brainchild of New York businessman Alfred Stanford, commodore of the Cruising Club of America. Early in April, Stanford offered the services of his members' fleet of motor yachts and sailing boats as a civilian force of U-boat observers. By now desperate for help of any kind, Admiral Andrews signed them up. The coast guard managed the program, with the civilian owners and civilian crewmen—most of them too old or unqualified to serve in the navy—sent out to sea with small-caliber guns and depth charges. The program got underway in May 1942, steadily expanding over that summer. Ultimately, more than 550 of these tiny auxiliaries were operating along the East Coast and Gulf of Mexico by the summer of 1942, but they neither attacked nor sank a single U-boat.

A far more effective ploy was the navy's recruitment of the Civil Air Patrol (CAP) to aid the USAAF and navy aircraft in their uphill struggle to search for U-boats offshore. Created six days before Pearl Harbor, the CAP came under the federal Office of Civil Defense, led by New York Mayor Fiorello H. LaGuardia. Manned by volunteer civilian pilots who owned their own single-engine aircraft, the Civil Air Patrol initially had been conceived as an auxiliary service that could courier documents and people and patrol America's land borders. But the eruption of U-boat attacks along the East Coast prompted Vice Admiral Andrews to recruit CAP for coastal patrol duties. The program grew rapidly, and by late spring several hundred private aircraft were making scheduled patrol flights along the East Coast and later into the Gulf of Mexico. While also failing to destroy a single one of Dönitz's marauders, CAP fliers did help in locating lifeboats and rafts, leading to the rescue of 363 survivors from sunken merchant ships; CAP aviators also called in 173 separate U-boat sightings. Since Admiral Dönitz had issued strict instructions to his U-boat commanders to crash-dive at the sight of any unidentified aircraft, the CAP aircraft significantly complicated Germany's campaign in American waters. But even this makeshift air force was not America's most effective stopgap in the Atlantic.[7]

The Atlantic Fleet initiated an even more serious U-boat countermeasure as the "Hooligan Navy" and Civil Air Patrol were getting organized. After months of delay and frustration, Vice Admiral Andrews and the Eastern Sea Frontier staff decided not to wait for the formal coastal convoy system to become organized in mid-May. As an interim step, ESF moved in mid-April to create an ad hoc series of protected anchorages along the East Coast and to organize small groups of available escorts to shepherd groups of merchant ships during daylight from one haven to the next. A pivotal site was a massive anchorage the navy built near Cape Lookout along the North Carolina shore sixty-two nautical miles southeast of Cape Hatteras, complementing an existing one near Ocracoke Island. Ships arriving there could pass the night behind torpedo nets, then make the run up to Hampton Roads by daylight. Admiral Andrews and his staff called these convoy escorts the "Bucket Brigade."

Within a week, the anchorage system was in place. The results were immediate. Total Allied ship losses during the second half of April 1942 showed a sharp downturn: U-boats sank only fifteen merchantmen totaling 76,896 tons during that period, a 50 percent drop from the twenty-four ships totaling 145,735 tons lost between April 1 and 15.

Apparently overlooking the sudden falloff of sinkings after the "Bucket Brigade" convoys began, the ESF staff at first lamented the total shipping losses as the month ended. "April was almost an exact repetition of the proceeding month," Lieutenant Elting E. Morison—who had succeeded Lawrance Thompson as the ESF war diarist—wrote in the command war diary. "Thus, once again, the Eastern Sea Frontier was the most dangerous area for merchant shipping in the entire world." Elsewhere, senior officials quickly grasped the shift. In London, Winston Churchill observed, "You can always count on Americans to do the right thing—after they've tried everything else."

In Paris, Admiral Dönitz bluntly acknowledged the increase in American coastal defense but indicated he was not yet ready to abandon U-boat deployments along the Atlantic littoral. "The decline in sinking figures is attributable to unfavorable conditions for attack during full-moon and high pressure weather," he penned in his war diary. "Boats cannot operate on the traffic routes right under land because they are constantly forced under water by the numerous sea and air patrols and have no chance to operate on the surface and charge their batteries." Nevertheless, he went on, "attacking conditions in the American area continue to be very good. [U-boat commanders] are all of the same opinion, namely that the American area will remain a highly favorable area for attacks for some months to come and that a high percentage of successes can be scored with very few losses." Whatever obstacles the Americans managed to throw up, the BdU staff remained confident that the odds were likely to remain in the U-boats' favor for the foreseeable future.

To that end, Dönitz and his operations staff added two top-secret U-boat operations to the campaign. One mission would require two U-boats to insert German saboteurs on the American mainland to attack vital industrial and transportation sites. The other called for three more U-boats to lay minefields in three major US ports. The Battle of the Atlantic along America's shores was about to enter a deadly new phase.[8]

9

TO AMERICA,
WITH MINES

ONE MORNING IN EARLY MAY 1942, AFTER FOUR WEEKS
spent supervising German shipwrights as they repaired his
storm-battered U-boat at the bunker complex in Brest, Kapitänleutnant Horst Degen found himself on the *BdU Zug*, an express
train reserved for U-boat personnel, to Paris. After a week of
growing impatience and anticipation, he had finally received
the summons to U-boat Force Headquarters at the avenue du
Maréchal Maunoury for an appointment with Admiral Karl
Dönitz and the senior BdU staff. Once there, Degen received
thrilling news: the admiral and operations chief Fregattenkapitän Eberhard Godt told him that his next patrol would begin
with a mine-laying operation at the mouth of the Chesapeake
Bay, where the Thimble Shoal Channel enters the Atlantic.

BdU had chosen the night of June 12–13, when a new moon
would help obscure the U-boats as they moved close inshore, for
the mine-laying operation. Two other U-boats would attempt to
lay minefields at the same time at the mouth of New York Harbor and Delaware Bay. Closing the main shipping lanes at those

three sites would strike a major blow against the Americans, especially if the mines managed to sink large ships in the narrow passages, thereby bottling up the major ports. After the frustrations of his first two patrols, Degen returned to Brest excited that Dönitz had picked U-701 for this "very special" operation.[1]

Around this time, Degen also learned that other elements of the U-boat Force had a completely different operation planned for the night of June 12–13. The German high command had ordered BdU to ferry eight German Abwehr (military intelligence) saboteurs by U-boat across the Atlantic and land them ashore in the United States. The mission—codenamed Operation Pastorius—called for the saboteurs to attack critical manufacturing sites, power plants, and transportation hubs using high explosives they brought along. Degen learned of the plan from twenty-nine-year-old Kapitänleutnant Hans-Heinz Linder, a fellow member of the Class of 1933 and close friend who commanded the Type VIIC U-202. He and U-584 commander Kapitänleutnant Joachim Deecke, also twenty-nine, were each to carry four agents and one-half of the explosives. Deecke, yet another classmate of theirs, had visited and befriended the Marston family in San Diego during the *Karlsruhe* port visit along with Degen eight years earlier. U-202's landing site was at the far eastern tip of Long Island, while U-584 would use a beach south of Jacksonville, Florida.

Dönitz and his staff were confident that the mining operation would be a success but regarded the saboteur infiltration as yet another sideshow foisted on the U-boats that would do little but add to the danger and distract the crews from their primary mission of sinking ships. Korvettenkapitän Günter Hessler, a senior BdU staff officer, later wrote, "The U-boat Command was averse to embarking these individuals in U-boats, for some of them were not actuated by patriotic motives. . . . But the task had to be undertaken since there was no other means of transportation to the United States." Aware that most of the saboteurs had been selected for the sabotage mission primarily because they had lived in the United States before the war, Hessler doubted their reliability, later recalling his fear at that time that they would readily betray the mission "to save their skins." His suspicions would prove correct.[2]

Dönitz's shift in U-boat tactics from direct attacks on Allied merchant shipping to mine-laying marked the BdU staff's recognition that the period U-boat commanders called *der Glückliche Zeit* (the happy time) was finally drawing to a close. For four months, the U-boats had operated at will from the Gulf of Maine to Florida, seemingly impervious to the ineffective American sea and air patrols. "But by the end of April," Dönitz later wrote, "it became apparent that the routing of shipping and the anti-submarine defense measures in the immediate vicinity of the American coast were becoming more efficient." The Atlantic Fleet's countermeasures were beginning to take their toll.

Dönitz and the BdU staff had not stood idly by as Admiral Adolphus Andrews and the Eastern Sea Frontier (ESF) frantically assembled the "Bucket Brigade" convoy escorts in late March. In addition to conducting early planning for the mine-laying and saboteur operations, BdU had introduced a new element into the mixture of U-boats aimed at significantly expanding the force's operational range. The first of a new type of U-boat specifically designed to replenish Type VII and IX boats at sea with fuel and food supplies entered operational service in late March, with nine more on the way. Under the command of Kapitänleutnant Georg von Wilamowitz-Moellendorf, the "milch cow" U-459 sailed from Heligoland on March 29 with a cargo of 720 tons of diesel fuel, 34 tons of lubricating oil, and 10 tons of fresh water. Arriving at its designated operational area five hundred nautical miles northeast of Bermuda on April 20, U-459 refueled twelve outbound Type VII and two Type IXB U-boats and three VIIs on return passage during a two-week period.

The impact of these refueling boats on U-boat deployments was dramatic. The ten outbound Type VII boats in the previous patrols had been at sea for an average of thirty-six days before being forced to return to France. Now, with up to fifty tons of additional diesel oil in their tanks from U-459, they would be able to patrol for an average of sixty-six days—more than four additional weeks at sea. Because of that dramatic development, Dönitz was able to dispatch seven of the shorter-range Type VIIs to the Caribbean, Gulf of Mexico, and northern coastal waters of Brazil, rich hunting grounds previously out of range for the 500-ton "medium" U-boats.

But any celebration at BdU Headquarters would have been premature. In the weeks that followed the deployment of the first "milch cow," U-boat commanders who had obtained the extra fuel and more time on station reported disappointing results as they patrolled from Cape Hatteras south to Florida. BdU kept a close eye on the tonnage-per-day rate, derived by simply dividing a U-boat's total tonnage of ships sunk by the number of days on patrol. In January, the daily average was 209 tons. This increased to 378 tons in February, then climbed to 409 tons in

March and 412 in April. None of the Type VII boats on extended patrols in American waters in May came even close to matching these earlier numbers. The daily tonnage formula ranged from 73.4 tons per day for U-751 (two ships totaling 4,555 tons sunk during sixty-two days at sea) to a high of 234.4 tons per day for U-333 (three ships sunk totaling 13,596 tons during fifty-eight days at sea). "Reports from the boats [operating along the US East Coast] showed that . . . extremely few ships were sighted," Hessler later observed. "As the days passed, it became evident that the [merchant ship] traffic situation had fundamentally changed."

During a face-to-face meeting with Adolf Hitler in his Wolf's Lair headquarters on Thursday, May 14, Dönitz admitted that American coastal defenses were becoming "considerable" but quickly added that the inshore campaign would continue. The admiral predicted the establishment of an American coastal convoy system in the near future, then briefed the Führer on the planned mine-laying campaign by U-701 and the other two boats.

Dönitz's prediction about coastal convoys came true much faster than he and his staff anticipated. Within hours of his meeting with Hitler that second Thursday in May, Convoy KS500, with nineteen merchant ships totaling 155,680 gross registered tons, departed Norfolk for Key West accompanied by seven escort warships. The easy times along America's coast were over.[3]

AMID ALL THE FRUSTRATIONS AND SETBACKS, there was one piece of good news for the 396th Medium Bombardment Squadron in the spring of 1942. The Fourth Air Force decided to replace the unit's underperforming B-18 Bolos with the newer Lockheed A-29 Hudson. Forty-four feet long with a wingspan of sixty-five feet, the Hudson was a militarized update of the Model 14 Super Electra, which at the time of its first commercial flight in October 1937 was lauded as a state-of-the-art passenger airliner. It had two main landing wheels and a small tail wheel that left the aircraft resting on the tarmac at a cant. The civilian model, flown by a pilot and copilot, could carry twelve passengers at a speed of 250 knots. It had a maximum range of about 2,000 miles, with a maximum altitude of 24,000 feet. Even for those who had yet to experience commercial flight, the A-29 would have been a clearly recognizable plane; on the outside, it was virtually identical to the Model 10 Electra that famed aviatrix Amelia Earhart had flown in her ill-fated 1937 quest to become the first woman to circumnavigate the globe.

While the A-29 may have superficially resembled a civilian aircraft, Lockheed engineers had significantly modified its airframe for combat. The Hudson's fuselage and wings were painted in a camouflage pattern of brown and tan swirls. Its armament included a pair of fixed, forward-firing .30-cal. machine guns in the upper nose, a retractable .30-cal. "tunnel gun" in the rear belly of the fuselage facing aft, and a rotating British-supplied Boulton Paul gun turret with twin .303-cal. machine guns protruding from the top of the fuselage just forward of the aircraft's twin rudders. The main armament, however, was not visible once loaded. The Hudson could carry in its eleven-foot-long internal bomb bay four 250-pound bombs plus another four 100-pound bombs. For antisubmarine patrols, the aircraft carried three 325-pound Mark XVII depth charges, plus a practice dummy depth charge for training should a patrol prove uneventful. The Hudson's four fuel tanks carried 643 gallons of avgas, which was enough fuel to fly at cruising speed for nearly eight hours.

The A-29 "was quite a bit faster, more maneuverable than the old B-18s," Harry Kane later recalled. "Of course, we had to check out in those again and get all accustomed to going in them." Kane was not the only airman who needed extensive training in order to use the new warplanes. The 396th by now had grown to thirty-six officers and 271 enlisted men, and all of the aircrews, armorers, and maintenance personnel required "transition training" to the new aircraft. "The A-29 . . . had a terrific tendency to ground loop" because of the powerful torque generated by its two 1,100-horsepower Pratt & Whitney R-1830 Twin Wasp engines, Kane said. Landings were equally challenging because the Hudson easily stalled at low speeds. "On landing they were very, very treacherous," he said. The Hudson had a strong tendency to bounce back into the air after touching down on the runway, and that could easily result in the aircraft stalling out and cartwheeling into the ground, Kane added.[4]

Kane's concern about the safety of the A-29 was not unreasonable. During the first half of 1942, an air crewman in the USAAF was nearly as likely to die in training as in combat. The Army Air Forces expansion was in high gear as the new service branch prepared to fight the Japanese and Germans overseas. At the beginning of the year, Lieutenant General Henry H. "Hap" Arnold, who had been promoted to three stars on December 15, 1941, had 417,526 uniformed personnel under his command, of which 30,040 were commissioned officers. Total personnel would double over the next six months as the USAAF passed the 840,000 mark in July; it would double again to 1.6 million personnel by year's end. At the same time, aircraft production was soaring as the American aircraft industry hit full stride in meeting President Franklin Roosevelt's goal of fielding nearly 240,000 combat, transport, and training aircraft. Inevitably, the legion of new pilots, navigators, radio operators, and crewmen made mistakes, many of them fatal. The number of midair collisions, crash landings, and aircraft vanishing into the mountains or disappearing at sea was as horrific as other statistics were inspiring. And since the number of USAAF units overseas remained miniscule (only 90,542 airmen were serving outside the continental United States by May 1942, and most of them were support personnel preparing for later unit deployments), most of the carnage was taking place at home. During the first six months of the war, the USAAF recorded 3,341 aircraft accidents inside the continental United States in which 763 airmen perished and 825 aircraft were wrecked. The daily average was astonishingly high: 4.5 aircraft destroyed and 4.1 personnel killed every day. For two of those months (March and April 1942), more airmen died in stateside training than in combat overseas.

Although the 396th had to adjust to a new type of aircraft, the squadron's mission remained the same. But the mood of the men in the squadron had also changed. On April 21, a cadre of twenty-five officers and 153 enlisted men was abruptly transferred from Sacramento to Naval Air Station Alameda on the eastern shore of San Francisco Bay. From there, they mounted daily patrols out into the North Pacific searching for the Japanese fleet. Fears of another Japanese attack from the sea had suddenly spiked in the wake of the Doolittle Raid against Tokyo three days earlier. Intent on avenging the country's losses at Pearl Harbor, Lieutenant Colonel James H. "Jimmy" Doolittle of the USAAF had led a group of sixteen B-25 Mitchell bombers launched from the carrier USS Hornet on a daring air raid over the Japanese capital and five other cities. Senior army officials—including Secretary of War Henry L. Stimson—had convinced themselves that the Japanese navy would retaliate for the American strike by attacking the West Coast. Army Chief of Staff General George C. Marshall warned Fourth Army commander Lieutenant General John L. DeWitt to be on his guard.

Fear and anticipation flowed down the army chain of command to individual squadrons such as the 396th, and the aviators flew out on patrols with a grim sense of purpose. For Kane and his fellow air crewmen, the patrols "consisted of flying up and down the Pacific coast, covering most of the state of California." When the squadron detachment returned to Sacramento on May 10, two additional antiaircraft regiments were being rushed to Los Angeles and the San Francisco Bay area, and army officials were issuing 350,000 gas masks and protective clothing to the West Coast troops. Well aware of the Japanese use of chemical weapons in China, the army was preparing for the worst.[5]

U-701 BEGAN ITS THIRD COMBAT PATROL on Tuesday, May 19, just five days after the first American coastal convoy set sail from Norfolk. Casting off late in the afternoon as a military band played from the U-boat bunker quayside and a small crowd of well-wishers—including U-202's Kapitänleutnant Linder—waved farewell, Degen backed U-701 out of the Brest bunker, turned around, and conned the boat out through the opening in the harbor's two long jetties, entering the Atlantic while two patrol boats kept station and a pair of Messerschmitt fighters circled overhead. The boat was back up to a full complement of four officers, one midshipman under training, and forty-one enlisted crewmen. Six new faces had reported aboard U-701 during its in-port period, including twenty-two-year-old *Fähnrich Ingenieur* (Engineering Midshipman) Günter Lange and five junior enlisted men.

The first leg of the deployment was short. U-701 made an overnight passage down the Brittany coast to the larger U-boat base at Lorient. Arriving early the next morning, shipyard workers loaded fifteen TMB seabed mines, three apiece, in its five torpedo tubes. First deployed in 1939, the TMB featured an aluminum cylindrical shell whose exterior dimensions allowed for three mines to fit inside each of the Type VIIC U-boat's five torpedo tubes. Although at 7.5 feet it was only one-third the length of a G7e torpedo, each mine carried a much more powerful explosive charge of 1,276 pounds of hexanite, nearly twice the size of a torpedo warhead. This was possible since no propulsion system was required. The mine utilized a timing clock to delay arming the weapon until the U-boat was safely out of the area and employed a sensor whereby the magnetic field of a ship passing overhead set off the explosive. Earlier in the war, U-boats had dropped TMB mines where the water was one hundred feet deep, but subsequent engineering tests showed that the weapon's lethality sharply increased in water eighty feet deep or less. Since channels for ships entering and departing American ports were dredged to a depth of around fifty feet or so, the only question regarding the effectiveness of the mine-laying operation was whether the U-boats could accurately drop their mines in the most highly traveled sectors of the narrow waterways.[6]

While in Lorient, Degen engaged in a minor deception operation of his own, telling dockyard officials that he had been unable to completely fill his diesel tanks before leaving Brest. "We wanted the expedition to last as long as possible, and that depended on how much diesel oil we could take," Degen recalled years later. "The authorities at Lorient did not ask silly questions when we told them that fueling was not done completely in Brest." U-701 got the additional tons of fuel oil without debate. As a result, Degen was able to make a three-day dash at high speed across the Bay of Biscay into the open Atlantic without cutting into the boat's normal fuel allotment.

The three-week transit of the North Atlantic passed in relative calm. The U-boat crew fell into the normal at-sea rhythm of practice crash dives, four-hour daytime watches and six-hour night watches at their workstations, and meals served in the crowded bow compartment. Herbert Grotheer and the other radiomen entertained their shipmates by playing popular music over the boat's intercom system as the men worked or relaxed off watch. Yet it was still far from a pleasure cruise: the danger of detection was constant, and crewmen maintained a rigorous work schedule in cramped and uncomfortable conditions.

Only two events broke the crew's daily routine. One day, Degen's lookouts spotted a neutral Portuguese fishing trawler as it headed northwest toward the Grand Banks off Newfoundland. Several days later, Degen and his lookouts sighted an 18,000-ton passenger liner heading east toward Europe. Visions of bagging such a large prize prompted Degen to reverse course and pursue the vessel. Alas, after several hours of chasing the prey, U-701 closed in after nightfall only for the lookouts to report that it was the Swedish American Line *Drottningholm*, sailing under a neutral flag. The liner was bearing German and Italian diplomats back to Europe after months of internment in the United States following Pearl Harbor and the American declaration of war against the Axis. Degen ordered his helmsman to resume the boat's westward course toward the United States.[7]

WHILE DEGEN AND HIS CREW CONCENTRATED on the routine day-to-day tasks of their westward passage in the first days of June, senior American admirals in Washington, DC, and Honolulu were grappling with a sudden major crisis in the Pacific. An imperial Japanese naval force of four aircraft carriers, 181 surface warships and auxiliaries, and several dozen submarines was steaming across the central Pacific to attack and occupy Midway Island, about 1,000 miles northwest of Hawaii. Elements of the Japanese fleet also planned a diversionary attack against US bases in the Aleutians. The US Pacific Fleet, still struggling to recover from the Pearl Harbor disaster, could assemble only three carriers and twenty-five surface escorts to block the Japanese. However, Pacific Fleet commander Admiral Chester W. Nimitz had one advantage that would prove pivotal. A team of navy code breakers had gleaned enough intelligence from decrypted Japanese naval messages to position the carriers USS *Enterprise*, USS *Hornet*, and USS *Yorktown* in place for an ambush against the four aircraft carriers headed for Midway.

Despite the navy's firm intelligence about the destination of the larger Japanese force, army leaders continued to fear that it would steam past Hawaii to strike the West Coast. As it turned out, though, the code breakers were correct. During four days of fighting between June 4 and 7, the Americans sank all four Japanese carriers and a cruiser and destroyed 248 carrier aircraft and their aircrews. American losses were smaller: the carrier *Yorktown*, a destroyer, and about 150 aircraft. Victory at Midway allowed the US Pacific Fleet to seize the strategic initiative in the Pacific.

The consequences of the American victory at Midway were far-reaching. The battered Japanese fleet, having lost four of the six carriers that attacked Pearl Harbor, limped back to Japan; Americans everywhere—when details of the victory emerged weeks later—had the opportunity to celebrate for the first time since December 7, 1941. Victory at Midway also cleared the path for Nimitz and Admiral Ernest King to take the offensive in the Pacific. In August 1942, the Marine Corps would land on Guadalcanal in the Solomon Islands, marking the first major American land offensive against Japan and beginning the steady rollback of Japanese advances in the Pacific.

One unnoticed and unheralded event that stemmed from the Pacific Fleet victory at Midway would have a direct and dramatic impact on U-701 and its men. With Japanese forces now tied up in the Pacific, on Monday, June 8, General DeWitt canceled the special alert triggered by fears of a Japanese attack, and the War Department began recalling the extra units it had rushed to the West Coast. At the same time, redeployment orders came down from Fourth Air Force Headquarters to Lieutenant Colonel D. O. Monteigh, commander of the 396th Medium Bombardment

Squadron. On Saturday, June 12, the squadron base at Sacramento was a beehive of activity. Monteigh had received orders to lead a cadre of thirty-four officers, fifty-five enlisted men, and all fifteen of his squadron's A-29 Hudson bombers on a cross-country aerial caravan to eastern North Carolina starting the next day. Upon arrival at the Marine Corps air station at Cherry Point, their new mission would be to hunt for German U-boats.[8]

U-701's CREW WENT TO BATTLE STATIONS shortly before sunset on Friday, June 12, but the men had been on edge since long before that point. They had been on full alert for the past four days, as U-701 slowly crept into American waters and came within range of land-based patrol bombers. The radio operators had entertained the crew by piping American radio broadcasts through the boat's internal loudspeakers. To great amusement, they heard several news reports announcing that Sunday, June 14, had been proclaimed "MacArthur Day," honoring General Douglas MacArthur on the forty-third anniversary of his appointment to West Point. Crewmen joked that their present to MacArthur would be fifteen magnetic mines.

On the U-boat's cramped bridge, however, the mood remained deadly serious. The duty watch officer and three enlisted lookouts took particular pains to scan their sectors of the horizon for any American warships or patrol planes. To their astonishment, the ocean and skies remained empty. "There were no airplanes and no coast guard cutters as U-701 drew nearer and nearer to the shore," Degen later recalled.

Then, suddenly, U-701 arrived. Several hours after dark on June 12, the bright lights of the Cape Henry and Cape Charles lighthouses rose above the western horizon, clearly marking the twenty-nautical-mile opening between the Virginia Beach shoreline and the southern tip of the Delmarva Peninsula.

Earlier in their journey, Degen, Leutnant zur See Erwin Batzies, Obersteuermann Günter Kunert, and Oberleutnant zur See Konrad Junker had spent hours reviewing a large nautical chart of the area. They came to two firm conclusions. First, the wide waterway separating the two capes was an illusion. "The chart clearly showed us that there was only one way into the gate . . . due to a big [underwater] bank that came down from Cape Charles," Degen explained years later. "It covered the direct westward entrance from the Atlantic into Chesapeake Bay." The chart showed that ships entering the bay had to round the shallow bank at its southern tip, then proceed north paralleling the Virginia Beach shoreline in order to reach the entrance to the dredged ship channel. Second, they would ignore the BdU operations order for the mine-laying mission. "Our operations order directed us to go straight to the entrance of [the Chesapeake] Bay; to dive there during the night and to observe during the day the exact ship traffic of incoming and outgoing ships," Degen wrote. But that meant U-701 would have to hide in water adjoining the dredged channel only thirty-six feet deep, leaving its conning tower just four feet below the surface. Dismissing the staff order as "suicidal," Degen opted to run straight into the channel after midnight, locate the ship channel through visual observation, drop the fifteen TMB mines, and get the hell back out. The only flaw in their new plan was a development neither they nor Admiral Dönitz knew about: the Eastern Sea Frontier already knew that several U-boats were on their way to the US East Coast to lay minefields.[9]

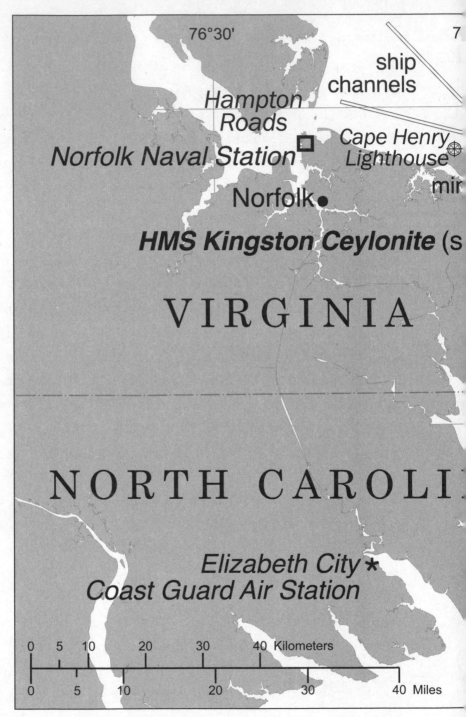

76°30'

7

ship
channels

Hampton
Roads

Cape Henry
Lighthouse

Norfolk Naval Station

mir

Norfolk•

HMS Kingston Ceylonite (s

VIRGINIA

NORTH CAROLI

Elizabeth City ★
Coast Guard Air Station

0   5   10   20   30   40 Kilometers

0   5   10   20   30   40 Miles

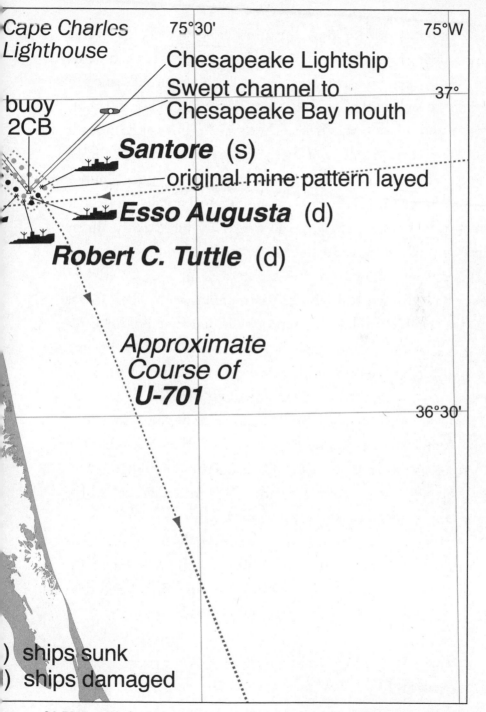

Cape Charles Lighthouse

75°30'

75°W

Chesapeake Lightship

Swept channel to
Chesapeake Bay mouth

37°

buoy 2CB

Santore (s)

original mine pattern layed

Esso Augusta (d)

Robert C. Tuttle (d)

Approximate
Course of
U-701

36°30'

) ships sunk
) ships damaged

U-701's mine-laying operation at the mouth of the Chesapeake Bay required the U-boat to come within several hundred yards of shore on the
surface before it reached the target area. ILLUSTRATION BY ROBERT E. PRATT.

THE FIRST WARNING that the Germans had decided on a mine-laying campaign in American coastal waters had come in April, when an agent working for US Army Intelligence in France revealed that BdU had initially decided to block American seaports during March. Vice Admiral Andrews at ESF Headquarters received a copy of the agent's report, which included "surprisingly detailed [map] overlays of the [proposed] minefields." Since the agent's previous reports had usually turned out to be accurate, the navy and Andrews's ESF staff took the threat seriously. However, April and May passed without incident.

Then came the next alert. On Tuesday, June 9, COMINCH issued a warning to all US Navy commands on the East Coast that a reliable intelligence report revealed that BdU had recently received a large supply of antiship mines. The following day, a third piece of intelligence seemed to confirm the German mine-laying threat beyond any doubt. In Santiago, Chile, a high-ranking official of the Chilean shipping line Compañía Sud Americana de Vapores tipped off the US embassy that the German ambassador had warned that country's foreign minister to keep all Chilean vessels away from New York Harbor because it would be mined in the very near future.

At his headquarters in lower Manhattan, Vice Admiral Andrews ordered an alert message sent out to all ports, naval districts, and operating units under his command. Beyond this, however, the Atlantic Fleet could only watch and wait.[10]

DEGEN HELD U-701 several miles off the coast until around midnight, then ordered the boat slowly ahead to close with the shoreline. Because the two lighthouses remained illuminated, the task of locating the entrance to Thimble Shoal Channel became nearly effortless. Kunert, the navigator, was on the conning tower bridge with Degen, Junker, and Batzies. His task was to take constant bearings of the Cape Charles Lighthouse. When the flashing light showed a bearing of due north, U-701 would turn ninety degrees to starboard, heading directly for the target area at the mouth of the Chesapeake Bay.

U-701 continued moving slowly westward toward the Virginia Beach shoreline for nearly an hour, aiming for a point of approach about five miles south of Cape Henry. "Besides our echo-sounding, we kept a sharp eye for Cape Charles and its guiding light," Degen recalled. Finally, Kunert called out that Cape Charles was bearing due north, and Degen ordered the starboard turn. The U-boat, with its diesel engines murmuring softly, came around until it was running parallel to the shoreline. Six months earlier, Kapitänleutnant Reinhard Hardegen and his lookouts on U-123 had gaped at the busy nighttime traffic along Brooklyn's Atlantic Avenue at the opening of Operation Drumbeat. Despite the ravages the U-boats had inflicted on Allied shipping along the US East Coast since then, Degen and his team were seeing the same "breathtaking" spectacle, he later recounted. "To the port we could see the dark shadows of dunes, with lights here and there . . . even cars and people and lighted houses. These Americans didn't seem to know there was a war going on!"

As the Cape Henry Lighthouse drew near, Degen knew that U-701 was very close to the channel entrance. He ordered the maneuvering watch to bring the boat's speed to dead slow and the torpedo mechanics to prepare to drop the mines. In the bow compartment, the torpedomen flooded the four torpedo tubes and opened the bow cap of the first tube. Then they released the locking bolt that anchored the forward-most TMB mine in that tube.

Degen was about to give the order to release the first mine when several lookouts stiffened. A small patrol boat was crossing the 1,000-foot-wide ship channel dead ahead of U-701. The vessel was totally blacked out, but the illumination from the shore cast enough light for the lookouts' night binoculars to spot it without difficulty. Degen and the others watched as the patrol boat reached the western side of the channel, then reversed course and headed east, passing from left to right just several hundred yards ahead. Degen ordered his helmsman to bear to the left for the western edge of Thimble Shoal Channel. Glancing at his watch, he saw that it was 0130 local time on Saturday, June 13. He spoke into the voice tube, and a jolt of compressed air ejected the first TMB mine out of the torpedo tube. It silently fell to the bottom of the channel fifty-two feet down.

For the next fifteen minutes, U-701 slowly zigzagged along the western side of the ship channel, dropping a mine every two minutes. Degen and the other lookouts did not let the patrol boat out of their sight. As the little patrol craft reached the middle of the channel again heading west, U-701 had laid seven of the fifteen mines. Degen then ordered the engine room to shut down the diesel engines and activate the silent e-motors. U-701 drew past the patrol boat's track and moved another hundred yards up the channel. Then Degen ordered a reverse course and began to zigzag along the eastern side of the channel. The boat slowly moved back toward the open ocean, dropping the remaining eight mines as it proceeded. When the last mine fell out of U-701's stern tube, Degen's watch read 0200 hours local. The mines were set, their internal clocks ticking off the preset sixty-hour interval before they armed themselves. It had taken just half an hour to do the job. U-701 silently moved back out into the Atlantic Ocean and headed south at high speed for its patrol area off Cape Hatteras.[11]

WHILE U-701 WAS DROPPING ITS MINES in the vicinity of the whistle buoy "2CB" that marked the entrance to the Chesapeake Bay, three other U-boats were engaged in equally dangerous inshore moves farther north. U-87 came in between Cape Henlopen, Delaware, and Cape May, New Jersey, that same moonless night and dropped fifteen TMB mines across the Delaware Bay channel. At the same time, U-373 edged into the shallow waters of Massachusetts Bay to block the ship channel at Boston. Both laid their minefields without detection.

Things went differently for the third boat, U-202, which barely avoided disaster. Departing Brest on Wednesday, May 27, Degen's close friend and classmate Kapitänleutnant Hans-Heinz Linder proceeded to Lorient, where four Abwehr agents, including thirty-nine-year-old team leader George John Dasch, boarded the U-boat. The team brought with them four small crates packed with TNT and other explosives, timers, and detonators. Fifteen days after leaving Lorient, late in the evening of June 12, U-202 crept through a thick fogbank toward the landing site on the eastern end of Long Island. Linder and his lookouts were peering through a thick fog and listening to the sound of waves breaking on the beach when U-202 touched bottom and grounded. Two sailors and the four saboteurs with their deadly cargo set out for the beach in an inflatable dinghy. After long minutes of struggling against the surf, the men reached the shore, leaped out into waist-deep water, and waded ashore. Linder and his lookouts were so preoccupied with landing the Abwehr team that they failed to notice U-202 had swung parallel to the beach as the tide went out. At last, however, the two sailors who had ferried the agents ashore signaled to U-202, and other crewmen hauled them back to the boat via a towline. What they reported to Linder threw the U-boat commander into a panic: a US Coast Guard patrolman had stumbled on Dasch and his team as they were burying the explosives. Discovery of U-202 by the Americans seemed inevitable. Fortunately, after two hours of terrified waiting, a miracle occurred. The tide shifted and was now coming back in. Linder sent every off-duty crewman to the stern to lighten up the bow, then put full power into both diesel engines and the two e-motors. U-202 suddenly broke free of the sand and began backing out into deep water. The crew erupted in cheers.[12]

LINDER'S BRUSH WITH THE US COAST GUARD along the shore of Long Island was just the beginning of the difficulties the latest wave of U-boats would face. Now convinced that a massive mine-laying operation was afoot, American commanders hastened to put their men on high alert about the incoming danger.

Vice Admiral Andrews could not have been more explicit in the warning he passed to his subordinates: he predicted that as defenses against the U-boats improved, "an effort would be made to mine the sea lanes and the approaches to the principal ports." Andrews recommended an intense effort at all harbors to sweep the channels. He reminded the port authorities that U-boats in May 1918 had dropped a total of fifty-seven mines at key harbor entrances from New York to Wimble Shoals, North Carolina. That brief campaign had caused the sinking of six ships totaling 35,592 gross registered tons, including the 13,680-ton armored cruiser USS San Diego, which sank off Fire Island. The clerical staff at ESF typed out multiple copies of the warning message, addressed them to the various naval commands, and delivered them to the post office, where they were postmarked June 13, 1942. Once again, however, ESF was too late. Up and down the eastern seaboard, the timers of forty-five German mines were already ticking.[13]

10

THE WAR
COMES HOME

I T WAS A PERFECT SUMMER DAY, AND THOUSANDS OF TOURISTS
and Tidewater, Virginia, residents had flocked to the Virginia Beach shore. The late afternoon sun beamed down from a cloudless sky, and a light northerly breeze wafted across the city boardwalk and the bright strip of sand where small waves gently brushed the beach.

Norfolk resident Frank Batten Jr. had not a care in the world that Monday, June 15, 1942. The fifteen-year-old had gone to the beach for the day with his family. As he waded into the surf shortly after 5 P.M., Batten gazed out at a long column of large merchant ships that seemed to fill the entire horizon. When it first appeared an hour earlier, the convoy had been arrayed in two columns of six vessels apiece, but now it was reorganizing into a single file to enter port. In the bright daylight, Batten and other observers could clearly see that all but two of the ships were massive oil tankers riding low in the water with full cargos. Five escort warships were also in sight. "The ships were so close to the beach that we felt we could almost swim out to them," Batten recalled years later.

Beachgoers were used to (by now) the sight of escorted convoys arriving and departing from the ports of Norfolk and Newport News. It had been four weeks since the Eastern Sea Frontier had inaugurated the coastal convoy system between Key West, Florida, and Hampton Roads, Virginia. Both the southbound convoys, identified with the letters "KS," and the northbound formations, which began with the letters "KN," were leaving port every three days and arriving at the other terminus within four to seven days, depending on the weather and other operational factors. This particular convoy, designated KN109, had gotten underway from Key West on June 11, passing through the Florida Strait along with five escorts and moving up the East Coast without incident. Navy officials were proud of their handiwork: during the past month, eight northbound KN convoys and eleven southbound KS convoys had sailed to their destinations with a total of 312 merchant ships under escort, totaling 2.3 million gross registered tons. Not a single vessel had been lost. This was about to change.[1]

Batten was idly watching the line of tankers when suddenly a massive explosion rocked the fifth ship in line. The giant oil tanker fell out of the formation and quickly began listing to starboard as a towering cloud of black smoke climbed into the sky. At that moment, Batten and the other swimmers experienced a basic physics lesson. While the thundering bellow of the explosion did not reach their ears for twenty-five seconds, the shock wave from the blast arrived in less than five. "The bottom of the ocean appeared to tremble," eyewitness G. F. Martin later told the *Virginian-Pilot*. "My feet were on the bottom and when the explosion occurred, there was a tingling sensation in my toes."

Her keel shattered by a mine laid by U-701 at the mouth of the Chesa-peake Bay, the 11,615-ton American oil tanker *Robert C. Tuttle* rests on the bottom of Thimble Shoal Channel. It was the first of four ships either damaged or sunk by U-701's minefield. The tanker was later successfully repaired and continued to serve until the end of the war. NATIONAL ARCHIVES AND RECORDS ADMINISTRATION.

As the master of the 11,615-ton American tanker *Robert C. Tuttle*, Martin Johansen had been on the ship's navigation bridge waiting his turn to pick up a harbor pilot when the explosion rocked the vessel at 1704 hours Eastern War Time. The two-year-old Atlantic Refining Company tanker was carrying 152,000 barrels of crude oil for a refinery in Philadelphia.

The blast threw Johansen and the other watch-standers to the deck. As he scrambled back to his feet, Johansen saw that the *Robert C. Tuttle* had apparently suffered fatal damage. The explosion—either a torpedo or antiship mine—had ripped a massive hole in the starboard side at the No. 2 tank about one hundred feet aft of the bow. Seeing that the *Robert C. Tuttle* was probably doomed, Johansen ordered the forty-seven crewmen and gunners to abandon ship. He grabbed the ship's codes and confidential papers and threw them over the side in a weighted metal box. Alerted that 2nd Assistant Engineer Ruben Redwine was missing, Johansen and Chief Engineer George Fithen made a last-minute search of the sinking ship without finding him. They and the forty-four remaining crewmen and gunners took to lifeboats and were quickly picked up by a navy patrol craft and taken ashore.

Reaction to the attack was swift. Within fifteen minutes, several navy patrol aircraft and a patrol blimp appeared overhead and circled the slow-moving line of ships. The growing crowd on the beach gasped and cheered as, one by one, the aircraft dove toward the ocean and dropped aerial depth charges at the suspected U-boat. Then another blast shook a second oil tanker.

The 11,237-ton tanker *Esso Augusta* had been in the lead position of the port column as Convoy KN109 approached the Chesapeake Bay entrance. The two-year-old Standard Oil Company tanker was carrying 119,000 barrels of diesel oil from a Texas refinery for ultimate delivery to the United Kingdom. When Master Eric Robert Blomquist had seen the *Robert C. Tuttle* explode, he immediately suspected that a U-boat had torpedoed it. Thirty seconds after the first explosion, Blomquist and his lookouts had seen a second blast about three hundred yards off the stricken tanker's port bow.

Blomquist had ordered his helmsman to put the wheel hard right and ordered the engine room to make maximum speed. The *Esso Augusta* began hastily zigzagging in a wide circle in order to avoid being struck. The ship was making sixteen knots by the time it came around to head for the Thimble Shoal Channel. Then a third explosion went off close astern. The shock wave tore off the tanker's rudder and sternpost, disabled the engines, and severed fuel and steam lines. The *Esso Augusta* slowly glided to a halt several miles offshore. Blomquist ordered his crew below to plug any leaks in the hull, and the British trawler *HMS Lady Elsa* drew near to attempt towing the tanker into port.

While this was going on, several of Convoy KN109's escorts were reacting to what they thought was a nearby U-boat. Sonar operators aboard the coast guard cutter *USS Dione* reported to commanding officer Lieutenant James Alger that the shallow water conditions and the loud noise from the ships' propellers made it impossible to detect anything. Alger estimated where a U-boat would most likely have been if it had launched two torpedoes that struck the two tankers, and the *Dione* raced several miles to seaward and dropped a spread of eight depth charges. Not far away, the escort *USS Bainbridge* was attempting the same thing. When its sonar operator called out a "mushy" contact, the destroyer sprinted in and dropped a pattern of eight depth charges of its own. Surprisingly, the attack netted nine explosions. The depth charges had set off another mine.

By now, word of the attack was spreading like wildfire throughout southeastern Virginia. People were racing to the beach by the thousands to witness the action offshore. Coast guard and navy personnel cleared a one-hundred-yard swath of the beach by the local coast guard station as crewmen raced out in surfboats to search for survivors from the two tankers. A hush fell over the crowd as the boat returned with the body of the

Robert C. Tuttle's second engineer, whom Johansen and Fithen had been unable to locate after the first explosion. Redwine had been blown overboard by the explosion and drowned.

At that moment came the worst blow of all. At 1915 hours, just as Redwine's body was being brought ashore, the seven-year-old antisubmarine trawler *HMS Kingston Ceylonite* was approaching the 2CB buoy that marked the entrance to Thimble Shoal Channel. The *Kingston Ceylonite* was not part of the escort for Convoy KN109 but rather one of several dozen Royal Navy trawlers dispatched to the US East Coast in April to beef up coastal defenses. Lieutenant William McKenzie Smith and his thirty-one-man crew were escorting the 3,478-ton American freighter *Deslisle*, which had been damaged in a torpedo attack off Jupiter Inlet, Florida, on May 5, and was being towed by the tug *Warbler*. Now, as it approached the channel, the *Kingston Ceylonite* triggered yet another mine. The 448-ton trawler vanished in a towering column of fire and seawater. Eighteen of its crew, including Lieutenant Smith, died instantly.

The men who perished aboard the *Kingston Ceylonite* would not be the last casualties of Horst Degen's minefield. Within hours of the initial explosions, Fifth Naval District officials realized that a U-boat had mined the ship channel. At daylight on June 16, Rear Admiral Manley H. Simons dispatched a small fleet of minesweepers to clear the area. Due to a misunderstanding, however, the minesweepers failed to clear a broad swath of the area to the east and northeast of Buoy 2CB. The error became apparent at 0750 hours the next day when the 7,117-ton American collier *Santore*, proceeding down-channel to join southbound Convoy KS511, set off another TMB mine. Although the twenty-four-year-old ship capsized and sank in less than two minutes, all but three of its forty-six-man crew managed to escape. United Press correspondent Walter Logan and a photographer were embarked on one of the convoy escorts and had a front-row seat for the incident. He later wrote, "I was standing on deck lazily watching a grimy old collier when she blew up in my face."

The crowds anxiously watching the initial spectacle from the beach that Monday evening had no idea exactly what was taking place just offshore. Like the harried crewmen on the *Dione* and *Bainbridge*, they were experiencing firsthand the fog and confusion of war. Many saw what they thought was a pitched battle between a marauding U-boat and the escort warships and patrol aircraft. Reporter Frank Sullivan documented the confusion in the *Virginian-Pilot*: "For several hours after the attack, bombs were dropped from the planes and the blimp in an attempt to force the submarine to the surface. Some of those on shore said the submarine appeared on the surface. There was a terrible explosion, they said, after a bomb was dropped, and the U-boat disappeared. From the shore, it appeared that the craft had been blown to bits."

In fact, at that time U-701 was patrolling more than two hundred nautical miles away to the south-southeast off Cape Hatteras, its crewmen still unaware of the havoc their mine-laying operation had caused.[2]

WHILE DEGEN'S MINES were still lying dormant in the Thimble Shoal Channel, the fifteen A-29 Hudsons of the 396th Medium Bombardment Squadron had been cruising from California to North Carolina to join in the coastal defense there. The cross-country flight from Sacramento to Cherry Point was far from uneventful. Fifteen of the 396th's aircrews left Sacramento beginning early on the morning of Saturday, June 13, and flew in loose formation for about four and a half hours before landing in Tucson, Arizona. Following a night of crew rest, the unit proceeded east for 825 miles, landing in Dallas, Texas. There, one of the Hudsons was involved in a landing mishap that rendered it unfit for flight, although the aircrew escaped unharmed. After a second night for crew rest, the fourteen remaining A-29s lifted off for the third leg of the trip, a 421-mile flight up to Memphis, Tennessee. There, a second Hudson sustained major damage upon landing, leaving its crewmen unhurt but forcing them to complete their journey to North Carolina ignominiously by ground transportation. The surviving thirteen Hudsons refueled at Memphis and took off for the final 647-mile leg of the trip, landing at the Marine Corps air base late in the day on Monday, June 15. They had only a few days to get organized on the ground, secure temporary housing, and service their planes before Lieutenant Colonel D. O. Monteigh drew up the schedule for the six daily patrol flights.

While Harry Kane and the other pilots in his squadron were excited to be hunting U-boats, their new base and the surrounding countryside proved a major letdown after Sacramento and the San Francisco Bay area. At that time, Cherry Point was a Marine Corps air station in name only, Kane recalled years later. Although formally commissioned as a Marine Corps base just four weeks before the squadron's arrival, the place was in actuality a set of runways surrounded by a major construction project.

"It was a very new base," Kane said. "In fact, there were hardly any paved streets. The runways were paved, the streets, as I recall them, were all dirt." The ranking Marine Corps officer at Cherry Point in June 1942 was Lieutenant Colonel Thomas J. Cushman, who had reported to the site ten months earlier with a staff of four enlisted men. Since then, the base cadre had grown to 603 Marine Corps personnel, with another 499 navy and USAAF personnel assigned to the patrol squadrons rushed there because of the U-boats offshore. Army and navy squadrons had been on temporary duty at Cherry Point since March 22, and the 396th was there to relieve two other army squadrons that had been temporarily assigned to Cherry Point since mid-May.

The Marine Corps had acquired the 10,000-acre Cherry Point site because it was only fifty miles from Camp Lejeune, an even larger Marine Corps base spread out on 156,000 acres of coastal land, also still under construction to accommodate the recently activated Second Marine Division. Located near the town of Havelock on the south shore of the New River, Cherry Point's advantage was that because of the local climate, it was one of the three areas in the United States with the greatest amount of annual sunshine—a plus for flying training operations. Its liabilities included vulnerability to Atlantic hurricanes and an abundance of malaria-carrying mosquitoes in the extensive swamps and marshes in the area. "It was desolate country," Kane said. The only way in or out, a narrow two-lane highway, was clogged with construction traffic around the clock as teams of workers hastened to assemble dozens of office buildings, barracks, hangars, and other structures to accommodate the 310 aircraft and sixteen squadrons of the Third Marine Aircraft Wing, scheduled for commissioning in November 1942. "We used to kid each other that it was the same as being overseas, being stationed at Cherry Point in early 1942," Kane added.

During the squadron's first three weeks of patrols off the Outer Banks, U-boat sightings were rare. However, the enemy was there in force. Of ten U-boats patrolling within the overall Eastern Sea Frontier boundaries during that time, five forayed within fifty nautical miles of Cape Hatteras for varying periods. Because of the stiffened air patrols and heavily escorted coastal convoys, only two U-boats managed to inflict any damage on coastal shipping, sinking four merchant ships totaling 25,909 gross registered tons and a 170-ton navy patrol craft and damaging two more merchant ships totaling 14,241 gross tons.

The aviators of the 396th found the patrols both tedious and tense. "We kept on just flying . . . which got quite boring, because you never would see anything, just freighters and . . . convoys," Kane remembered. Occasionally, a Hudson aircrew would come upon the aftermath of a U-boat attack. On one flight, Kane and his crew passed over a freighter that had been torpedoed an hour or so earlier. Descending to get a closer look, the pilot saw that the merchantman's main deck was crowded with about fifty cars and trucks. "There I was without a car," he said years later, "and I could see all those cars just slowly going under the water."

On another patrol, Kane and his crew spotted a large storage tank floating in the water. Deeming it a navigation hazard, Kane alerted his crew and dove at the object several times, firing the Hudson's two fixed forward machine guns in an unsuccessful attempt to sink it. Upon return to base, Kane reported his attempt to Lieutenant Colonel Monteigh. To Kane's consternation, the squadron commander verbally rebuked him and threatened to charge him $1 for each of the ninety rounds of ammunition he had expended. Sure enough, when Kane's next paycheck arrived, it was $90 short.

Kane resumed his place in the patrol schedule, disappointed by the bureaucratic response to his effort but not so chastened that he avoided taking any initiative. In fact, on one midday patrol he found himself deliberately flouting the USAAF's formal instruction that aircraft fly at an altitude of one hundred feet above the water as they hunted for U-boats. That decision would have unforeseeable consequences for Kane and his crew.[3]

By MID-JUNE 1942, the Allied struggle against Germany and Japan remained desperate, and the fight against the U-boats was nearing a critical juncture. Allied military planners were well aware that an acute shortage in merchant ship tonnage, caused in great part by the U-boat campaign in American waters, was emerging as a major handicap to any future operations against Nazi Germany and its Axis partners. Without a solution, the United States, Great Britain, and their allies could not hope to thwart, much less roll back, the ongoing Axis campaign that was continuing on several fronts. Whereas the Japanese navy was withdrawing from the central Pacific after its June 4–5 defeat at Midway, Nazi Germany was very much on the move. By mid-June 1942, the German army was preparing to launch a massive mechanized force out of the Ukraine toward the Caucasus Mountains to seize the rich oil fields at Baku on the Caspian Sea. A second army group was preparing to lay siege to the city of Stalingrad in the south-central Soviet Union, a move that threatened to cut that country in half. Germany was also at the brink of scoring a major victory in the Mediterranean and North Africa. Field Marshall Erwin Rommel's Afrika Korps launched a major attack against the British army in Tunisia on June 12, while at the same time the Luftwaffe and a number of Italian naval units repulsed a major naval attempt by Britain to reinforce its bastion at Malta.

The sense of impending crisis prompted President Franklin Roosevelt to invite Prime Minister Winston Churchill and his staff back to Washington, DC, for the second time since Pearl Harbor. After a twenty-seven-hour island-hopping flight across the Atlantic in a Boeing 314 flying boat, Churchill and his delegation arrived in Washington on Thursday, June 18, for what was termed the Argonaut Conference. The British delegation's agenda included persuading the Americans to forgo a planned invasion of France; identified as Operation Sledgehammer, the invasion was tentatively scheduled for later in 1942, but Churchill and his generals believed that the hastily cobbled-together plan was "certain to lead to disaster." As an alternative, they argued for a reconsideration of Operation Gymnast, the planned Anglo-American invasion of French Northwest Africa.[4]

To their surprise, the British found their American counterparts at one another's throats over the U-boat offensive. The havoc wrought by Horst Degen's minefield in the Chesapeake Bay channel four days earlier prompted Army Chief of Staff General George C. Marshall to unleash an uncharacteristically harsh attack against Chief of Naval Operations Admiral Ernest King. In a memorandum to King on Friday, June 19, the day after the British delegation arrived in Washington, Marshall wrote,

The losses by submarines off our Atlantic seaboard and in the Caribbean now threaten our entire war effort. . . . I am fearful that another month or two of this [rate of ship losses] will so cripple our means of transport that we will be unable to bring sufficient men and planes to bear against the enemy in critical theaters to exercise a determining influence.

In his reply to Marshall, King chastised the USAAF for clinging to its doctrine of offensive "hunter-killer" air patrols while minimizing defensive convoy escort flights. The offensive patrols favored by pilots and aircrews, King wrote, had "time and time again proved futile" against the U-boats. The only efficient way to kill the enemy submersibles at sea, King added, was to go "continuously and relentlessly" after those drawn to escorted convoys. He ended by requesting that Marshall transfer a force of 1,000 radar-equipped aircraft to patrol for U-boats. Marshall refused.

Even FDR was drawn into the mêlée. Pressured by Churchill, Secretary of War Henry Stimson, General Marshall, and others, Roosevelt that week complained to King in a private letter about the delays in organizing the coastal convoy system: "I think it has taken an unconscionable time to get things going, and further, I do not think that we are utilizing a large number of escort vessels which could be used, especially in the summertime. We must speed things up." The president conveniently overlooked two of his own earlier decisions that had helped create the dire situation now confronting the Allies. Shortly after the British declaration of war against Germany in September 1939, the navy's General Board—a high-level advisory panel of senior rear admirals, which at that time included Ernest King—had urged Roosevelt to give highest priority to developing an effective warship for convoy escort duty. King got the board to recommend mass construction for the navy of the *Treasury*-class coast guard cutter design as a cost-effective alternative to using multimission destroyers for convoy protection. FDR rejected the plan. Roosevelt also rebuffed a subsequent proposal that the navy build a fleet of destroyer escorts modeled after a Royal Navy frigate design. Like the *Treasury*-class cutters, the "DE's" would be simpler and less expensive than destroyers but would carry the necessary armaments to fight U-boats. After Pearl Harbor, the president continued to give the destroyer escort such a low priority that the first warships of that design would not enter fleet service until well into 1943.

Despite their concern, the Argonaut Conference participants could not focus solely on the U-boat threat; events in the war's other theaters demanded too much of their attention. On Sunday, June 21, three days into the conference, the Americans and British alike were stunned when word came that 35,000 British and Commonwealth soldiers had surrendered the Tunisian city of Tobruk to the Afrika Korps. It now appeared possible that the Germans might rout the rest of the British army in North Africa and seize control of Egypt, severing the vital Suez Canal lifeline and cutting Great Britain off from its Asian colonies. The Argonaut Conference disbanded on June 24 with no firm consensus as to the next strategic move to take against the Axis. The U-boats, meanwhile, grimly pressed on.[5]

11

HUNTER AND
HUNTED

It took U-701 two days to reach Cape Hatteras after
laying the minefield off the Chesapeake Bay. Fearing detection from land-based patrol aircraft, Kapitänleutnant Horst
Degen ordered a high-speed run to deeper waters offshore and
then submerged the boat shortly before sunrise on Saturday, June
13, just hours after jettisoning his deadly cargo in the Thimble
Shoal Channel. While U-701 ran quietly on its two e-motors,
Degen organized the boat for the planned inshore patrol. His
torpedo gang transferred four torpedoes—two hanging from the
steel I beams overhead in the bow compartment and another
pair stored below the deck plates—to the forward torpedo tubes.
Next, they retrieved the spare torpedo below the e-motor compartment for the solitary stern tube. The procedure took two
hours. "Everybody was happy to get rid of those big 'cigars,'" De-
gen later recalled. "Now that they were pushed into the shooting
tubes, the sailors were able to rig up a table and sit down for their
meals." But even as they enjoyed their newfound elbow room,
the crew remained on high alert; at sunset, Herbert Grotheer

decrypted a message from U-boat Force Headquarters ordering U-701 to remain totally submerged in daylight hours because of the ramped-up defenses reported by other boats.

Degen's work, however, was far from done. Waiting for the cover of darkness, he undertook the risky task of transferring the two G7a torpedoes from their topside storage canisters. Shortly after midnight on Sunday, June 14, he ordered a working party up on deck to unload the two torpedoes. The first went down the bow hatch without difficulty, but during the second loadout at the stern, a cable jammed. The men worked feverishly to untangle the loading mechanism. "We would have been dead ducks if someone had come upon us on the surface with our open hatches, tangled ropes and a dozen men on deck," Degen recalled. Several hours passed as the cursing sailors tried one option, then another, without success. Finally, as the sun peered above the eastern horizon, the working party managed to clear the rig, lower the second torpedo inside U-701, and secure the hatch. Degen ordered the boat to dive. All together, U-701 had nine torpedoes, five ready to fire from its torpedo tubes and four spares: two more G7e electrics and the pair of compressed-air G7as. Although five fewer torpedoes than the standard loadout of fourteen, this was nevertheless enough to engage the Allied shipping he hoped to find.

Four hours later, U-701 got a nasty lesson in America's beefed-up aerial defense tactics. Traveling on the surface, Degen's lookouts spotted a multiengine bomber quickly closing in on the boat. He ordered a crash dive and reached a depth of 150 feet when several depth charges exploded close by. The shock waves shattered instrument dials and slightly damaged the main periscope. Degen decided to keep the boat submerged until his men could complete repairs and darkness once again concealed their presence. Several hours later, lookouts sighted the flashing light of the Diamond Shoals navigational buoy. Degen and his men were ready to hunt but, to their dismay, found the ocean empty of ships.

Disappointed though they might be, Degen and his lookouts were not surprised to find the shipping lanes devoid of merchant vessels. They had braced themselves for a grueling ordeal. The instructions from Admiral Karl Dönitz to remain submerged by day meant that U-701 had to move about one hundred miles offshore before sunrise each day to reach that part of the continental shelf where the depth of the water fell to three hundred feet and made concealment possible. The forty-six men confined inside U-701's pressure hull accepted the need to remain invisible, but they suffered for it. The residual heat inside the boat from its batteries and e-motors, combined with the high water temperature outside, quickly spiked the thermometer above one hundred degrees Fahrenheit. In addition, the boat's air-cleansing system was proving inadequate to rid the boat of carbon dioxide gas. For up to seventeen hours each day, the crew stewed in this hellish environment, slowly waiting for the hours to pass and the safety of darkness to finally arrive before they could surface and ventilate the boat.[1]

For the next three days, U-701 hunted in vain for Allied merchant ships. Spotting a southbound 8,000-ton freighter after nightfall on Tuesday, June 16, Degen chased the target for several hours, approaching close enough to fire two of his G7e electric torpedoes. Both missed, and Degen abandoned the effort.

The next night, Degen moved inshore to hunt near Cape Hatteras, then shifted southwest toward Cape Lookout and entered Onslow Bay near the southern end of his designated patrol area. The boat's four radio operators kept a twenty-four-hour watch, listening on their headphones for the distant sounds of a freighter's propeller churning through the water. The passive sonar system could pick up propeller noises from merchant ships up to dozens of miles away and enable Degen to get a bearing on the target to begin the hunt. In the shallows off the North Carolina Outer Banks, however, excellent sound propagation and the results of earlier U-boat attacks would send U-701 sprinting miles toward a suspected target, but once there, the crew would find only shipwrecks.

Ample targets passed by during that frustrating three-day ordeal, but the belated formation of the coastal convoy system by the Atlantic Fleet and Eastern Sea Frontier had moved them beyond U-701's reach. During that time, two coastal convoys— one northbound from Key West and another southbound from New York and Hampton Roads—passed through the Outer Banks area with a total of thirty-four merchant ships displacing 249,316 gross registered tons. Under heavy escort, the two formations rounded Cape Hatteras in daylight when U-701 was hiding on the seabed over one hundred miles to the east.

On Wednesday, June 17, Degen decided to bend BdU's restriction on daylight operations and moved closer to shore. Instead of finding a fat merchantman, however, U-701 stumbled on a small patrol boat that quickly became a major headache. Patrolling at periscope depth at around 1000 hours, Degen spotted a small trawler heading directly toward the U-boat that then passed by about five hundred yards away. The presence of the small warship—one of the civilian vessels converted to serve as a patrol craft in the navy's coastal defense system—forced U-701 to cancel its daily surfacing to ventilate the boat, and conditions inside worsened.

The next day, U-701 was somewhat farther out from Cape Hatteras than on previous days, but the ubiquitous trawler made another appearance, patrolling roughly parallel to the Outer Banks. For a second day, Degen and his crew were unable to ventilate the boat. He decided that he had to take the trawler out.[2]

By ALL ACCOUNTS, the patrol craft USS YP-389 was unfit for hunting U-boats. The navy had acquired the 110-foot Boston fishing trawler on February 6, 1942, and rushed to convert it into a coastal patrol vessel. Its armament consisted of a World War I–era 3-inch/23-cal. cannon, two equally antiquated Lewis .30-cal. machine guns, and a pair of tiny depth charge racks that held two three-hundred-pound depth charges apiece. It lacked sonar and radar. Its maximum speed was just nine knots—half the top speed of a Type VIIC U-boat on the surface. Its manual steering and round-bottomed hull made maneuvering difficult at best and impossible in rough seas. Its crew consisted of three officers and twenty-one enlisted men, all naval reservists who had received scant instruction in antisubmarine warfare tactics.

After serving as an inshore patrol craft for three months, the YP-389 received a transfer to Morehead City, North Carolina, for service along the Outer Banks. YP-389's commander, Lieutenant Roderick J. Philips, requested an engine overhaul but could only get minor repair work accomplished. Arriving at Morehead City on Tuesday, June 9, Philips learned that his vessel would be one of several small craft assigned to patrol a defensive minefield off Ocracoke Island and Cape Hatteras. Its primary duty would be to warn passing merchant ships of the danger and prevent them from getting too close to the mines.

On June 14, the *YP-389* left Morehead City on its first patrol, which passed without incident—except for the disheartening discovery that the 3-inch gun would not fire. Upon return to port, Philips had the gun inspected by a chief gunner's mate, who concluded that it needed a new firing pin. The operations department at Morehead City ordered a replacement but rebuffed Philips's request to remain in port until the gun was fixed. On Thursday, June 18, *YP-389* returned to Cape Hatteras lacking its most important weapon.

Shortly after midnight on Friday, June 19, *U-701*'s lookouts again spotted the silhouette of the small patrol craft as it proceeded southwest along the Outer Banks. As with earlier sightings, when the vessel reached a point near the Diamond Shoals light buoy, it reversed course and began heading northeast. It was the moment Degen and his crew had been waiting for. Degen quietly passed the order, and his 88-mm gun crew silently climbed up the conning tower ladder, descended to the main deck, and readied the *Schnelladekanone* for firing. At Degen's order, *U-701* slowly gained speed and closed in behind the target on its starboard quarter.

Lieutenant Philips was serving as officer of the deck in the *YP-389*'s tiny pilothouse atop the stern living quarters. His quartermaster and a signalman were also there, and two other sailors were standing lookout. "It was a quiet night, clear, very dark at the time, the moon had gone down," Philips later said. Then, suddenly, a hail of tracer bullets crashed into the patrol craft from about three hundred yards off.

On U-701, Degen and his lookouts watched intently as the 88-mm gun crew and two machine gunners on the bridge fired without letup into the 170-ton patrol craft. "Our gunners pumped shell after shell into that poor vessel," Degen later recalled. "Not a single shell failed to reach its destination. Because of our ceaseless firing the cutter was almost lost within the first fifteen minutes."

Philips did what he could to save YP-389, but it was hopeless from the start. He sounded general quarters, which brought the rest of the crew up on deck. The murderous gunfire instantly cut several of them down. Philips then got on his vessel's radiotelephone and alerted the coast guard station at Ocracoke that he was under attack. The voice on the other end promised to scramble boats and aircraft, but by that time the YP-389 was ablaze in several areas from incendiary rounds that had struck the hull and small superstructure. Two of his men were manning the .30-cal. machine guns and returning fire, but they could not see the U-boat. In desperation, Philips told his helmsman to keep the U-boat astern and raced aft to drop the patrol craft's four depth charges in a desperate attempt to drive off the attacker. Although he succeeded in rolling them into the water, their explosions occurred too far from the U-boat to damage it or force it to give way.

When Philips saw that the U-boat had now closed to within 150 yards, he realized that the situation was hopeless and ordered his crew over the side in lifejackets. The *YP-389* was still making nine knots, so after Philips and his men abandoned ship, the burning vessel continued for another half mile until a shell from the U-boat struck the engine room and destroyed its diesel motor.

Concerned that the flames from the burning trawler might attract aircraft or other patrol vessels, Degen ordered U-701 to break off the engagement. After an hour, the distant bloom of fire quietly went out. Three hours later, an Ocracoke patrol craft arrived on scene and picked up Philips and his men. Of the twenty-four crewmen aboard, six had been killed, and another twelve were injured.

By the time of Philips's rescue, U-701 was well out to sea, preparing to lurk underwater for another seventeen hours. Degen was glad that he had gotten rid of the patrol craft that had caused so much nuisance but felt slightly ashamed of the brutal attack. However, his morale and that of his men soared several hours later when a message arrived from BdU reporting that the Chesapeake Bay minefield had caused the sinking of four enemy ships earlier in the week. "Congratulations to U-701," the message continued. "Well done!"[3]

DURING THE WEEK THAT FOLLOWED U-701's destruction of *YP-389*, Degen boldly kept the U-boat on patrol relatively close to shore, even though the moon was waxing toward full and the danger of detection increased dramatically with each passing night.

As the days passed, Degen and his crew became frustrated by the heat, incessant aerial patrols, and absence of targets. On

Sunday, June 21, Degen spotted a formation of thirteen merchant ships in his periscope, most likely southbound Convoy KS512, but was unable to intercept it for a submerged daylight attack. The coastal convoy system was proving its effectiveness. During the week of June 19 to 26, four convoys with eighty merchant ships totaling 583,475 gross registered tons passed through U-701's patrol area off Cape Hatteras without sustaining a single loss.

Finally, the U-boat's luck seemed to turn. In the late afternoon of Thursday, June 25, U-701's hydrophone operator heard the distinctive sound of a ship's propeller churning through the water. Raising the periscope, Degen spotted the silhouette of a midsize freighter steaming north without escort within sight of the beach. He ordered his crew to battle stations and began calling off the range and bearing of the target.

The 7,256-ton Norwegian freighter *Tamesis* was carrying a cargo of 9,300 tons of copper, tin, and palm oil from Angola to New York as it headed toward Cape Hatteras. Master Even A. Bruun-Evensen would have been well aware of the risks in steaming in those dangerous waters without escort as he had passed through the area twice since the U-boats began operating off the US East Coast five months earlier. Fifty crewmen and seven passengers were aboard—and all of them, too, had doubtless heard the terrifying reports of the U-boats roaming along the North American coastline.

Shortly after 2000 Eastern War Time, a female passenger standing on the starboard bridge saw a long, black object heading for the *Tamesis* at what she described as "a rapid rate." Before she could call out her sighting to any crewmen, the torpedo struck the ship on its starboard side at the No. 4 hatch. The explosion threw up a tall column of water on either side of the hull. Bruun-Evensen ordered passengers and crew to abandon ship in four lifeboats. The hours passed with no follow-on attack since Degen, anxious to escape before any warships could respond, had broken off contact after the first torpedo. Early the next morning, most of the crew reboarded, and Bruun-Evensen beached the listing ship in Hatteras Inlet. The ship was later towed to New York for repairs.

Two days later, U-701 struck again. Shortly after sunrise on Saturday, June 27, Degen's hydrophone operator picked up multiple propeller sounds. It was southbound Convoy KS514 with thirty-one merchant ships. Guarding the formation were seven warships, including the destroyer USS *Broome* and six smaller vessels. Degen ignored the threat from the escort group and closed in for a submerged attack. The formation was twenty-nine nautical miles south-southeast of Cape Hatteras when one of two torpedoes fired from U-701 struck the 6,985-ton British tanker *British Freedom*. Master Frank Morris initially ordered the fifty-five-man crew to abandon ship in three lifeboats, but after fifteen minutes, he noticed the tanker showed no sign of sinking despite a thirty-foot hole in its side. Reboarding, they restarted the ship's engines and broke away from the convoy to return to Norfolk.

Several of the escorts, meanwhile, had rushed in to attack the U-boat. The patrol craft USS *St. Augustine* straddled U-701 with a spread of five depth charges. The shock temporarily disabled both e-motors and shattered glass instrument dials in the conning tower. Rather than attempting to finish off U-701,

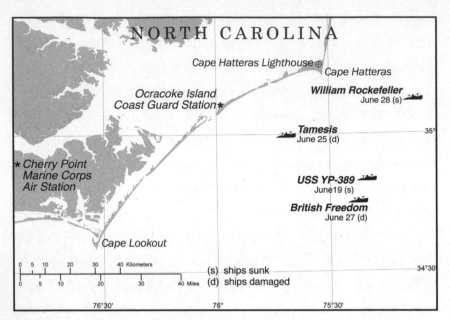

Like many U-boats, U-701 found the area east of Cape Hatteras to be a rich hunting ground for Allied merchant ships. Illustration by Robert E. Pratt.

however, the escorts—apparently concerned that other U-boats might pounce on the formation—quickly broke off their attack to return to the merchant ships. Because of the strong escort presence, Degen decided to abandon the convoy, and his men spent several hours repairing the minor damage caused by the depth charges. They did not have to wait long for their next victim, which would turn out to be the richest prize of all thus far in their patrol.

Master William R. Stewart no doubt thought his ship was safe as it passed Diamond Shoals and headed northeast toward Cape Hatteras at midday on Sunday, June 28. The 14,054-ton American oil tanker *William Rockefeller* was carrying a cargo of 135,000 barrels of fuel oil from Aruba to New York under a seemingly strong escort. Upon arriving off Ocracoke Lighthouse the previous afternoon, the ship had moored for the night in the protected anchorage. When the *William Rockefeller* departed the next morning, a coast guard patrol boat escorted the tanker, and three patrol planes circled overhead. On board, a six-man Naval Armed Guard gun crew stood by a solitary 3-inch gun mounted on the stern deck. None of those defenses, however, would help in the encounter that followed.

Degen and his crew were waiting for the *William Rockefeller*'s approach. Earlier that morning, U-701's hydrophone operator detected what he called a "heavy" engine noise approaching from the south. Sitting at the periscope control in the conning tower when the report came in, Degen quickly raised the periscope above the surface and gasped aloud. "There it approached," he later said, describing the sight, "the unique chance for a submerged U-boat torpedo attack against a big tanker that was lying deep in the water because she was full to capacity with oil."

Judging that the tanker's closest point of approach would be 1,000 yards, Degen ordered his torpedo gang to prepare to launch a pair of G7e electric torpedoes. On the command "Los!" (Release!), Oberleutnant zur See Konrad Junker turned the firing handle, and U-701 shuddered from the twin blasts of compressed air that expelled the torpedoes. Degen recalled thinking, "Endless seconds, waiting, waiting . . . was this to be a failure?" He was about to fire a third torpedo when there was an enormous eruption. Raising the periscope again, Degen looked out at a scene of complete devastation.

Stewart was in the *William Rockefeller*'s chart room marking the ship's current position when, at 1216 hours EWT, one of Degen's torpedoes struck amidships on the port side. The blast ripped a twenty-foot hole in the ship and sprayed burning oil over the rear half of the hull. The master sounded the general alarm, and Chief Engineer Edward Synder shut down the engine, closed the fuel oil valves, and activated a steam smothering system to suppress the fire. However, when Stewart emerged on deck to assess whether the ship could be saved, he found that the entire crew had panicked and abandoned ship without orders. In their haste, the men had fouled the rigging for the lowering of two of the tanker's four lifeboats, forcing several of them to jump overboard into the oil-coated water.

Stewart finally climbed down into a lifeboat and studied his stricken ship, which was burning fiercely amidships but had not settled lower in the water and remained on a level keel. He argued with the officer commanding the coast guard patrol craft that had picked up the crew that the ship was not in danger of sinking and should be reboarded. But when told that a number of his crewmen needed urgent medical attention after swallowing oil in the water, Stewart acceded, and the patrol boat took the crew into Ocracoke Harbor, arriving at about 1700 hours EWT. There, a coast guard officer told Stewart that they would have to wait until the next day to inspect and possibly reboard the ship but assured him it was under close observation by another patrol craft out of Norfolk.

At dusk, Degen called down into the control room and invited a handful of sailors to climb up and get a quick glimpse through the periscope of the burning oil tanker. Several men were taking turns looking through the eyepiece when three sharp, nearby explosions suddenly rocked their boat. Realizing

The fate of the 14,054-ton oil tanker *William Rockefeller*, torpedoed by U-701 on June 28, 1942, remains clouded in doubt. Horst Degen claimed to have watched the tanker sink hours after U-701 torpedoed it, but the US Coast Guard reported its aircraft bombed and sank the burnt-out derelict the next day to prevent its becoming a hazard to navigation. NATIONAL ARCHIVES AND RECORDS ADMINISTRATION.

that at least one patrol plane was attacking, Degen ordered his planesmen to take them down deep. U-701 silently moved away from the area. After two hours, Degen again ventured up to periscope depth, where he saw the distant tanker still ablaze but guarded by at least two escort ships. Degen tried to approach the damaged vessel on four separate occasions that afternoon, but the escorts picked up U-701 on sonar each time and drove it away.

Later that night, Degen noticed that the two escorts were no longer in sight. U-701 closed in on the surface and circled the burning vessel from 1,000 yards out. "What we saw was hell on board that tanker," Degen recalled. "The night was bright like a sunny day due to the enormous fire." In a daring, almost reckless move, Degen invited a group of crewmen up onto the cramped U-boat bridge to watch the stricken ship. Shortly after 2330 hours EWT, he fired a coup de grâce, and the tanker swiftly sank. "The bow rose high into the sky like a torch in a terrible nightmare," he said. "It stood up there for a few moments, then suddenly the whole ship went down by the stern in a giant glide, hissing all over. The giant fire went out instantly and we found ourselves in a completely dark night." This account remains controversial, since the US Coast Guard reported that its aircraft had found and bombed the burnt-out tanker the next day to prevent its becoming a hazard to navigation. In any event, the *William Rockefeller* was U-701's last victim.

SIX WEEKS INTO THEIR THIRD WAR PATROL, the men of U-701 had every reason to be proud of their accomplishments. The boat's record was four ships sunk by torpedo, gunfire, or mines totaling 21,789 gross tons and another four vessels totaling 37,093 tons seriously damaged. The mining operation at the mouth of the Chesapeake Bay had been an unparalleled success, in contrast to the missions of the other two U-boats assigned to lay mines along the North American coast during the same period. U-373's minefield off Delaware Bay sank a solitary 396-ton tug, while U-87's mines laid near Boston sank nothing. The attacks on the *Tamesis*, *British Freedom*, and *William Rockefeller* had left U-701 with only two remaining torpedoes, but U-701 still had sixty-five cubic meters (17,000 gallons) of diesel fuel in its tanks. Degen intended stay on patrol and to hunt at least one more ship before breaking off for the return to France.[4]

Within a week of the sinking of the *William Rockefeller*, however, the crewmen of U-701 could not have helped wishing their patrol was over. By day, the boat lurked deep underwater out where the continental shelf dropped off to several hundred feet, its crew gasping and vomiting in the overheated, putrid air inside the pressure hull. The hydrophone operator heard no sounds of passing merchant ships, and quick glimpses through the periscope confirmed that the ocean was empty. In desperation, Degen resumed a daily surfacing maneuver to ventilate the boat, even though the American air defenses were becoming visibly stronger with each passing day. On Monday, July 6, Degen sent a sober message back to BdU Headquarters in Paris:

SITUATION CAPE HATTERAS; SINCE 28 JUNE TIGHT-
ENED SEA AND AIR PATROL. DURING THE NIGHT OF
2 JULY, 2000 GRT FREIGHTER WITH 3 SUSPICIOUSLY
REMOTE ESCORT VESSELS, PROBABLY A TRAP. OTH-
ERWISE OUTSIDE AND WITHIN THE 200-METER LINE
NOTHING MORE SEEN.

It was the last message that Admiral Dönitz and his staff ever received from Horst Degen and U-701.[5]

SHORTLY AFTER 0945 EWT ON TUESDAY, JULY 7, Lieutenant Harry Kane and his four aircrewmen donned their flight suits, boots, and lifejackets and walked out onto the tarmac of Cherry Point to begin yet another patrol flight off the coast. Another five-man aircrew followed behind them, heading for a different aircraft. The sun was already well up in the east, promising another

scorching summer day. The five airmen had already flown at least
ten missions since the 396th Medium Bombardment Squadron
arrived at the Marine Corps air station, and this one gave no
indication of being any different from the previous ones.

The airmen walked up to the port side of the Lockheed A-29
Hudson, ducking under the left wing before reaching the main
cabin hatch in the side of the fuselage. Entering the cabin, the
five fliers began the long-practiced routine of preflight inspection. Corporal George E. Bellamy entered the aircraft first.
The thirty-year-old bombardier was one of the older men in
the squadron; his flight station was in the spacious nose of the
bomber, where a small moveable seat allowed him to handle
the sensitive bombsight that guided the plane's aerial depth
charges to their target. Kane followed the corporal into the aircraft, walking up the canted metal floor plates to the small access
door leading to the flight deck. Seating himself in the left-hand
seat, Kane opened up his satchel and took out the aircraft's flight
manual. Meanwhile, twenty-four-year-old navigator Lieutenant
Lynn A. Murray and twenty-two-year-old radio operator Corporal Leo P. Flowers entered the Hudson. Murray followed Kane
into the flight deck and lowered the foldaway seat on the right-
hand side. Flowers sat down at the radio station in the cramped
radio compartment immediately aft of the pilot's station. Flight
engineer Corporal Presley L. Broussard, also twenty-two, remained outside to observe the engine start-up procedure.

Kane, as a Brooklyn native, was the only city boy on the
aircrew. Bellamy was a native of Overton, Texas. Murray came
from a family that had settled in North Dakota at the turn of
the twentieth century. Flowers was a native of San Bernardino,
California, and Broussard was from Delcambre, Louisiana. De-

spite their varied backgrounds, the five men had been flying together as a team for months and had become professionally close as they proceeded through their extensive transition training and subsequent U-boat patrols.

Kane briskly proceeded through the engine start checklist. "Master battery switch on," he began. Kane's eyes moved down the checklist, hands grasping the proper switch or button as he continued. "Brakes locked. . . . Landing gear lever down. . . . Wing flap lever neutral."

Another half dozen checklist items went by as the pilot checked the tail wheel position, bomb bay door, automatic pilot, and other flight instruments. Finally, Kane cracked the two engine throttles to the position of 1/10 open, reached down in front of him, and grasped the hand fuel pump, giving it three strokes. Turning the master ignition switch to the on position, he then engaged the starter and booster for the left engine. The fourteen-cylinder Pratt & Whitney R-1830 sputtered into life, its three-bladed propeller quickly blurring as he powered it up to 1,000 rpm. He then repeated the process for the starboard engine, and the Hudson was soon ready for taxiing. Finally, Broussard climbed into the cabin and belted himself in. Kane began taxiing toward the main runway.

At 1015 hours, Kane's Hudson and a second aircraft were barreling down the Cherry Point runway. When they reached altitude, the planes flew in loose formation until they reached a point about twenty-five miles off the coast. Once there, in accordance with the squadron patrol plan, the two planes separated. Kane banked A-29 No. 9-29-322 to the right and headed southwest toward Cape Lookout. The second Hudson headed northeast to parallel the coast on its way up to Norfolk.[6]

AT ABOUT 1400 EWT ON JULY 7, Degen decided to ventilate
the boat for its daily cleansing. After confirming with Grotheer
in the hydrophone compartment that the nearby ocean was
empty of ships, he ordered U-701 up to periscope depth. A quick
360-degree scan of the sky revealed no aircraft passing overhead.
Degen called down, and his designated lookouts—Junker, the
first watch officer (1WO); Günter Kunert, the navigator; and
Oberbootsmaat (Boatswain's Mate 2nd Class) Kurt Hänsel—
came climbing up the ladder from the control room.

"Blow all tanks! Diesels full speed ahead," Degen ordered. As
U-701 broached the surface, he reached up and twisted the conning tower hatch wheel, then popped the circular hatch open.
The four men quickly climbed up onto the narrow bridge. Down
below, Chief Engineer Karl-Heinrich Bahr ordered the engine
room watch to start the two Germaniawerft diesel motors. Instead of opening the bridge-mounted air intakes that normally
fed air directly to the two engines, the crew deliberately left
them shut. The two diesel engines roared as Bahr ordered full
power, and a rush of clean air swept through the bridge hatch
into the sweltering U-boat. U-701 slowly advanced on a course
of 320 degrees, heading in the direction of the Outer Banks some
thirty to thirty-five miles away.

Degen was concerned about Junker, a former Luftwaffe officer
who had transferred into the U-boat Force. Many of the men
disliked the twenty-five-year-old for his officious and overbearing
manner. "He was very arrogant," Gerhard Schwendel said years
later of the 1WO. "He always wanted to command the crew."
But Degen was bothered by something else. Earlier that morning
he had caught Junker not paying close attention while on look-

out duty. "He was looking around and playing about," Degen later recalled. "I told him, 'You must pay more attention. You can't carry on like that.' I warned him seriously." Those words would prove prophetic.[7]

LOCKHEED HUDSON NO. 9-29-322 had been in the air for more than four hours when Kane brought it back from Charleston on a northeast course to the area off Cape Hatteras, flying about thirty miles offshore. Although USAAF tactical doctrine directed the patrol aircraft to fly at an altitude of just one hundred feet above sea level, Kane had opted to take advantage of current weather conditions. Spotting a cloud layer at 1,200 feet, he decided to conceal the aircraft in the thin layer on the assumption that he and his crew could see much farther off than at the lower altitude while remaining hidden from any U-boat lookouts. Kane edged his Hudson up to 1,500 feet, placing the bomber just above the base of the clouds. Since there were gaps between the clouds, the aircrew was mostly concealed from view from below but, at intervals, could scan the ocean for any U-boats. "I was mostly in [the clouds] . . . for two or three minutes and I'd break out for thirty seconds," Kane explained, "and then I'd be back in them for two or three minutes. . . ."

At about 1412 EWT, Kane glanced out his left-hand window and spotted a tiny, feather-like line on the water about ten miles away. He called out on the aircraft's intercom for the other crewmen to view the sight. After several minutes, Kane changed the aircraft's heading to due west and went in for a closer look. He nosed the bomber higher up in the cloud layer and instinctively pulled back on the throttles to reduce the engine noise.[8]

On U-701's narrow bridge atop its partially submerged conning tower, Degen, Junker, Kunert, and Hänsel peered through their Zeiss binoculars, each man tracking a ninety-degree sector of the ocean and sky. The boat continued to plow through the moderate waves, its bow and stern still just below the surface, but the twin propellers were thrashing a noticeable wake behind it.

Suddenly Hänsel, the forward lookout, called out a surface sighting: the funnel and two mastheads of an Allied freighter sunk in shallow waters had just appeared on the western horizon. At that moment, Bahr called up on the voice tube to report that the ventilation process was complete.

"Let's go down! Take her down!" Degen shouted. In the engine room, the duty watch-standers shut off the diesel engines and activated the two e-motors, while in the control room, Bahr ordered the ballast tanks blown and a down angle on the diving planes. U-701 began easing below the choppy surface.

Kunert and Hänsel disappeared down the hatch opening, and Degen was waiting for Junker—who was standing at the aft end of the bridge—to step forward and climb down, when the 1WO suddenly stiffened and pointed, shouting, "Airplane, 200 degrees, coming in from port aft!" Junker leaped down the hatch opening. Horrified, Degen looked up and saw an enemy bomber plummeting out of the cloud layer. He jumped down the hatch and cranked it shut as the U-boat submerged.

Degen stood in the cramped control room with Junker, Hänsel, and Kunert as the duty watch-standers pushed U-701 nose first into the depths. It was silent and tense; the only sound was the high-pitched whine as the boat's two e-motors ran at full speed. Degen turned to Junker and said in a near-whisper, "You saw it too late."

"Yes."

BY THE TIME KANE'S HUDSON got within five miles of the object, he and the other crewmen knew they had spotted a surfaced U-boat. When he saw it suddenly begin to submerge, Kane fire-walled the throttles and shoved the control yoke forward. The bomber dove at the target, which was now cloaked in a swirl of bubbles and foam. Kane shouted at Bellamy to open the aircraft's bomb bay doors as he yanked back on the yoke and leveled off at fifty feet above the water, hurtling at 225 knots toward the U-boat's location.

As the A-29 came up over the U-boat, Kane could clearly see that it was still close to the surface. He judged the right moment and stabbed the bomb-release override button on the control yoke. He felt a slight thump-thump-thump as the aircraft's load of three 325-pound Mark XVII depth charges fell free. Kane threw the A-29 into a steep climbing turn and craned his neck looking down at the water. He watched as the three depth charges exploded. The first fell twenty-five feet short of the U-boat's blurred outline, but the second and third straddled its hull at the stern. Three columns of seawater erupted more than fifty feet high, then slowly collapsed back down into the boiling surf.[9]

12

THE ORDEAL

MANY OF THE CREWMEN ON U-701 RECEIVED NO WARNING that their boat was on the brink of destruction. In one moment, Gerhard Schwendel, Herbert Grotheer, and *Mechanikergefreiter* (Seaman 1st Class) Werner Seldte were among a group of a dozen or so off-duty crewmen relaxing in the bow compartment as the diesel motors sucked sweet, fresh air throughout the boat. In the next instant, they heard distant shouts ordering a crash dive. They felt the blast of compressed air as the ballast tanks emptied and the sudden lurch as the U-boat pitched down by the nose in a frantic attempt to go deep. But before they could even react to the emergency, three sharp explosions rocked the boat, throwing several of them to the deck. The compartment lights went out, and in the dim illumination of the emergency lighting system, the crewmen heard the most terrifying sound imaginable in such a scenario: the harsh bellow of seawater thundering inside the pressure hull. Seconds later, a wave shot through the open bulkhead hatch, sweeping loose equipment, personal possessions, and several crewmen against the forward bulkhead.

Within the span of a few seconds, the crew's world had been upended. "A petty officer was washed forward and got stuck between the torpedo tubes. We became aware of him because of his groaning," Schwendel recalled. Reacting instantly, he reached up from his position in a bunk and grabbed his emergency breathing apparatus, a *Dräger Tauchretter* escape device that consisted of an air-storage bag, compressed-oxygen cylinder, and mouthpiece. He half-waded, half-swam across the bow compartment, pushing aside debris, as the space steadily flooded.

Schwendel and his fellow crewmen fought against the surging water, but to no avail. "Water was rushing in the bow compartment through the watertight bulkhead passage with enormous power," Seldte later said. "We tried to close the bulkhead hatch, but it was impossible." In less than a minute, the bow compartment had nearly completely flooded, leaving only a small air pocket in which the struggling crewmen tried to keep their heads up. What air was left in the boat became overheated due to the soaring water pressure as U-701 fell to the seabed.

In the control room, the situation was equally dire. "The water inside rose by the second, and within half a minute the whole boat was filled up to the hatches, and the inner air was pushed against the overhead by the outer pressure," Horst Degen said. At last, U-701's shattered hull came to rest on the sand about 110 feet below the surface, tilting about twenty degrees to starboard.

Degen, Günter Kunert, and Kurt Hänsel climbed up into the mostly flooded conning tower as others struggled behind them. There was less than a foot of air in the tower, and the water pressure there also created "a terrible heat," Degen said. Shouting for the others to prepare to abandon ship, Degen grabbed the circular hatch wheel and turned it. With the water pressure inside the boat nearly equal to that outside, the hatch opened easily, and the three swam up out of the conning tower in a veil of air bubbles. Even at a depth of over one hundred feet, there was enough light for Degen to see the dim outline of U-701 on the seabed as he slowly rose toward the surface. Thanks to their underwater escape training back in Germany, even the crewmen lacking the *Dräger* devices knew that to avoid contracting decompression sickness ("the bends"), they had only to restrict their rate of ascent to the same speed as the air bubbles escaping the stricken U-boat. One of the last sailors to swim up the conning tower hatch was Fireman 1st Class Ludwig Vaupel. As he waited for the men ahead of him to exit the boat, Vaupel saw Oberleutnant Konrad Junker clinging to a stanchion with his head in the air pocket, apparently making no effort to prepare to escape. Vaupel picked up an escape lung and handed it to the first watch officer, but the officer shook his head and said, "Go on, get out!" Neither Vaupel nor any of the survivors of U-701 ever saw Junker on the surface, and years later Degen himself would say, "I still to date do not understand why 1WO Konrad Junker, who was standing next to me in the control room, did not come up to the surface at all."

Word spread quickly throughout U-701 that the men should abandon ship. While other crewmen in the bow compartment tended to the seriously injured sailor, the senior enlisted man present, *Obermaschinist* (Machinist Chief) Walter Fritz, asked for a volunteer to see what was happening in the control room three compartments aft. Seldte nodded. Donning his *Dräger* apparatus, he plunged into the debris-filled water and struggled through the open hatch. Groping his way to the rear end of the petty officer's compartment, he found Second Watch Officer Leutnant zur See Erwin Batzies, clinging to a stanchion in what remained of Degen's semiprivate cabin, where there was a small air pocket. "He looked all right and composed," Seldte recalled years later. "He ordered the crew in the bow compartment to try to make it to the central operations room, to evacuate the boat from there." Seldte reversed course, returned to the bow compartment, and relayed Batzies's order to Fritz. However, several crewmen who attempted to make it to the control room quickly returned, saying the way was now blocked. Seldte himself made the attempt and briefly became trapped in the completely flooded petty officers' compartment.

Stifling a growing panic, Seldte dove to the deck plates and saw a faint light glimmering ahead of him. Emerging into the control room, he found it empty except for two crewmen huddled in the shrinking air pocket. One was incoherent from an injury, and the second, while seemingly unharmed, did not reply when Seldte told him to swim out of the boat through the conning tower hatch. Seldte was racking his brains for what to say next to the man when a loud hissing erupted and the air pocket began to disappear as water pressure built up inside the boat. Seldte left the pair behind and swam up the conning tower hatchway; in less than a minute he was on the surface.[1]

CIRCLING SEVERAL HUNDRED FEET OVERHEAD, Harry Kane and his aircrew intently studied the disturbed water below where their three depth charges had detonated. "We didn't know that we'd gotten the submarine," Kane said. Even when they saw a plume of diesel oil and what appeared to be small pieces of debris emerge from the turbulence, the Americans thought these might be part of a ruse by the U-boat commander to trick them into abandoning the hunt. But after several minutes, they saw tiny figures popping up to the surface. Slowing the Hudson down to near-stalling speed, Kane and his crew counted about sixteen Germans in the water below, many of them lacking lifejackets or the smaller *Dräger* devices.

Kane got on the bomber's intercom and issued a terse order. All five crewmen tore off their own lifejackets, and in the next several passes, threw them out of the plane to the struggling swimmers. Then Kane ordered Corporals Leo Flowers and Presley Broussard to jettison the aircraft's inflatable life raft, which was mounted on the inside of the main cabin door. "They were beaten," Kane later said of the Germans. "They couldn't hurt anyone anymore. We couldn't leave them to drown like rats. They were like us, they'd had a job to do and they'd done it."[2]

DOWN ON THE SURFACE, Degen was trying to organize the control room survivors but became distracted when he saw the twin-engine bomber fly past at a very low altitude. As he watched, a figure in the cockpit waved down at them, and a few seconds later, several objects fell into the water nearby. One of the crewmen swam over and retrieved two lifejackets. Degen counted six flotation devices: one lifejacket and three *Dräger* sets from the U-boat and the two lifejackets the Americans had just tossed down (they never saw the life raft from Kane's aircraft). He ordered his crewmen to string them together in a circle and to quiet down, hang on, and conserve energy. The A-29 circled around one more time, and its crew dropped three smoke floats into the water. These gestures gave Degen and the other fifteen crewman hope that they would soon be rescued.

Unfortunately, two of the men in Degen's group were non-swimmers; they quickly became exhausted and panicked as they clung to the ring of flotation devices. The ocean was choppy with a strong breeze, which splashed the men as they floated. Despite Degen and others' pleading that they relax, the pair quickly began swallowing and choking on seawater, which further weakened them. After forty-five minutes, both men drowned. As the sun slowly descended toward the western horizon, two more men perished. Both had been injured in the attack. They too quickly became drained of energy and succumbed to the waves.

Degen's group had shrunk to twelve by sunset when another pair of men abandoned the group. Even though he had estimated U-701 was at least thirty nautical miles from the coast at the time of the attack, Fähnrich Günter Lange and Oberbootsmaat Kurt Hänsel decided to strike out for the semi-submerged shipwreck that Hänsel, as forward lookout, had sighted moments before the sinking. Degen warned the two that they would be swimming against the Gulf Stream and encouraged them to remain with the group, but they refused and started off together. "We never saw those two men again," Degen later recalled.

Just before sunset, Degen and the others spotted a large convoy passing by about four miles from their position, much too far away to spot the tiny group clinging to their flotation gear.

They also saw several aircraft flying high overhead, brightly illuminated by the setting sun. "They were too high to notice us," he said. The smoke floats had long since gone out. Darkness fell. Degen exhorted his men to have faith that they would be rescued and told them what an incredible story they would be able to recount to their families, once they were saved, after such an amazing adventure. "We talked it over how lucky we had been by going towards the coast and not eastward to the open ocean, and how all of us would have been lost immediately had we not hit the bottom at 60 meters depth," Degen recounted. "Thinking of these facts and the situation put much of us at ease as far as a [hoped-for] rescue."[3]

LIEUTENANT KANE AND HIS CREW were desperate to obtain help for the German sailors stranded in the water below them. Nine minutes after their attack, Kane instructed radio operator Flowers to transmit a report on the sinking. At 1424 Eastern War Time, Flowers raised Cherry Point on the radio and sent, "Sub sunk position 393376," which translated into 34:23N 075:10W. At 1442 hours, as the A-29 continued to circle the area, Flowers dispatched a follow-up report: "Please send other aircraft to 393376, we are running low on gas. There are men in the water. Send help."

One hour after sinking the U-boat, Kane sighted a freighter steaming about five miles away and turned toward it. Coming upon the vessel, Kane identified it as a Panamanian-flagged merchant ship. Flowers climbed up into the cockpit with a flashing light and signaled to the ship in Morse code: "Submarine sunk in this area, survivors in the water. Please send a small boat." The ship's captain signaled back, "Congratulations," but did not alter course to assist. Kane later theorized that the Panamanian skipper was fearful that other U-boats might be in the area and refused to put his ship in harm's way.

Several minutes after receiving Flowers's second message, Cherry Point called back and ordered Kane to repeat the details of the attack and sinking. Flowers did so as Kane turned the bomber and headed back toward the survivors. At this point, more frustration: with a sea state creating waves six to eight feet in height, Kane and his crew could not find the smoke floats or any sign of the Germans. Meanwhile, they sighted another A-29 from their squadron flying by. Flowers tried to raise the aircraft on the radio, but his transmission was blocked by a loud, continuous signal from a shore station that effectively jammed the channel. Cherry Point finally radioed Kane a second time and instructed him to send a series of bursts on a frequency of 314 kilocycles so that other aircraft could home in on his position. Nearly two hours had now passed since the sinking.

Finally, other units began to join the search. Kane and Corporal George Bellamy both sighted coast guard patrol boat *USCGC-472*, which was steaming about thirty-seven nautical miles from Cape Hatteras Lighthouse on a bearing of ninety-six degrees. Flowers used his blinking light to alert the patrol craft, and it turned to head for the sight of the sinking. Kane also heard from Cherry Point that a navy patrol plane and four more A-29s from the 396th Medium Bombardment Squadron were scrambling to join the hunt. But the sun was going down, and spots of bad weather hampered the efforts. All proved unsuccessful.

Kane made one more attempt to locate the men in the water, but the white caps flecking the ocean made it impossible to identify anything, and his fuel state was becoming critical. He finally had to break off to return to Cherry Point, landing an hour later with just five minutes' worth of fuel in his aircraft's last tank.[4]

DEGEN AND THE OTHER SURVIVORS spent a long night in the water. Their plight eased somewhat when the surface of the ocean grew calm, making it less difficult to cling to the flotation gear and possible for the men to save energy. Then an hour after sunrise on Wednesday, July 8, they sighted a coast guard vessel approaching from the north. "As far as we could see, she was going to directly hit our position, but suddenly she zigzagged away and passed at a distance of about 1,000 meters," Degen said. The cutter was close enough that the Germans could clearly see its crew on the bridge but too far away for the Americans to see or hear them. Once more the ocean had picked up, and the men were lost in the waves and white caps. It was a devastating blow to their morale, compounding the feeling of desperation that came with their increasingly sunburnt skin, their weakening physical states, and their growing hunger and thirst. Even worse, the group floated through a patch of heavy oil, which burned their mouths and nostrils when an errant wave doused them with the substance.

As the harsh summer sun climbed high in the sky, five more men in Degen's group gave up and drowned. Others had become delirious from exposure and the lack of food or water.

An unexpected event that afternoon brought the tiniest bit of relief. One of the men spotted a lemon and a coconut floating by. Degen tore the fruit in half and passed it around. "Each man was able to suck from that sour fruit, which burned like hell in our throats, but still gave a little stimulus," Degen said. Another crewman, Ludwig Vaupel, managed to break an opening in the coconut shell by boring two holes with a safety pin found on Degen's clothing. Each survivor was able to swallow some of the very sour coconut milk. Then Vaupel managed to break the shell apart by striking it repeatedly against the metal oxygen flask on his *Dräger* escape lung. Each man avidly chewed on a piece of the coconut meat. This proved disastrous. Because by now the men could not breathe through their nostrils due to the saltwater irritation, they immediately gagged on the coconut pieces.

By evening, the group had dwindled to only seven men. As the darkness cloaked them for a second time, Degen quietly exhorted the others to keep warm by hugging their neighbors, massaging their limbs, and stretching muscles that ached beyond measure. Close to midnight, three more sailors gave up and slipped beneath the surface. Even those with enough physical stamina to continue hanging onto their makeshift raft found themselves hallucinating.

At sunrise on Thursday, July 9, Degen's group was down to just four men lingering at the edge of consciousness. Only Degen, Kunert the navigator, Radioman Grotheer, and Machinist's Mate Vaupel were left of the sixteen men who had fled through U-701's conning tower hatch. With the rising sun once more came "a murderous heat," Degen remembered. Although the water was again calm, during the night their circle of tied-together

A US Navy blimp circles overhead as a coast guard PH-2 seaplane rescues the seven survivors of U-701 after their discovery on July 9, 1942. US NAVY PHOTOGRAPH.

flotation devices had come apart, and Degen had floated some distance away from the other three. All were too far-gone to consider any attempt to reconnect.

It was midday when Herbert Grotheer heard a strange humming sound and sensed a large shadow falling across the spot where he floated on the water. He blearily opened his eyes and looked around. He saw Kunert and Vaupel slumped lifelessly in their flotation gear. Degen was several hundred feet away, barely conscious in a lifejacket. Grotheer heard the thrumming sound again and looked up. A large US Navy blimp was hovering above him. As he watched, a door to the cabin attached to the underside of the dirigible opened and a man called out, "Who are you?"

Grotheer replied in a hoarse croak, "Ich bin von einem Deutschen U-Boot."

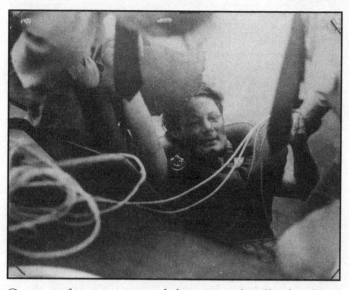

Crewmen from a navy amphibian aircraft pull a dazed and exhausted Bruno Faust into the plane after sighting U-701's seven survivors on July 7, 1942. US Navy photograph.

The man disappeared inside the cabin and then returned with a second crewman. They wrestled a large shape out through the hatch. A large inflated life raft splashed down into the water. Summoning his last reserve of energy, Grotheer scrambled into the raft, followed by Kunert and Vaupel. Scarcely believing their good fortune, the three men settled down. Then the man overhead shouted again and pointed: "One man over there!" Paddling with their hands, the three Germans reached an unconscious figure kept breathing by the American life jacket that supported his head out of water. It was Degen. Once the three crewmen had managed to pull Degen into the life raft, the dirigible's crew threw down a package containing a first aid kit, two loaves of bread, water, and canned vegetables and fruit.

Lieutenant Harry Kane points to the location of his attack on U-701 as his four air crewmen watch. From the left, Corporal George E. Bellamy, bombardier; Corporal Presley C. Broussard, flight engineer; Lieutenant Lynn A. Murray, navigator; and Corporal Leo P. Flowers, radio operator. NATIONAL ARCHIVES AND RECORDS ADMINISTRATION.

Several hours later, a coast guard PH-2 seaplane piloted by Commander Richard L. Burke landed near the raft and picked up the four survivors. To their astonishment, three other crewmen from U-701 were already aboard. As the seaplane droned through the air toward the Norfolk Naval Air Station, the survivors exchanged accounts of what had befallen them. Gerhard Schwendel, Werner Seldte, and Bruno Faust were the only survivors from a group of about twenty crewmen who had escaped from the bow compartment through the torpedo-loading hatch. It had taken them nearly a half hour to unlock the hatch and get it completely open. By that time, the Gulf Stream had carried the conning tower group nearly a mile away, well out of eyesight or hailing distance. The blimp had apparently come upon the second group some time before finding Degen and the three men with him. A crewman aboard the coast guard seaplane told them that when they were finally sighted forty-nine hours after Kane's attack, they had drifted nearly 110 nautical miles northeast from the site where the U-boat had gone down.[5]

For the three days that passed after the sudden sighting, attack, and destruction of U-701, Harry Kane and his aircrew resumed their regular schedule of coastal patrols, generally aware that other units were still searching for the U-boat's surviving crewmen. Upon returning to Cherry Point on the evening of July 7, Kane became vexed, then furious, when navy and Marine Corps officials at the base at first refused to believe his account of the sinking. Given the intense rivalry between the navy and the US Army Air Forces over land-based antisubmarine patrol bombers and the fact that navy pilots had already sunk three U-boats, while the army score to date had been zero, it was not unusual that the navy pilots at Cherry Point immediately debunked Kane's claim of a U-boat kill. "The navy was there and the navy, to my knowledge, didn't care to say that the . . . Army Air Corps had sunk the submarine," Kane said. "They wouldn't believe me."

Then on Thursday, June 11, Kane was suddenly ordered to the office of Lieutenant Colonel Monteigh.

"We're going to Norfolk," the squadron commander said. "We want you to go with us."

Not knowing why, Kane and his four crewmen climbed into one of the squadron's A-29s, with the lieutenant colonel in the pilot's seat. Arriving at the Norfolk Naval Air Station, the army fliers were driven to a hospital on base where they were surprised to see a number of civilians—Kane thought they were either FBI or Naval Intelligence agents—standing around with submachine guns. A small group of officials stood close by. Two of them introduced themselves to Kane and his men as Navy Secretary Frank Knox and Vice Admiral Adolphus Andrews from Eastern Sea Frontier Headquarters. They entered a large hospital bay, where Kane saw a heavily sunburned man dressed in pajamas and a hospital robe sitting in a chair. One of the officials bent over and muttered something in German to the man, who looked at Kane, then struggled painfully to his feet. He threw Kane a sharp military salute.

"Congratulations," Horst Degen said in clear English. "Good attack."[6]

EPILOGUE

ON SUNDAY, JULY 12, 1942, THREE DAYS AFTER THEIR dramatic rescue at sea, the seven survivors of U-701 left Norfolk under armed guard for a US Army detention camp at Fort Devens, Massachusetts. For the next two months, army and navy interrogators grilled Horst Degen and his men about every aspect of their U-boat service, from their *Baubelehrung* "familiarization training" and workups in the Baltic to the boat's three war patrols in the North Atlantic.

Of particular interest to the American intelligence officers were the saboteur landing missions carried out by the two U-boats during the new-moon period in mid-June. The Abwehr mission to infiltrate the eight saboteurs into the United States to destroy critical economic targets such as manufacturing plants, transportation nodes, and other sites, was already a failure. Within a day of landing at Amagansett on the night of June 12–13, George Dasch and Ernst Berger, two of the four agents landed from U-202, decided to betray the mission and turn themselves in to the FBI. Dasch contacted the FBI several days later, and by Saturday, June 27, the bureau had arrested all eight infiltrators and seized their two caches of explosives at Amagansett, Long Island, and Ponte Vedra Beach, Florida. However, the FBI and Naval Intelligence were desperate to confirm that no other saboteur teams were running free.

American intelligence officials at that time remained suspicious that a third U-boat might have carried a pair of German naval agents who were to be landed in the vicinity of New York or New Jersey, presumably to report on the arrival and departure of merchant shipping. One of the captured saboteurs told his interrogators that the third U-boat with the two-man team had left Lorient during the same two-day period of May 26–28 as had U-202 and U-584. The Americans strongly suspected that U-701 had done this. Unfortunately, in his initial interrogation sessions, Degen had refused to divulge the date U-701 had left for American waters, as part of his tactic to prevent his captors from learning of his mine-laying operation off Virginia Beach.

After several weeks of veiled threats from interrogators that he might face a special tribunal and the death penalty on charges of aiding the saboteurs, Degen finally admitted that U-701 had left Lorient on May 19, but stressed that his operational area had been restricted to the mid-Atlantic littoral. In a conversation with a fellow POW secretly recorded by Naval Intelligence agents in early August 1942, Degen confessed to Oberleutnant zur See Oskar Bernhard, a survivor from U-352, that he had "no wish to sit in an electric chair" as had six of the eight captured saboteurs executed just the previous week in Washington, DC. A Naval Intelligence report on the two prisoners' conversation noted, "Degen seems to be trying to justify himself before Bernhard for the information he has given the interrogators. Seems to be a trifle worried."[1]

Naval Intelligence agents were equally interested in the U-boat Force's mine-laying operations. They were well aware by the time of Degen's rescue that Admiral Karl Dönitz had dispatched at least two boats with mines to the Chesapeake Bay and the mouth of Delaware Bay. U-87's attempt at the entrance to Massachusetts Bay was unsuccessful and thus had not been detected.

Degen knew vaguely about the Abwehr agent infiltration but provided little useful information to the Americans. And he and

his six crewmen com-
pletely stonewalled
the US Navy about
their mining mission.
The final Office of
Naval Intelligence
report on U-701 er-
roneously concluded
that the U-boat had
proceeded straight
to Cape Hatteras on
June 12 to hunt Al-
lied shipping with its

Wearing POW dungarees, Degen (at far right) and the six other survivors from U-701 prepare to leave Norfolk for a secure confinement facility in Massachusetts after recovering from their ordeal in the Atlantic. US NAVY PHOTOGRAPH.

torpedoes. Degen's role in mining the Thimble Shoal Channel would not be known for another forty years.[2]

AFTER U-701 DID NOT ANSWER requests for situation reports on July 12 and 13, Admiral Dönitz declared the U-boat to be presumed lost at sea. Subsequently, U-boat Force Headquarters learned from a letter mailed by a POW from U-352 that an aerial attack had sunk U-701 and that Degen and six crewmen had survived.

Eight days after the U-701's loss, BdU dispatched two more U-boats to attack shipping off the Outer Banks. One was U-402, a veteran Type VIIC boat commanded by thirty-one-year-old Kapitänleutnant Siegfried von Forstner. During his first three patrols commanding U-402, von Forstner sank three ships totaling 11,135 gross registered tons and damaged a fourth for another 11,951 gross tons. Also ordered to Cape Hatteras was the Type VIIC U-576, commanded by a classmate of Degen's, twenty-nine-year-old Kapitänleutnant Hans-Dieter Heinicke. On four previous patrols, Heinicke and his crew had sunk three Allied merchant ships totaling 13,387 gross registered tons. Patrolling independently from Cape Lookout to north of Cape Hatteras, the two U-boats found heavily defended coastal convoys and saturation coverage by land-based air patrols. The solitary targets that had made the "happy time" so exceptional were now a distant memory.

The convoy system that American planners had been so slow to adopt was proving its worth. In the early morning hours of Saturday, July 11, Heinicke sighted northbound Convoy KN117, consisting of fourteen merchant ships totaling 89,949 gross tons. Escorting the formation were two destroyers, a coast guard 165-foot patrol vessel and two smaller PC craft. Unable to close for attack, Heinicke broke off the chase.

Both U-402 and U-576 came under aerial attack during the next two days. Eastern Sea Frontier logs show that during this time, land-based coast guard, army, and navy aircraft made four separate air attacks against sighted U-boats. Von Forstner sent a message to BdU on July 14 to report heavy damage and a battery explosion as a result of one attack and that he was aborting his patrol. Heinicke sent a similar message. Only one of them would make it back to France.

On Wednesday, July 15, U-576 was south-southeast of Cape Hatteras when Heinicke's lookouts spotted southbound Convoy KS520. This formation consisted of eighteen merchant ships totaling 107,840 gross tons en route to Key West and an escort of five warships, including the destroyers USS *Ellis* and USS *McCormick*, and four smaller vessels. At 1600 hours Eastern War Time, Heinicke closed and fired a spread of four torpedoes at the convoy. One struck and damaged the 8,310-ton American freighter *Chilore*, a second hit and damaged the 11,147-ton Panamanian tanker *J. A. Mowinckel*, and a third sank the 2,063-ton Nicaraguan freighter *Bluefields*. Escorted by the corvette USS *Spry*, the captains of the *Chilore* and *J. A. Mowinckel* sought to beach their damaged ships in shallow water near Cape Hatteras but instead blundered into the navy's defensive minefield. Both were extensively damaged, and the *Chilore* later sank while being towed to Norfolk.

Heinicke did not have long to celebrate. Reaction from the convoy's defenders was swift and deadly. U-576, most likely as a result of earlier damage, became destabilized after firing the torpedoes and broached the surface in the middle of the convoy. Naval Armed Guard gunners on the American freighter *Unicoi* opened up with their 5-inch gun, and two navy OS2U-3 Kingfisher aircraft dropped a pair of Mark XVII depth charges that straddled the U-boat. As with U-701, the depth charges ripped open U-576's pressure hull, and it quickly sank. Unlike the men of U-701, Heinicke and his crew were out in several thousand feet of water, and none of them escaped.

Four days later, on July 19, Admiral Dönitz—unaware that U-576 had been destroyed—recorded in his command war diary,

> In the sea area off Hatteras successes have dropped considerably. This is due to a drop in the traffic (formation of convoys) and increased defense measures. . . . Of the boats stationed there in the recent period only two, U-754 and U-701, have had successes. On the other hand U-701 and U-215 have apparently been lost, and U-402 and U-576 badly damaged by depth charges or bombs. This state of things is not justified by the amount of success achieved. The two remaining boats (U-754 and U-458) will therefore be removed.

For six long months, the U-boats had waged a ruthless campaign against Allied shipping in American coastal waters. Refocusing their efforts from the central North Atlantic to the entire North American East Coast, the U-boats later expanded the campaign to the Caribbean Sea and Gulf of Mexico as well. From mid-January to late June, the U-boats rampaged practically unopposed along the East Coast, sinking 226 Allied merchant ships totaling 1,251,650 gross registered tons.

While no part of the Atlantic seaboard escaped the violence, the shallow waters off the North Carolina Outer Banks experienced the full fury of the onslaught. Within one hundred nautical miles of Cape Hatteras, twenty-one U-boats carried out twenty-two patrols from their bases in occupied France between mid-January and mid-July. For seventeen weeks of the twenty-

six-week period after the Type IXB U-123 moved down from the
New York area on January 19 to hunt Allied merchantmen off
the coast of the Outer Banks, there was at least one U-boat in
the vicinity—and for seven of those weeks, there were anywhere
between two and four U-boats on patrol in the area.

The U-boats had concentrated their efforts along the Outer
Banks for one particular reason: until late June 1942, it was a
relatively safe place to operate. By July 1942, that was no longer
the case. Admiral Dönitz understood as much; his July 19 redeployment order signaled that the deadly and vicious U-boat
campaign along the US East Coast was finally over. The Battle
of the Atlantic, however, was not.[3]

AFTER TEN WEEKS OF PATROL MISSIONS from Cherry Point, the
396th Medium Bombardment Squadron returned to California
on August 22, 1942. Another bombing squadron took its place
carrying out maritime patrols. Although Lieutenant Harry Kane
and his flight crew would not participate in the later phases of
the Battle of the Atlantic, no end was in sight for that battle or
the war itself. The squadron would remain in Sacramento for another three months and then be transferred to Naval Air Station
Alameda once more to conduct maritime patrol missions off the
West Coast. Throughout the period, small groups of officers and
enlisted men transferred out to form cadres for newly created
squadrons, just as the first men to join the 396th had done in
January 1941.

Harry Kane returned to the West Coast with more than the
distinction of being the first US Army Air Forces pilot to sink a

German U-boat, a feat for which he and his crewmen received the Distinguished Flying Cross. Kane had acquired something even more precious during his unit's time at Cherry Point. Just four days after arriving in North Carolina, Kane and a squadron mate, Lieutenant Ed Goray, had decided to hitch a ride to Atlantic Beach a dozen miles from the base. After a half day at the beach, they caught a bus up to Morehead City. As they strolled down the main street, a woman approached and introduced herself as the mother of a USAAF flier. It turned out that Kane and her son had served together on the West Coast. "She said, 'Well, you two boys, I'd like you to meet some young girls here in town,'" Kane recalled later. "And she said, 'I know quite well one of them is having a house party.'" As he entered the summerhouse of Mr. and Mrs. Walter D. LaRoque, Kane eyed a young woman walking down the stairs. She was Marguerite LaRoque, their daughter. Kane turned to his friend and said, "That's the girl I'm going to marry."

Kane did not allow his continuing wartime responsibilities to get in the way of his romance. In the spring of 1943, Kane and the rest of "A Flight" of the 396th transferred to Alaska, where as a newly promoted captain, he flew maritime patrols along the Aleutians for the next year. In mid-1944, Kane transferred to a USAAF flying school in Oklahoma, finishing out his war service as an instructor pilot. By then, Harry and Marguerite had been wed.[4]

HORST DEGEN AND THE OTHER SIX survivors of U-701 were also on the move in the fall of 1942. When their formal interrogations ended that September, they were transferred to several temporary POW camps. Degen spent two years at Camp Blanding, about thirty miles southwest of Jacksonville, Florida, before he and other POWs were transferred to Camp Papago Park in eastern Phoenix, Arizona. At the time of their rescue, only thirty-three other U-boat crewmen were in captivity, all of them survivors of U-352, which had been sunk on May 9. Nevertheless, the prisoner population at Papago Park would grow to its capacity of 2,500 as the war progressed and as more and more German army POWs from Western Europe were transferred to American soil. Indeed, Papago Park was among the first of what would become a network of 175 POW camps that ultimately held 425,000 German prisoners of war, mostly from the German army.

Arriving at Camp Blanding in late 1942, Degen and his fellow survivors from U-701 found conditions at the camp luxurious compared with day-to-day life on a U-boat. The conditions were the same in Arizona. Inmates were not required to work, the camp had a theater where the guards showed movies twice a week, a camp choir practiced, and the prisoners were allowed to publish a camp newspaper. At Papago Park, Degen's knowledge of English led US Army officials to appoint him as a trustee who worked in the camp's administrative office. An army officer would later praise Degen as "one of our most trusted and helpful prisoners of war." Degen was able to make contact with the San Diego family whose dinner guest he had been as a naval cadet in 1934. Writing Hamilton and Elsa Marston shortly after his transfer to the Arizona camp in August 1944, Degen explained that while life as a POW was "not so very pleasant," he had come to accept his situation and looked forward to returning to Germany when the war ended. He did not mention one cause for dismay that haunted him throughout his four years as a POW: because American policy was to segregate officers and enlisted men, Degen never saw the other six U-701 survivors until after their repatriation to Germany in the summer of 1946.[5]

WHILE THE BATTLE OF THE ATLANTIC was over for Kane and the 396th Medium Bombardment Squadron, and while the war itself was over for Horst Degen and his men, the deadly fight between the U-boat Force and Allied merchant shipping steadily escalated out in the open ocean. During the six-month campaign along the US East Coast, in the Caribbean and Gulf of Mexico, and along South America's northern shoreline, Admiral Dönitz and the BdU staff could deploy on average only fifty-one U-boats on any given day. With the coming of spring and summer, the logjam of newly commissioned U-boats trapped in the Baltic ice during the fierce winter of 1941–1942 finally broke up, and the U-boat Force steadily grew in size. The daily at-sea average surpassed 100 boats in September 1942 and would peak at 118 by mid-1943.

The next phase of the Battle of the Atlantic occurred in late 1942 as Dönitz unleashed dozens of U-boat wolf packs across the North Atlantic convoy routes between North America and the British Isles. With the British code breakers still shut out of the four-rotor naval Enigma communications system, and with B-Dienst cryptologists in Berlin regularly breaking Allied merchant and naval codes, the U-boats enjoyed a distinct advantage in the race between the two sides' intelligence services to anticipate, locate, and destroy the enemy at sea. Merchant

After the US Navy organized an effective coastal convoy system along the East Coast in late spring 1942, the U-boat Force shifted operations back to the deep North Atlantic and set the stage for the ultimate Allied victory in the spring of 1943. Here, the coast guard cutter *USS (CG) Spencer*, on April 17, 1943, has attacked and sunk the Type IXC U-175 with depth charges within sight of Convoy HX233 south of Iceland. CLAY BLAIR COLLECTION, AMERICAN HERITAGE CENTER, UNIVERSITY OF WYOMING.

ship losses soared in the last four months of 1942: worldwide, the U-boats sank 96 ships totaling 461,794 gross tons in September, 89 ships for 583,690 gross tons in October, and 126 vessels comprising 802,160 gross tons in November. The tally for December through February 1943 showed a marked decline, but only because the fierce winter storms during that three-month period halted the fight on both sides. The coming of spring in 1943 brought a resumption of the conflict in all its fury and a full-fledged crisis in Washington, London, and Ottawa as Allied leaders feared the possibility of an outright German victory at sea. Still, one positive development for the Allies occurred in December 1942. Bletchley Park finally broke back into German naval Enigma. This set the stage for a renewed stream of intelligence data that would enable the Allies to locate the U-boats, muster their defenses against them, and ultimately prevail at sea.

The stunning Allied turnaround against the U-boats culminated in a series of convoy battle victories in May 1943, which destroyed forty U-boats in that month alone and forced Admiral Dönitz to withdraw his forces from the North Atlantic. This retreat set the stage for a successful Allied invasion of Western Europe the following year. Made possible by the uninterrupted flow of men and matériel across the Atlantic, the Allies' invasion of Normandy and the eleven-month land campaign that followed broke the Nazi regime and forced its unconditional surrender.*

For the U-boat crews who enjoyed *der Glückliche Zeit* in North American waters during the first six months of 1942, the succeeding phases of the Battle of the Atlantic would bring a crushing string of defeats. After the decisive battles that forced the U-boats out of the transatlantic convoy routes, Admiral Dönitz made several attempts to employ new weapons and technologies to offset the U-boats' deepening inferiority to Allied defenses. All failed: within a few weeks the Allies neutralized a new wake-homing torpedo designed to sink convoy escort warships; a U-boat "snorkel" that allowed the air-breathing diesel engines to run while submerged rendered the boats too slow to

---

* This was described in detail in the author's book *Turning the Tide: How a Small Band of Allied Sailors Defeated the U-boats and Won the Battle of the Atlantic* (New York: Basic Books, 2011).

operate effectively; and the introduction of two new high-speed U-boat designs came too little, too late to have any significant impact on the war at sea. By late 1944, the once-feared German U-boat Force had been driven back into the Baltic and Norwegian fiords with the Allied liberation of France and the loss of the Brittany ports.

Even with all of these setbacks, there was no letup for the battle-scarred German U-boat crews. Officially volunteers fighting for a regime that tolerated no dissent, they were in it for the duration. As the Battle of the Atlantic dragged on for nearly another three years after the campaign along the East Coast ended, U-boat service became for most crewmen a death sentence. Of the 4,631 German U-boat men who served aboard the ninety-five U-boats involved in the North American campaign, 3,479 officers and enlisted men—75 percent—were killed at sea. Of the 1,152 survivors, 249, or 22 percent, were rescued by their attackers and spent the rest of the war as POWs. Only 903 officers and enlisted men would survive and return home to Germany to see the final collapse of the Third Reich. Only nine of those ninety-five U-boats avoided destruction at sea: three were rendered ineffective after being bombed in port, another four were scuttled in port to avoid capture by the Allies, and the ill-fated U-505 was captured by a US Navy hunter-killer group west of Africa on June 4, 1944. Only one U-boat, U-155, was still operating at sea on May 5, 1945, when it received Admiral Dönitz's order—by that time he had succeeded Adolf Hitler as head of state—to surrender to the Allies.

Like their German U-boat enemies lurking off the North Carolina Outer Banks, the men of the 396th Medium Bombardment

Squadron found that there remained much more of the war to fight after their temporary East Coast assignment. In early December 1942, the squadron transitioned to the B-25D Mitchell bomber and spent much of 1943 conducting practice combat missions in the new aircraft. In late October 1943, the unit transferred to Hawaii, and by Christmas Eve it was operating out of an airstrip at the former Japanese bastion of Tarawa in the central Pacific, captured by the Second Marine Division just four weeks earlier. During the first four months of 1944, the squadron flew multiple raids against Japanese bases in the Marshall Islands about five hundred miles away. The unit—whose personnel strength by then was about four hundred men—suffered fifty combat fatalities and another thirty-eight men wounded in action during that period. As the US military ground its way across the Pacific toward the Japanese homeland in 1944–1945, the squadron followed and, at war's end, was operating out of the Philippines.[6]

After his discharge from the US Army Air Forces in late 1945, Harry and Marguerite Kane settled in her hometown of Kinston, North Carolina. The war had transformed the sleepy tobacco and cotton trading center into a modern American city. What Kane had jokingly called a "desolate country" in mid-1942 was now thriving due to new manufacturing plants and the proximity of a major military air base. Kane founded the Coastal Plains Distribution Company in Kinston and became an active member of the local business community. In the years immediately after the war, they had three children, Harry III, Randy, and Marguerite. They became socially prominent members of the community, joining several clubs and organizations. During the summer, they could stay at the LaRoque family beach house at Atlantic Beach near Morehead City.[7]

HORST DEGEN'S HOMECOMING could not have been more different from that of American servicemen returning from the war. Traveling by train across the United States, then by ship to a resettlement camp near Hamburg, he came home in June 1946 to a devastated Germany with millions of people dead or missing. Allied bombing, including a 1943 raid that triggered a firestorm that killed at least 42,000 civilians in one night, had devastated his new hometown of Hamburg. But Degen did not wait to resume his life. Within a week of his release at Hamburg on June 6, 1946, Horst met and quickly proposed to Lotte Dressler, the thirty-year-old widow of a German officer who had died on the Russian front in 1943. He became stepfather to her two young sons, Rolf and Rainer, and in 1948 they had a son of their own, Günther. For several years, Horst managed his wife's family's business, a fifty-eight-year-old wine and spirits wholesaler in the city of Lüneberg outside Hamburg. After the family sold the company in 1964, Degen joined a local Ford Motor Company dealership and enjoyed a full career as its administrative manager, retiring in 1978. Horst Degen did not discuss his wartime experiences with his family, preferring to put that dark chapter of his life behind him. But it would not stay buried forever.[8]

On a warm evening in late May 1968, Horst Degen was watching the evening news on TV at home with his son, Günther, when a news bulletin ripped through his heart like a dagger. The news anchor reported that American naval ships involved in a frantic search for the missing nuclear attack submarine USS Scorpion had come across what some believed was the wreck of a German U-boat. The US Navy announced that another nuclear submarine had found the submerged hull in about 180 feet of water. At the time, Degen recollected U-701 as having gone down in about 200 feet of water (not the actual depth of 110 feet as later determined), and his initial reaction was that the US Navy had found his U-boat. He later recounted his reaction to a local magazine reporter. "For a moment, I was stunned. Then my son, who was sitting next to me, heard me murmur, 'Son, that could be my boat.' And suddenly I again was living through . . . the two most horrible days of my life and the two darkest nights." Details he had long suppressed now flooded Degen's mind: the depth charges splitting open U-701's pressure hull, the desperate swim up to the surface, early hopes of rescue that faded into endless hours clinging to the flotation devices, watching his shipmates descend into madness or quietly give up and slip under the waves, and the unexpected miracle of rescue. With those long-buried memories free once more, Degen sat down and penned a thoughtful letter of condolence to the US Navy for the loss of its shipmates—an experience whose horrors few others could comprehend as well as he. Several months later, the US Navy announced that the mysterious wreck was not a U-boat but the capsized hull of a freighter that had fallen victim to a U-boat.[9]

A NEWS STORY OF AN ENTIRELY DIFFERENT stripe triggered wartime memories for Harry Kane. In the fall of 1979, the sixty-one-year-old businessman came upon an account of sport scuba divers who liked to explore two submerged U-boat wrecks off the North Carolina coast. Discovery of the hulk of U-85 about forty-four nautical miles north-northeast of Cape Hatteras and

U-352 only fifteen nautical miles south of Cape Lookout got Kane to wondering, Why hasn't anyone found the wreck site of U-701? After requests for information from the US Naval Historical Center drew a blank, Kane became interested in seeing if he could locate the U-boat himself. He decided that he should seek out its former commander for any information or insights that might help. After several unsuccessful attempts through the German Red Cross and a German military veterans organization, in October 1979 Kane wrote a letter to the editor of the *Hamburger Abendblatt* seeking the newspaper's help in locating Horst Degen. To Kane's great surprise and pleasure, the newspaper found Degen and gave him Kane's address in North Carolina. Thirty-seven years after their confrontation at sea, the two veterans began a lengthy and engaging correspondence.

Degen and Kane avidly shared details of their encounter that the other did not know about and exchanged photos, documents, and holiday gifts. Kane explained that his success in surprising U-701 on the surface was due to his deliberate violation of USAAF tactical doctrine to fly at an altitude of just one hundred feet above the surface of the ocean. In a follow-up letter, Kane revealed that his A-29 was nearly out of fuel when reaching Cherry Point after hours of trying to attract rescue ships to the scene. "If anyone ever mentions to you that I did not stay [over the water] as long as possible trying to find you again, don't believe them," Kane wrote. Degen in turn was candid about the fatal role that his "drowsy" first watch officer played in letting the A-29 sneak up on U-701. "If we had dived three minutes earlier, you wouldn't have got us," Degen wrote. After Degen mailed Kane a copy of his unpublished 1965 memoir of U-701's last patrol, Kane replied that he had realized an "absolutely fascinating" fact. Both he and Degen had traveled a total of 6,000 miles—Kane from California and Degen from France—to reach the scene of their fateful engagement, and they had arrived within hours of one another in mid-June 1942.

Early on in their correspondence, Degen apologized to Kane for the gushing tone that the Hamburg newspaper had taken in an article recounting the meeting between the U-boat commander and army pilot at the Norfolk Naval Hospital on July 11, 1942. "I would like to bring to your attention the somewhat funny article in the *Hamburger Abendblatt* concerning the great 'friendship' between you and me!" Degen wrote. "I was a little embarrassed. It sounds as if we both had become friends in a way that would not be so very correct in wartime." Nevertheless, as the two men continued their correspondence in the winter of 1979–1980, their interest in one another's accounts grew stronger. Often Kane or Degen could not wait for the reply from his most recent letter and would dash off another update. By the spring of 1980, the two veterans had indeed become fast friends. Harry Kane was more determined than ever to find U-701, and that year he found a group of scientists with the knowledge, equipment, and interest in naval history to make the search possible.[10]

SIX YEARS BEFORE HARRY KANE tracked down Horst Degen at his home in West Germany to solicit his help finding U-701, a fellow North Carolinian had made an unprecedented underwater discovery not far from where the U-boat went down. Dr. John

G. Newton, superintendent of the Duke University Marine Laboratory, led a team that included Dr. Harold "Doc" Edgerton of the Massachusetts Institute of Technology and Gordon P. Watts Jr., then an underwater archeologist with the North Carolina Department of Cultural Resources. They were searching for the Union ironclad USS *Monitor*, which had foundered off Cape Hatteras on December 31, 1862, nine months after its historic "battle of the ironclads" with the Confederate warship CSS *Virginia* in Hampton Roads. Using state-of-the-art side-scanning sonar, the team surveyed a seventy-square-mile area south-southeast of Cape Hatteras, locating nearly two dozen shipwrecks. One of them proved to be the long-lost navy ironclad.

When Kane contacted Newton and told him of his correspondence with Horst Degen, the scientist became interested in adding U-701 to his roster of shipwrecks under investigation. After reviewing the US Navy file on U-701 and Degen's recollection of the U-boat's position, course, and speed at the time of Kane's attack, the team, with Kane as an observer, set sail in August 1980 for a three-week survey of the underwater tract that promised to be the boat's final resting place. Despite their pleas to Degen to join them on the hunt, the former U-boat commander politely declined, citing personal health reasons, but wished them luck in the search. Alas, the U-boat went undetected. U-701 would remain lost for another decade.[11]

While Kane was disappointed that the research group hadn't found the long-lost U-boat, he and his wife, Marguerite, had a very rewarding experience two years later in July 1982 when they visited Horst and Lotte Degen in West Germany. It was the fortieth anniversary of the two war veterans' dramatic encounter in

Forty years after their wartime encounter off
Cape Hatteras, Harry Kane (left) and Horst
Degen (right) met at Degen's home in Lüne-
berg, West Germany, in the summer of 1982.
COURTESY OF MARGUERITE KANE JAMESON.

the North Atlantic, and they were meeting face-to-face for only
the second time in the four intervening decades since their brief
and violent confrontation off Cape Hatteras. Degen's first words
to his friend confirmed that, for the two of them, battle was no
longer the defining event that had brought them together. In
the interceding years, Degen had no doubt reflected on the fact
that, at the moment of his rescue, he was wearing an American lifejacket with the name "Bellamy" stenciled on the back.
It was thrown out of the A-29 Hudson by Corporal George E.
Bellamy, Kane's bombardier. Now, in a departure from his first
words to Kane in the Norfolk hospital—"Congratulations, good
attack"—Degen grasped Kane's hand in a firm handshake and
said, "Thank you, Harry, for saving my life."[12]

More than seven decades after the Battle of the Atlantic, scientists from the National Oceanic and Atmospheric Administration (NOAA) regularly survey wartime shipwrecks along the North Atlantic coast. Here, NOAA archeologist Russ Green captures imagery of U-701 during a 2011 inspection of the U-boat. COURTESY OF NOAA/PHOTOGRAPHER JOE HOYT.

U-701 still rests on the North Atlantic seabed several dozen miles off Cape Hatteras more than seven decades after its daring patrol off the US East Coast. Half covered by sediment, its interior blocked by accumulated sand, the Type VIIC U-boat lies at a twenty-degree tilt, unmoved by the steady flow of the Gulf Stream current. Buried with the boat are at least a half dozen of its crewmen who never got out after the aerial depth charges ripped open the pressure hull. Not far away are the decaying hulls of two of its victims, the patrol vessel YP-389 and oil tanker SS *William Rockefeller*, along with at least three other U-boats and scores of Allied merchant ships, as well as scores of Allied sailors and merchant seamen who went down in the fiery conflict that raged nonstop for six months in 1942.

Sport diver Uwe Lowas discovered U-701 in May 1989 after solving the riddle of the U-boat's location, which had perplexed so many people over the years. Taking Degen's recollection that moments before the attack, lookout Kurt Hänsel had sighted a partially submerged shipwreck dead ahead on the U-boat's course of 320 degrees, Lowas delved into the archives for a merchant ship that matched the description of a half-sunk freighter whose superstructure remained visible, with a solitary funnel bracketed by two cargo cranes. Lowas and colleagues Reinhart Lowas and Alan Russell came up with the 6,160-ton British freighter *Empire Thrush*, which was torpedoed by U-203 several hours after sunrise on Tuesday, April 14, 1942, about eight miles north of Diamond Shoals. Taking the reverse bearing from the shipwreck, Lowas used a towed magnetometer and found a large metallic contact on the seabed that turned out to be the hulk of U-701.

News of the discovery, which Lowas and his colleagues kept close to their vests for many months, brought final closure to the two elderly veterans who had shaped the U-boat's story. Lowas informed Harry Kane of the finding several months before the pilot's death at the age of seventy-two on September 30, 1990. Two years later, on July 7, 1992, Lowas and four other divers went down to the wreck site of U-701 and released a memorial wreath from Horst Degen commemorating the fiftieth anniversary of the sinking. At Degen's request, they did not affix the wreath to the hull but instead released it over the site to allow it to drift with the Gulf Stream as its surviving crewmen had done for forty-nine hours so long ago. The gesture no doubt brought comfort to Degen in his final years before he too passed at the age of eighty-two on January 29, 1996.[13]

ACKNOWLEDGMENTS

My fascination with the saga of the German U-boat U-701—its daring mine-laying mission, its hunt for Allied shipping off Cape Hatteras, and its destruction by an Army Air Forces A-29 Hudson bomber—goes back a very long way, and my thanks to those who helped me create this account are many.

First and foremost, I want to thank my wife, Karen Conrad, whose loving support sustained me throughout the long months of research and writing.

Once more, the team at Perseus Books Group and its imprint, Basic Books, demonstrated their full commitment to this author's project. My deepest thanks to Basic publisher and editorial director Lara Heimert and editor Alex Littlefield. I've said this before, but it bears repeating: they and the rest of the people at Perseus/Basic Books—particularly, Perseus CEO David Steinberger and Basic managing editor Chris Granville—have created an organization that brings out the best in the writers they work with. I also want to thank copy editor Jennifer Kelland, for her hard work polishing my prose, and illustrator-cartographer Robert E. Pratt, for his excellent charts and illustrations. I also must thank my agent, Deborah Grosvenor, for her unstinting support for this book project.

In the summer of 1974, while I was working as a newspaper reporter in Tidewater, Virginia, I first heard anecdotes about a bizarre combat incident that had taken place at the mouth of the Chesapeake Bay just three decades earlier. A German U-boat had managed to elude coastal defenses and lay a minefield across the Thimble Shoal Channel, seriously damaging two ships and destroying two others. Because of wartime censorship, details of the incident remained buried.

In that era long before the Internet and Google, it took a sustained effort to find people decades after an event and thousands of miles away. Thanks to renowned German naval historian Jürgen Rohwer, I was able to locate Horst Degen at his home in Lüneberg, West Germany, and, through him, to find Harry Kane in his hometown of Kinston, North Carolina. Officials at the Naval Historical Center—today part of the Naval History and Heritage Command—were most helpful in providing a copy of the 1942 Office of Naval Intelligence report on the sinking of U-701.

Five years later, George Hebert, my editor at the *Ledger-Star* newspaper in Norfolk, strongly supported my interest in writing a comprehensive account of the incident and provided me with the time and resources to research and write a major three-part series on U-701 that appeared in the *Ledger-Star* in July 1982, the fortieth anniversary of the sinking. Nearly three decades later, that journalism project now forms the foundation of this book.

While I was finishing up my history of the 1943 crisis in the Battle of the Atlantic, *Turning the Tide*, a chance encounter occurred that opened the door for a book about the tale of U-701. Retired US Navy Captain Jerry Mason—whose website, U-boat Archive (www.uboatarchive.net), is a rich resource for historical documents concerning the World War II U-boat Force—had been a keen supporter of *Turning the Tide*. When that project was finished, we were chatting on the phone one day, and he asked me if I planned to write another book. I told him that I had written a major series thirty years earlier on a U-boat that had mined the Chesapeake Bay and was thinking that if I could find sufficient information on the incident, a book-length project might be possible.

"What U-boat was involved?" Jerry asked.

"U-701," I replied.

"Oh—Horst Degen's boat," he said.

I was stunned.

"Jerry, the Germans commissioned 1,168 U-boats before and during the war," I said. "I can't believe that you have memorized the names of the commanders of every single one!"

Jerry laughed. "No," he said. "I'm a good friend of his son."

That was how I was introduced to Dr. Günther Degen, a retired professor of literature in Dusseldorf, Germany, and his English wife, Caroline who became friends and strong collaborators in this project. Günther and Caroline helped organize, and joined Karen and me on, a fascinating and productive research trip across Germany in the fall of 2011. In the town of Suhl, Gerhard Schwendel, the last living survivor of U-701, provided a detailed and gripping account of his wartime experiences on the U-boat, interrupted only by a sumptuous meal prepared by his daughter, Elke Reif. As I was polishing the draft manuscript of this book in late September 2013, I was saddened to learn that Herr Schwendel had passed away two days after celebrating his ninety-first birthday. In the North Sea city of Cuxhaven, the Deutsches U-boot Museum is the largest single repository of information on the German U-boat Force. There, archive founder Horst Bredow—a World War II

U-boat veteran who established the archive in 1947 and remains its managing director—provided substantial documentation about the German U-boat Force and U-701. Retired German navy Captain Peter Monte, an associate of Herr Bredow, led a tour of the archive and gave generously of his time translating numerous technical documents into English. At the Baltic seacoast village of Laboe near Kiel, visitors can climb inside U-995, the last surviving Type VIIC U-boat. It has been restored as a museum ship adjoining the Laboe Naval Memorial to the 27,490 German submariners who perished in the war. The staff members of the naval memorial were most helpful.

In Saint-Nazaire, France, Luc Braeuer was a generous host and tour guide at the wartime U-boat bunker complex, which survived a massive Allied aerial bombing campaign and remains intact to this day. Braeuer is cofounder of Le Grand Blockhaus, a museum located in the nearby coastal town of Batz-sur-Mer and dedicated to the wartime history of Saint-Nazaire.

Günther Degen also turned over invaluable private papers from his father's collection, including an extensive correspondence between Horst Degen and Harry Kane conducted by the two veterans in 1979 and 1980.

Marguerite Kane Jameson, the daughter of Lieutenant Harry Kane, was another strong supporter of the project and provided key papers and information concerning her father and her family's history.

My particular thanks to British code-breaking expert and author Ralph Erskine for his patience in teaching me the intricacies of the German naval Enigma system and the British campaign to penetrate the U-boat Force's encrypted communications—a major element in the ultimate Allied defeat of the U-boats.

Since the discovery of the Civil War–era ironclad USS *Monitor* in 1976, the study of submerged shipwrecks has become a major field of scientific inquiry. Gains in underwater diving and salvage technology have also raised concern among scientists, environmentalists, and government officials over the need to safeguard historical shipwreck sites from damage and plundering. The hulk of U-701, resting not far from the *Monitor*, has become a part of that broad effort. My particular thanks go to David Alberg, superintendent of the Monitor National Marine Sanctuary, for his support and for providing underwater photos of U-701. Among Alberg's colleagues, I want to thank National Oceanic and Atmospheric Administration marine archeologists Joseph Hoyt and John Wagner, as well as Syracuse University emeritus dean Dr. Cathryn R. Newton.

I owe a debt to many other people who have provided help and support for this book. In Washington, DC, researcher Candice Clifford diligently retrieved hundreds of documents at the National Archives relating to U-701 and the A-29 Hudson that sank it. Rear Admiral Jay DeLoach, then commander of the Naval History and Heritage Command, provided important papers from the late Frank Knox, wartime secretary of the navy under President Franklin D. Roosevelt. At the National Air and Space Museum's Udvar-Hazy Center, archivists Brian Nicklas and Mark Kahn were most helpful in providing flight manuals and other technical documents for the Lockheed A-29 Hudson.

At the American Heritage Center at the University of Wyoming in Laramie, researcher Ginny Kilander once more assisted in retrieving documents from the extensive U-boat archive donated to the center by the late Clay Blair, author of the encyclopedic two-volume history *Hitler's U-boat War*. In San Diego, naval historian and retired navy Captain Bruce Linder helped locate ancient news reports involving Degen's port visit on the cruiser *Karlsruhe* and Kane's 1942 patrol flight that inadvertently triggered what became known as the "Battle of Los Angeles." Thomas P. Lauria at the Air Force Historical Research Agency at Maxwell Air Force Base in Montgomery, Alabama, provided detailed information on the 396th Medium Bombardment Squadron and its parent unit, the 41st Bombardment Group, as well as other US Army Air Forces units. Ranita Gaskins at the Learning Resources Center at Lenoir Community College in Kinston, North Carolina, was most helpful in locating family papers of Marguerite LaRoque, who married Harry Kane in 1943.

In London, naval researcher Tony Cooper retrieved fascinating intelligence reports by the Admiralty's Operational Intelligence Centre in January 1942 that confirm the Allies were aware of the planned U-boat campaign against Allied merchant shipping in American coastal waters.

Once more, the website Uboat.net, created and managed by Icelander Gudmundur Helgason, was a major source of information about the U-boats and their campaign in American waters in 1942. If you want to become a student of the U-boat campaign, that website and Jerry Mason's U-boat Archive are the best places to begin. I also want to thank the folks at the Internet-based travel site Indo.com for the use of their marvelous latitude-longitude calculator, which transforms the tedious and frustrating effort of computing distances and directions for events at sea into a simple and efficient routine (www.indo.com/distance).

And last but not least, a grateful thanks to my friends at Sunnyside Grill for their friendship and logistical support (good company, great food, and unlimited iced tea): Glenn Bowker, Nathan and Kelly Morgan, Julie Layne, Pam Battles, Misty Folds, and Sherri Varner. Go Steelers!

As ever, these people deserve a large share of the credit for this book. Responsibility for its accuracy, however, is mine alone.

Ed Offley
Panama City Beach, Florida

GLOSSARY

10th Fleet—Special US Navy command established in Washington, DC, headquarters in May 1943 to direct the control and routing of convoys, coordinate and direct all antisubmarine operations against U-boats, and supervise all US Navy antisubmarine warfare training and development.

1WO—first watch officer; the second in command of a U-boat.

2WO—second watch officer; a junior officer on a U-boat.

ABC-1 Conference—See *Conferences*.

Arcadia—See *Conferences*.

Atlantic Conference—See *Conferences*.

B-Dienst—Funkbeobachtungsdienst; German navy cryptologic service.

Ballast tanks—Tanks outside the pressure hull of a submarine that, when flooded with water, enabled the submarine to dive.

Baubelehrung—"Boat familiarization"; U-boat Force program that assigned officers and enlisted crewmen to a U-boat under construction from the time its keel was laid through commissioning for the purpose of training and getting used to all aspects of the boat.

BdU—*Befehlshaber der Unterseeboote*; commander-in-chief of U-boats (Admiral Karl Dönitz); the abbreviation was also commonly used to identify the admiral's staff or U-boat Force Headquarters.

BdU Zug—Special passenger train for U-boat personnel on leave.

Bletchley Park—A mansion and grounds northwest of London in Buckinghamshire, England, officially termed the Government Code and Cypher School, where cryptanalysts "broke" intercepts of encrypted German wireless radio traffic.

Bombe—Nickname for the electromechanical device at Bletchley Park used to solve the German Enigma cipher key settings.

CNO—Chief of naval operations; the senior uniformed officer in the US Navy. Prior to World War II, the CNO was the service's chief planner but subordinate to the commander-in-chief, US Fleet, at the time the highest-ranking admiral. The positions were merged early in World War II, with Admiral Ernest J. King holding both titles.

COMINCH—Commander-in-chief, US Fleet; senior-most US Navy admiral; position merged in 1942 with chief of naval operations under Admiral Ernest J. King.

Conferences

- ABC-1 Conference—American-British-Canadian Conference held by American, British, and Canadian senior military staff in Washington from January through March 1941 to develop a joint strategy against the Axis.
- Arcadia—Code name for US-British leadership conference in Washington from December 22, 1941, to January 14, 1942.
- Argonaut Conference—Second meeting of Anglo-American leaders in Washington, DC, during June 21 to 27, 1942.
- Atlantic Conference—Meeting between President Franklin D. Roosevelt and British prime minister Winston Churchill and their military staffs on naval warships in Placentia Bay, Newfoundland, from August 9 to 12, 1941. During the meetings the Allied leaders assigned top priority to defeating the U-boat threat in the Atlantic.

Dräger Tauchretter—Underwater breathing apparatus used by U-boat crewmen.

Enigma—German communications encryption device that used mechanical rotors to scramble a clear-text message and to reverse encryption back to clear-text at the receiving station. The formal name for the German naval cipher machine was the *Schlüssel M*, or *Marine Funkschlüssel-Maschine*. Other terms relating to the Allied-German struggle over penetrating the enemy's encrypted communications include

- Bombe—Electromechanical machine used to simulate Enigma settings and decrypt messages.
- Short signal—*Kurzsignale*; a code that used brief letter-numeral designations to provide routine reports such as weather conditions, fuel state, etc.
- Triton—Advanced naval Enigma using four changeable rotors in the machine rather than the three operational in February 1942.

ESF—Eastern Sea Frontier; the New York–based US Navy Headquarters responsible for coastal defense and convoys from Maine to the Florida-Georgia border (original name was North Atlantic Naval Coastal Frontier).

Flak—German acronym for *Flieger-Abwehr-Kanone*; term for antiaircraft gun or gunfire.

Führerprinzip—Leader principle; fundamental basis of political authority in the Third Reich that mandated that the leader's (Hitler's) word was supreme and above all written laws. This gave Hitler absolute authority over all political and military decisions, however small.

General quarters—US Navy signal that combat with an enemy is imminent.

GRT—Gross registered tonnage; measurement of a ship's total internal volume expressed as one "register ton" for each one hundred cubic feet.

Guerre de course—French for a war on seaborne trade or shipping.

HF/DF—High-frequency direction finding ("huff-duff"); a system of shore stations and/or ship-mounted direction-finding gear to pinpoint U-boat locations via intercepted bearings to the source of high-frequency radio transmissions.

Hydrophone—Underwater sound-detection device employed by both U-boats and surface warships; in German, *Gruppenhorchgerät*, or GHG.

Knight's Cross—*Ritterkreuz*; variation of the German Iron Cross decoration for valor in combat. There were six grades of the decoration, and to receive a higher class, one had to have previously earned the next-lowest medal. The levels and numbers awarded to U-boat sailors were

- Iron Cross Second Class (unknown number)
- Iron Cross First Class (unknown number)
- Knight's Cross with Oak Leaves (146 awarded)
- Knight's Cross with Oak Leaves and Crossed Swords (29 awarded)
- Knight's Cross with Oak Leaves, Crossed Swords, and Diamonds (5 awarded)
- Knight's Cross with Golden Oak Leaves, Crossed Swords, and Diamonds (0 awarded).

Knot—Unit of speed equivalent to one nautical mile (1.1516 statute miles) per hour.

Kommandantenschüler—"Commander pupil"; the phase of a U-boat commander's instruction when the officer makes a U-boat war patrol as an observer in training.

Kriegsmarine—Term for the German navy used between 1935 and 1945.

KTB—*Kriegstagebüch*; German daily war diary kept by ships and U-boats at sea and by shore-based headquarters staffs.

Lend-Lease Act—See *Treaties and other agreements*.

Luftwaffe—Term for the German air force used between 1935 and 1945.

Milch cow—U-boat designed as a refueling tanker for other submarines.

Military operations, Allied

- Chariot—British commando attack on Saint-Nazaire, March 28, 1942.
- Gymnast—Proposed 1942 Allied invasion of Northwest Africa (cancelled and replaced by Torch).
- Sledgehammer—Proposed 1942 invasion of France (cancelled and replaced by Roundup).

Military operations, German
- Pastorius—U-boat operation in which U-202 and U-548 landed eight saboteurs ashore at Amagansett, Long Island, and Ponte Vedra, Florida, in June 1942. All were captured, and six were executed after trial by a US military commission.
- Paukenschlag (Drumbeat)—U-boat offensive against the US East Coast, January 1942.

Ocean meeting point—specified location where a convoy rendezvoused with its assigned escort group; also known by specific area: WESTOMP for Western OMP, EASTOMP for Eastern OMP, HOMP for Halifax OMP, and ICOMP for Iceland OMP.

OIC—Operational Intelligence Centre; British Admiralty unit responsible for tracking U-boat operations from a wide variety of sources, primarily decrypted communications intercepts.

ONI—Office of Naval Intelligence (US Navy)

Organisation Todt—A Third Reich civil and military engineering group founded by Nazi leader Fritz Todt, who became the Reich minister for armaments and munitions in 1940. The group constructed the modern German autobahn system and, later, a series of massive U-boat bunkers in Germany, France, and Norway.

Pastorius—See *Military operations, German*.

Paukenschlag (Drumbeat)—See *Military operations, German*.

Periscope—Extendable, tube-like optical device containing an arrangement of prisms, mirrors, and lenses that enabled a U-boat to view the surface of the sea or the sky from a submerged position.

Pressure hull—Cylindrical steel hull containing personnel and essential operating systems designed to withstand many atmospheres of water pressure when a U-boat is submerged.

Q-ship—A decoy merchant ship full of flotation cargo and carrying concealed cannons to lure a U-boat into close range for attack.

Radar—"Radio Direction and Ranging," also RDF; a detection system that uses electromagnetic waves to identify the range, altitude, direction, and/or speed of both moving and fixed objects such as aircraft and ships.

Schnelladekanone—"Fast-firing cannon"; the 88-mm main deck gun on a Type VIIC U-boat or the 105-mm deck gun on a Type IX U-boat.

Snorkel—Breathing apparatus installed on U-boats late in World War II to enable them to use their diesel engines while running submerged.

Special Intelligence—Code for intercepted and decrypted German military communications; also called Ultra.

Tonnage war—Admiral Karl Dönitz's strategy to sink Allied merchant ships at a rate faster than new construction could offset the losses; also known by the French phrase *guerre de course*.

Torpedoes, German

- G7a—21-inch-diameter torpedo with compressed-air propulsion motor; carried a six-hundred-pound warhead with a maximum range of 7.5 nautical miles.
- G7e—21-inch torpedo with electric propulsion from lead batteries; carried a six-hundred-pound warhead with a maximum range of 1.6 nautical miles.

Treaties and other agreements

- Atlantic Charter—Declaration of US and British war objectives following the Atlantic Conference of August 1941 between President Franklin D. Roosevelt and British prime minister Winston Churchill at Placentia Bay, Newfoundland. This laid the foundation for the United Nations.
- Lend-Lease Act—Approved by Congress in March 1941, this program initially enabled the United States to send military aid to Great Britain while still remaining officially neutral; later expanded to forty-four Allied nations, with the Soviet Union receiving the second-largest share. A total of $50 billion worth of equipment was distributed during the war.

Uboot-Zieloptik—Surface-target aiming binoculars with luminous reticules attached to a bridge post that automatically fed target line-of-sight bearing and range to a calculator inside the U-boat conning tower; in turn, this fed attack course headings into the gyroscopes of the torpedoes; contracted to UZO.

Unrestricted submarine warfare—A form of naval warfare in which submarines are allowed by their senior commanders to attack civilian merchant ships without warning.

Vorhaltrechner—U-boat electromechanical deflection calculator in the conning tower that fed attack headings into the gyrocompass steering mechanism in each torpedo, determining its course upon firing (see *Uboot-Zieloptik*).

Western Approaches Command—Royal Navy Headquarters established in Liverpool in November 1941; responsible for defense of transatlantic convoys.

Wolf pack—*Gruppe*; formation of deployed U-boats directed from BdU Headquarters to hunt for a specific Allied convoy or to patrol a specific area of the ocean.

Zentrale—U-boat control room; located at the center of the boat beneath the conning tower.

APPENDIX

EQUIVALENT WORLD WAR II
NAVAL OFFICER RANKS

U.S. Navy	Royal Navy	German Navy
Fleet Admiral	Admiral of the Fleet	Grossadmiral +
Admiral	Admiral	Generaladmiral
Vice Admiral	Vice-Admiral	Vizeadmiral
Rear Admiral	Rear-Admiral	Konteradmiral
Captain	Captain	Kapitän zur See
n/a	n/a	Fregattenkapitän *
Commander	Commander	Korvettenkapitän
Lieutenant Commander	Lieutenant-Commander	Kapitänleutnant
Lieutenant	Lieutenant	Oberleutnant zur See #
Lieutenant (junior grade)	Lieutenant (junior grade)	Leutnant zur See
Ensign	Sublieutenant	Oberfähnrich zur See
Midshipman	Midshipman	Fähnrich zur See

+ English translation: Grand Admiral
* English translation: Junior Captain
# English translation: Senior Lieutenant

Sources: U-boat.net; Showell, Jak Mallmann, *Hitler's Navy: A Reference Guide to the Kriegsmarine, 1935–1945*, Seaworth Publishing, London, 2009.

NOTES

INTRODUCTION: THE BATTLE OFFSHORE

1. North Carolina geography and marine environment elements from John Roach, "Shoring Up N. Carolina Islands: A Losing Battle?" *National Geographic News*, November 10, 2003.

2. Allied merchant sinkings within one hundred nautical miles of Cape Hatteras compiled from "Ships Hit by U-boats in WWII," Uboat.net, www.uboat.net/allies/merchants, and "U-boat Fates," Uboat.net, www.uboat.net/fates.

3. US aerial defenses weak and disorganized from Eastern Sea Frontier War Diary (hereafter "ESF War Diary") for February 1942, ch. 3.

4. Aircraft types operating from MCAS Cherry Point cited in various unit histories; aerial patrol pattern described in Harry J. Kane, "Oral History Interview, Harry J. Kane," East Carolina University Manuscript Collection, Oral History Interview No. 71, September 29, 1978 (hereafter "Kane Oral Interview"); MCAS Cherry Point described in "History of U.S. Marine Corps Air Station Cherry Point, North Carolina—1941–1945," compiled by Florence K. Jacobs, 1st Lt. USMCWR, Air Station Historical Officer, undated.

5. The scene aboard U-701 is constructed from descriptions of underwater conditions off North Carolina by former Kapitänleutnant Horst Degen in his unpublished 1965 memoir *U-701: Glory and Tragedy* (unpublished manuscript, November 1965); underwater VLF communications receiving capability comes from former radioman second class Martin Beisheim, interviews, March and April 2009.

6. Details of the third war patrol of U-701 from "U-701," Uboat.net, www.uboat.net/boats/u701.htm, and Degen, *Glory and Tragedy*.

7. Patrol flight description from Kane Oral Interview.

CHAPTER 1: PREPARING TO FIGHT

1. Kane description of his aviation cadet training from Kane Oral Interview; *Tamiami Champion* daily direct schedule from New York to Lakeland in mid-1941 from "The *Tamiami Champion* (West Coast)," Streamliner Schedules, www.streamlinerschedules.com/concourse/track2/championwc194106.html.

2. FDR "your boys" statement and military growth figures from "Text of President Roosevelt's Addresses in Boston and Hartford," *New York Times*,

October 31, 1940; army growth from Geoffrey Perrett, *There's a War to Be Won: The U.S. Army in World War II* (New York: Random House, 1991), 26–27.

3. Military draft details from Norman Polmar and Thomas B. Allen, *World War II: America at War* (New York: Random House, 1991), 724; Kane comments on the draft from Kane Oral Interview.

4. Harry Kane's early life from Marguerite Kane Jameson interview, July 8, 2011; description of army flight training from Kane Oral Interview.

5. Degen comments on Hitler Youth from an intercepted conversation between Degen and Sorber of U-210 in an American POW camp on August 16, 1942, on file with the National Archives and Records Administration (NARA), Record Group 38 (hereafter "ONI Eavesdropping Report").

6. Degen family background courtesy of Dr. Günther Degen; testing for Naval Academy recounted by Reinhard Hardegen, an academy classmate of Degen's, in Michael Gannon, *Operation Drumbeat* (New York: Harper & Row, 1990), 18–19.

7. Description of *Karlsruhe* cruise from transcript of ONI recording of conversation between Degen and Oberleutnant zur See Heinz Sorber, a POW from U-210, August 15, 1942, NARA, Modern Military Branch, Adelphi, MD, Record Group (RG) 38; additional details of *Karlsruhe* port visits from articles in the *Seattle Times*, *San Diego Union*, and *Boston Globe* during March through May 1934.

8. Details on U-552 from "U-552," Uboat.net, www.uboat.net/boats/u552.htm.

9. Of thirty-four U-boats that transferred from Germany to Lorient and Saint-Nazaire between July 1940 and March 1941, five were subsequently transferred back to Germany to serve as training boats, and another five—U-31, U-32, U-47, U-99, and U-100—were lost in combat.

10. The U-boat expansion plan from January 1941 reflected a prolonged struggle between the admirals and other German military branches for priorities in steel, other vital materials, skilled shipyard workers, and funds to build the U-boat Force. See Günter Hessler, *The U-boat War in the Atlantic: 1939–1945* (London: H. M. Stationery Office, 1989), 1:106–108.

11. Kane's flight school experiences derived from Kane Oral Interview and Thomas H. Greer, "Individual Training of Flying Personnel," in *The Army Air Forces in World War II*, vol. 6: *Men and Planes*, ed. Wesley F. Craven and James L. Cate (Chicago: University of Chicago Press, 1955), http://www.ibiblio.org/hyperwar/AAF/VI/AAF-VI-17.html.

12. BT-13 Valiant specifications from "Vultee BT-13A Valiant," Combat Air Museum (Forbes Field, Kansas), www.combatairmuseum.org/aircraft/vultee.html.

13. Barksdale Field history from Barksdale Air Force Base website at Wikipedia, http://en.wikipedia.org/wiki/Barksdale_Air_Force_Base#Origins; twin-engine aircraft procurement during 1940–1941 from "Army Air Forces Statistical Digest (World War II)," US Air Force, June 1947 (hereafter "USAAF Statistical Digest").

14. Kane graduation date from Kane Oral Interview.

15. Christmas crew gathering recounted by U-701 survivor Gerhard Schwendel to Günther Degen.

16. U-701 movements from the U-boat's *Kriegstagebüch* (daily war diary) from July 16, 1941, through February 9, 1942 (hereafter "U-701 KTB 1"); crew size from "Report of Interrogation of Survivors of U-701 Sunk by U.S. Army Attack Bomber No. 9-29-322, Unit 396 B.S. [Bombardment Squadron] on July 7, 1942," published in "Post-mortems on Enemy Submarines," Office of Naval Intelligence, ONI 250-G, 1942, National Archives and Records Administration, College Park, Maryland, Records Group 38, 48 (hereafter "ONI U-701 Report").

17. Degen and U-701 activities in April–December 1941 from U-701 KTB 1. Description of U-552 interior based on the Type VII U-30, described in Clay Blair, *Hitler's U-boat War*, vol. 1: *The Hunters: 1939–1942* (New York: Random House, 1996), 57–62.

18. U-552 movements from KTB; details of *Commander Horton* from "Commander Horton," Uboat.net, http://uboat.net/allies/merchants/885.html.

19. Convoy HX121 details from ConvoyWeb.org.uk at http://www.convoy web.org.uk/hx/index.html (click "HX121" in box to the left); attack on *Capulet* in U-552 KTB, with additional details in Blair, *Hitler's U-boat War*, 1:271–272; Topp quote from Degen interview in ONI U-701 Report.

20. U-552 tonnage from "U-552," Uboat.net, www.uboat.net/boats/u552.htm; U-701 construction and commissioning from Kenneth Wynn, *U-boat Operations of the Second World War*, vol. 2: *Career Histories, U-511–UIT-25* (Annapolis, MD: Naval Institute Press, 1998), 125; "We all grew up . . ." from Peter Cremer, *U-boat Commander* (Annapolis, MD: Naval Institute Press, 1984), 30.

21. Adaptation of crew to U-boat conditions from Cremer, *U-boat Commander*, 23; U-701 flaws from ONI U-701 Report, 5; delays in shipyard from U-701 KTB 1.

22. U-boat training described in Grand Adm. Karl Dönitz, *Memoirs: Ten Years and Twenty Days* (New York: Da Capo Press, 1997), 13–16; U-701 training details from U-701 KTB 1 and "U-701," Uboat.net, www.uboat.net/boats /u701.htm.

CHAPTER 2: THE GATHERING STORM

1. Navy situation on December 31, 1941, described by Thomas B. Buell, *Master of Sea Power: A Biography of Fleet Admiral Ernest J. King* (Boston: Little, Brown and Company, 1980), 40; COMINCH powers established in Executive Order 8984, December 18, 1941; "Nothing was ready" from Buell, *Master of Sea Power*, 153.

2. General Board history and function from Buell, *Master of Sea Power*, 123–125; King career events from Buell, *Master of Sea Power*, and Samuel Eliot Morison, *The Two-Ocean War: A Short History of the United States Navy in the*

Second World War (Boston: Little, Brown and Company, 1963), 102–103; King commands Patrol Force from Buell, *Master of Sea Power*, 132–134.

3. ABC-1 report kept from King in Buell, *Master of Sea Power*, 137, and Patrick Abbazia, *Mr. Roosevelt's Navy: The Private War of the U.S. Atlantic Fleet, 1939–1942* (Annapolis, MD: Naval Institute Press, 1975), 137.

4. Creation of Support Force from "Commander Task Force Twenty-Four" in *Administrative History of the U.S. Atlantic Fleet in World War II* (Norfolk, VA: Commander-in-Chief, US Atlantic Fleet, 1946), vol. 2; three destroyer squadrons from Abbazia, *Mr. Roosevelt's Navy*, 143; Casco Bay base and South Atlantic patrol from Buell, *Master of Sea Power*, 139; events in spring and summer of 1941 from Buell, *Master of Sea Power*, 142–144; also Abbazia, *Mr. Roosevelt's Navy*, 199; destroyers meet Convoy HX150 from Abbazia, *Mr. Roosevelt's Navy*, 255.

5. The destroyer USS *Niblack* had encountered a U-boat back in April 1941 while rescuing survivors from a torpedoed merchant ship; it drove the U-boat away with depth charges. The incident received scant attention publicly; USS *Greer* incident from Abbazia, *Mr. Roosevelt's Navy*, 142; USS *Kearny* incident from Blair, *Hitler's U-boat War*, 369–370.

6. USS *Reuben James* sinking from Abbazia, *Mr. Roosevelt's Navy*, 293–299; Knox and Roosevelt reactions from Bertram Hulen, "Our Stand Clear, Officials Insist," *New York Times*, November 2, 1941; Associated Press, "Knox Assails Acts That Pass 'Piracy,'" *New York Times*, November 2, 1941.

7. American leaders feared Japan attack in Far East from Ronald H. Spector, *Eagle Against the Sun: The American War with Japan* (New York: Vintage Books, 1985), 96; B-Dienst message from "German Navy Reports of Intercepted Radio Messages," NARA RG 457, cited in Gannon, *Drumbeat*, xv; B-Dienst telegram stuns Hitler from Blair, *Hitler's U-boat War*, 1:435; Oshima and Ribbentrop talks from "Hiroshi Oshima," Wikipedia, www.en.wikipedia.org/wiki/Hiroshi _Oshima.

8. Raeder and Dönitz urge unrestricted U-boat campaign from Blair, *Hitler's U-boat War*, 1:360; also Abbazia, *Mr. Roosevelt's Navy*, 230; *Führerprinzip* from Heinrich Winkler with Alexander Sager, *Germany: The Long Road West: 1933–1990* (New York: Oxford University Press, 2007), 37.

9. Jodl repeated Hitler's comment on Japan and the United States to his interrogators at Nuremberg in 1945 and details of the Rainbow Five leak both cited in Thomas Fleming, "The Big Leak," *American Heritage* 38, no. 8 (December 1987).

10. Hitler meets with military commanders in Fleming, "The Big Leak"; Roosevelt radio address on December 9, 1941, from Mount Holyoke College World War II archive at https://www.mtholyoke.edu/acad/intrel/WorldWar2 /radio.htm; Hitler's December 11 Reichstag speech from "Germany's Declaration of War Against the United States," Institute for Historical Review, www .ihr.org/jhr/v08/v08p389_Hitler.html; Hitler takes over army command from Fleming, "The Big Leak."

11. Details of HMS *Duke of York* arrival in Norfolk from "Telegram: Prime Minister Churchill to President Roosevelt," in "The Conference at Washington, 1941–42" (hereafter "Arcadia Proceedings"), in US State Department, *Foreign Relations of the United States*, posted at the University of Wisconsin Digital Collections at http://digicoll.library.wisc.edu/cgi-bin/FRUS/FRUS-idx ?id=FRUS.FRUS194143; HMS *Duke of York* history from "HMS *Duke of York*," Wikipedia, www.en.wikipedia.org/wiki/HMS_Duke_of_York_(17).

12. FDR-Churchill first meeting and impressions from Jon Meacham, *Franklin and Winston: An Intimate Portrait of an Epic Friendship* (New York: Random House Trade Paperbacks, 2004), 4–5; evolution of relationship from Meacham, *Franklin and Winston*, 47; details of Arcadia Conference from Arcadia Proceedings, Buell, *Master of Sea Power*, 162–171, and Blair, *Hitler's U-boat War*, 1:445–447; Japanese attacks in Far East from Polmar and Allen, *World War II*, 11–13.

13. Churchill remarks on shipping crisis and FDR expansion of shipbuilding from Blair, *Hitler's U-boat War*, 1:446–447; Troopship convoy to leave New York on January 15, 1942, from Arcadia Proceedings, January 11, 1942, 190–193; Churchill on "greatest importance" of prompt arrival of troops from notes by Lt. Gen. Henry H. Arnold in Arcadia Proceedings, January 4, 1942, 168.

14. Description of BdU Headquarters in Lorient from Jak Mallmann Showell, *Hitler's U-boat Bunkers* (Port Stroud, UK: History Press, 2002), 101; also Gannon, *Drumbeat*, xv; BdU staff felt "relief" from Hessler, *The U-boat War*, 2:1; BdU reaction to diversion of U-boats and December 10 figures from Hessler, *The U-boat War*, 1:87–92; "an opportunity" to hunt Allied shipping along the American coast from BdU KTB for December 9, 1941; Hessler on US defenses from *The U-boat War*, 2:2.

15. Dönitz request for twelve Type IX boats from BdU KTB for December 9, 1941; BdU only allowed six large U-boats from BdU KTB for December 10, 1941; nautical miles to Newfoundland and Cape Hatteras from Hessler, *The U-boat War*, 2:2; U-boats assigned to North America and sailing dates from Blair, *Hitler's U-boat War*, 1:727, Appendix 4.

CHAPTER 3: FIRST MOVES

1. U-701 movements, weather conditions, and short signal message text sent on December 31, 1941, from U-701 KTB1, courtesy of Uboat Archive at www.uboatarchive.net, 5; threading the passage and U-701 course track from U-701 Daily KTB1, 2–4; background of Degen subordinates from ONI U-701 Report, 4; nine U-boats lost from "German U-boat Casualties in World War II," in *United States Submarine Losses in World War II* (Washington, DC: Naval History Division, Office of the Chief of Naval Operations, 1963).

2. Schwendel description of Degen from 2011 interview with the author; Hamburger Hof incident recalled by Degen to Oberleutnant zur See Heinz Sorber from ONI Eavesdropping Report.

3. Kane recollection of the B-18 from Kane Oral Interview; squadron activation and early history from "Unit Historical Data Sheet, 396th Bombardment Squadron (M) of 41st Bombardment Group," 1943; also "History of the 396th Bombardment Squadron (M), Headquarters, 41st Bombardment Group (M)," Hammer Field, Fresno, California, 1942 (hereafter "396th History"); B-18 Bolo specifications from "History: B-18 Bolo Bomber," Boeing, www.boeing.com /boeing/history/mdc/bolo.page; B-17 specifications from Paul Eden, ed., *The Encyclopedia of Aircraft of WWII* (London: Aerospace Publishing, 2004), 48.

4. Loss of Weinitschke from U-701 KTB1 entry of December 31, 1941; additional details from a February 13, 1942, letter from Degen to Weinitschke's parents explaining the event of his loss; Schwendel comment from 2011 interview; New Year's message from BdU in U-701 KTB1.

5. U-boat Force size on January 1, 1942, from BdU KTB for February 1, 1942; number of U-boats in the North Atlantic from Blair, *Hitler's U-boat War*, 1:718; U-boats should "spread" out once in their patrol areas from BdU KTB for December 10, 1941.

6. Tension among crew from Schwendel 2011 interview; sighting of convoy from U-701 KTB1 entry for January 2, 1942; Convoy HX166 identified from analysis of convoy traffic at ConvoyWeb.org.uk; unsuccessful attack from U-701 KTB1; sinking of *Baron Erskine* from U-701 KTB1, Schwendel 2011 interview, and "Baron Erskine," Uboat.net, www.uboat.net /allies/merchants/1239.html; closest land to site of sinking from Indo.com latitude-longitude calculator; firing of all but two torpedoes and subsequent movement from U-701 KTB1 for January 7–13, 1942; Cremer description of hurricane from Cremer, *U-boat Commander*, 38–39.

CHAPTER 4: WAR IN THE ETHER

1. Locations of U-701 and U-653 and numbers of U-boats in the Atlantic on January 7, 1942, from BdU KTB for that date; Feiler background information from Rainer Busch and Hans-Joachim Röll, *German U-boat Commanders of World War II* (Annapolis, MD: Naval Institute Press, 1999) 66; radio network for U-boat communications described in Gannon, *Drumbeat*, 68; daily staff meeting at BdU operations center including Hessler duties as A 1 operations officer from Gannon, *Drumbeat*, 67–69.

2. German surface raider *Atlantis* seizure of British codebooks from David Kahn, *The Codebreakers* (New York: Scribner, 1996), 465–466; reading Naval Cypher No. 3 from Michael Gannon, *Black May* (New York: Dell Publishing, 1998), 56; B-Dienst provided 50 percent of all intelligence to BdU from David Kahn, *Seizing the Enigma* (New York: Random House, 1991), 262–263.

3. Naval Enigma machine design and operating procedures from Kahn, *Seizing the Enigma*, 195–198, 285–290; also Gannon, *Drumbeat*, 425–426.

4. Rejewski solution of Enigma from Kahn, *Seizing the Enigma*, 62–67; Bletchley Park opening, Kahn, *Seizing the Enigma*, 88; OIC role in tracking

U-boats from Patrick Beesly, *Very Special Intelligence: The Story of the Admiralty's Operational Intelligence Centre, 1939–1945* (London: Hamish Hamilton Ltd., 1977), 22–23, 96–99.

5. U-boat Situation Report, week ending January 5, 1942, Operational Intelligence Centre, from the British National Archives, Kew, United Kingdom, declassified from Most Secret.

6. U-boat Situation Report, week ending January 12, 1942, Operational Intelligence Centre, from the British National Archives, Kew, United Kingdom, declassified from Most Secret.

7. British-American intelligence sharing from May 1941 from Gannon, *Drumbeat*, 165.

CHAPTER 5: OPERATION DRUMBEAT

1. U-123 attack on *Cyclops* from U-123 KTB for January 12, 1942, provided by U-boat Archive at www.uboatarchive.net; also Gannon, *Drumbeat*, 203–209, and "Cyclops," Uboat.net, www.uboat.net/allies/merchants/ships/1243 .html; Dönitz instructions for simultaneous attack from Gannon, *Drumbeat*, 80; exception for 10,000-ton ships from Dönitz, *Memoirs*, 198; *Cyclops* casualties from Wynn, *U-boat Operations*, 1:99.

2. Profiles of other Paukenschlag U-boats and their commanders from Wynn, *U-boat Operations*, vols. 1 and 2, and Busch and Röll, *German U-boat Commanders*.

3. Eastern Sea Frontier boundaries from Eastern Sea Frontier War Diary, December 1941, Appendix 1, U-boat Archive, www.uboatarchive.net/ESFWar DiaryDec41.htm.

4. Andrews biography from "Vice Admiral Adolphus Andrews," Naval History and Heritage Command, www.history.navy.mil/bios/andrews_adolphus .htm; Morison and Stimson comments about Andrews from Gannon, *Drumbeat*, 175; Rollins and burning waste can incident from Alexander W. Moffat, *A Navy Maverick Comes of Age: 1939–1945* (Middletown CT: Wesleyan University Press, 1977), 48–50.

5. Rainbow Five war plan responsibilities of Eastern Sea Frontier from ESF War Diary for December 1941, 5; U-boat campaign against Atlantic coast in 1918 from William Bell Clark, *When the U-boats Came to America* (Boston: Little Brown & Company, 1929), 302–305; King letter from ESF War Diary for January 1942, ch. 3, 6.

6. Many of the warships transferred to the Pacific Fleet after Pearl Harbor were actually returning to their original assignment, including the carrier USS *Yorktown* and the three older battleships. All had been transferred to the Atlantic in mid-1941 when tensions over the U-boats had spiked; see Abbazia, *Mr. Roosevelt's Navy*, 172; for King warning on coastal threat from U-boats, see King to CNO Stark, undated but written between December 14 and 30, 1941, in NARA RG 80, CINCLANT, Box 108.

7. Roster of Atlantic Fleet destroyers in December 1941 and January 1942 from Blair, *Hitler's U-boat War*, 1:750–753; location of destroyers on January 12, 1942, from analysis of individual destroyer histories and deck logs for that date by the author; deck logs from NARA RG 24, filed by ship's names.

8. Status of patrol craft and airplanes assigned to Eastern Sea Frontier from ESF War Diary for January 1941, Appendix 2.

9. OIC messages routed to ESF Headquarters and Lieutenant Braue decrypting procedure from Gannon, *Drumbeat*, 173; U-boat dispositions on January 12, 1942, from "Operational Intelligence Centre Special Intelligence Summary" for that date, PRO ADM 223/15, declassified from Most Secret, Public Records Office, Kew, United Kingdom. The previous assessment on January 5 dispatched from the British OIC to US Navy Headquarters, which unmasked U-653's radio deception operation, also noted "a concentration of six U-boats off Cape Race, St. John's and Argentia" but at that time had no evidence of their ultimate mission.

10. Discovery of the COMINCH alert message of January 12, 1942, by naval historian Michael Gannon in 1987 in the archives of the National Security Agency is one of the more explosive revelations to emerge from all of World War II, since it, for the first time, explicitly confirmed that the US Navy had detailed, advance information that could have allowed it to preempt the U-boat attacks.

11. Combat-ready status of destroyers on January 12, 1942, based on analysis of ship deck logs for that date (NARA RG 24): the USS *Benson*, USS *Bernadou*, USS *Dallas*, USS *Du Pont*, USS *Gwin*, USS *Lea*, USS *Monssen*, and USS *Upshur* were at the Boston Navy Yard, while the newly commissioned USS *Ellyson* was undergoing system checks at Newport. In addition, another six combat-ready destroyers were at Casco Bay, Maine, two destroyers were at the Brooklyn Navy Yard in New York, and at least two more were in Norfolk. Another four destroyers were in port undergoing repairs or maintenance, and their ability to get underway on short notice was uncertain. Distance to U-123 at 2200 EWT on January 12 calculated from U-boat position report for that date and time in U-123 KTB at the U-boat Archive; distance determined by latitude-longitude calculator at Indo.com.

12. Details of USS *Gwin* passage from Boston to New York taken from the ship's deck logs for January 13, 1942, from NARA RG 24, Box 3891; U-123 movements from the U-boat's KTB for January 13–14, 1942.

13. Details of *Norness* and its sinking from Gannon, *Drumbeat*, 217–220; "M/T Norness," Warsailors.com, www.warsailors.com/singleships/norness.html; and "Norness," Uboat.net, www.uboat.net/allies/merchants/1248.html. There is no indication from the *Gwin's* deck log of any message regarding the *Norness*.

14. Details of Convoy AT10 from Blair, *Hitler's U-boat War*, 1:445–447, 757; escort ships from "AT10," Convoy Web, www.convoyweb.org.uk/at/index.html; besides the *Gwin*, the destroyers in Task Force 15 included USS *Charles F. Hughes*, USS *Eberle*, USS *Grayson*, USS *Hilary P. Jones*, USS *Ingra-*

ham, USS *Lansdale*, USS *Livermore*, USS *Ludlow*, USS *Mayrant*, USS *Meredith*,
USS *Monssen*, USS *Roe*, USS *Rowan*, USS *Stack*, USS *Sterrett*, USS *Trippe*, and
USS *Wainwright*. The destroyers *Charles F. Hughes*, *Hilary P. Jones*, *Ingraham*,
and *Lansdale* at the last minute were reassigned to Task Force 16, which left
New York on January 21 escorting Convoy BT200 with eight troopships bound
for the Pacific; reduction of army troops for Iceland from Stetson Conn, Rose
C. Engelman, and Byron Fairchild, *United States Army in World War II: The
Western Hemisphere—Guarding the United States and Its Outposts* (Washington,
DC: Office of the Chief of Military History, Department of the Army, 1964),
533–534.

CHAPTER 6: HORRIFIC LOSSES

1. U-701 operating conditions on January 15, 1942, from U-701 KTB
1 for that date; U-552 sinking of *Dayrose* from "Dayrose," Uboat.net, www
.uboat.net/allies/merchants/1250.html; comments on weather possibly delay-
ing U-boats from BdU KTB for January 14, 1942.

2. U-123 movements and actions and Hardegen description of sights in
the early hours of January 15 from U-123 KTB for that date; Hardegen later
comments from Reinhard Hardegen, *Battle Stations! (Auf Gefechtsstationen!)*
(Leipzig: Boreas-Verlag, 1943); von Schroeter on bridge from Gannon, *Drumbeat*, 233.

3. Disclosure of the *Cyclops* and *Norness* attacks cited in articles in the
New York Times: "10,000-Ton Ship Sunk by U-boat off Canada," January 14,
and "Ship Found Awash: Rescue Craft Rushed to Tanker When Plane Reports
Plight," January 15; Long Island residents spot glow from *Coimbra* fire from Gannon, *Drumbeat*, 234; the ESF report on the *Coimbra* stated that the wreckage was
sixty-one nautical miles from the Ambrose Light at the entrance to New York,
but it was much closer to Long Island's eastern coast: twenty-seven nautical miles
from Southampton confirmed by latitude-longitude calculator at Indo.com.

4. Actions at Eastern Sea Frontier after *Coimbra* sinking from ESF Enemy
Action Diary for January 14–15, 1942; the website Uboat.net, citing U-123's
war diary, put the *Coimbra* sinking at a slightly different location about sixteen
nautical miles farther out to sea than that of the American patrol plane report;
this is most likely due to navigational imprecision.

5. Long Island officials quoted in "Navy Has No Word—Check Fails to
Confirm Report of New Victim of U-boat off Coast," *New York Times*, January
16, 1942; delay of thirty-seven hours for navy confirmation from ESF War Diary and "New U-boat Victim Confirmed by Navy," *New York Times*, January
17, 1942; rescue of *Coimbra* survivors from "Coimbra," Uboat.net, www.uboat
.net/allies/merchants/1251.html.

6. Interim U-boat kills during January 1942 from individual U-boat sites at
Uboat.net; U-701 patrol activities after January 18, lack of successes, and hunt
for *Spreewald* survivors from U-701 KTB 1.

7. U-701 crew in "luxury" from Schwendel 2011 interview; Thompson comments on inadequate coastal defense from ESF War Diary for January 1942, ch. 2, 3–4; Andrews plea for aircraft and King's reply from ch. 3, 3; Office of Censorship and "Code of Wartime Practices" from Michael S. Sweeney, *Secrets of Victory: The Office of Censorship and the American Press in World War II* (Chapel Hill: University of North Carolina Press, 2001), 47–48.

8. Navy communiqué over "one-way" U-boat trips from Associated Press, "Sinkings Indicated—'Some Recent Visitors Will Never Enjoy Return Trip,' Says Spokesman," *New York Times*, January 24, 1942; Ladislas Farago, a civilian employee at the Office of Naval Intelligence during World War II, later accused navy public affairs officers of fabricating the quote; ironically, Mason himself, just six weeks later, sank the Type IXC U-503, killing all fifty-one crewmen, piloting the same aircraft; article on Mason (unidentified in the text) from "'Sighted Sub; Sank Same,' Radios a Modern Perry in Naval Plane," *New York Times*, January 30, 1942; four weeks later, the navy, on February 26, publicly identified Mason as the pilot and announced that he had been promoted as a result of his actions.

CHAPTER 7: PARANOIA

1. Introduction of M4 Enigma from Blair, *Hitler's U-boat War*, 1:493–494; B-Dienst penetration of Naval Cypher No. 3 from Kahn, *Seizing the Enigma*, 211–212.

2. Twenty-six times longer to decrypt from Kahn, *Seizing the Enigma*, 210; merchant ship losses compiled from "Ship Losses by Month," Uboat.net, http://www.uboat.net/allies/merchants/losses_year.html; the nine U-boats that patrolled during March 7–14 were six Type VIICs (U-94, U-96, U-332, U-404, U-587, and U-588) and three Type IXs (U-124, U-155, and U-158); U-boats patrolling during March 16–31 included three more Type IX boats (U-105, U-123, and U160) and five more Type VIICs (U-71, U373, U-552, U-571, and U-754); ships and tonnage sunk compiled from "Allied Merchants Hit" at Uboat.net.

3. Ingersoll limited offer of destroyers and fourteen destroyers in Eastern Sea Frontier in ESF War Diary for March 1942.

4. Churchill comment on US Navy and cable to Hopkins from Winston S. Churchill, *Memoirs of the Second World War* (abridgement of the six volumes of *The Second World War*) (New York: Houghton Mifflin Co., 1959), 111–119; Winn visit to Main Navy from Beesly, *Very Special Intelligence*, 109; British-flagged vessels lost in US coastal waters and the Caribbean through mid-April 1942 (the time of Winn's visit) compiled from "Allied Merchants Hit" at Uboat.net.

5. I-17 bombardment of refinery from "The Shelling of Ellwood," California State Military Museum, www.militarymuseum.org/Ellwood.html; one unofficial account alleges that Commander Nishino, while master of a Japanese-flag oil tanker in the late 1930s, had experienced a humiliating incident while vis-

iting the Ellwood oil field. He reportedly was walking up the steep slope from the beach to a welcoming ceremony when he slipped and fell into a prickly pear cactus, which embedded a number of cactus spines in his posterior. Embarrassed by the loud catcalls from oil workers as the spines were plucked out, Nishino allegedly vowed to get revenge; army buildup on West Coast from Conn, Engleman, and Fairchild, *United States Army in World War II*, 82–84.

6. Number of personnel from 396th History; Kane comments from Kane Oral Interview; plot of course track compiled by the author based on Kane description; description of LA "battle" from "Los Angeles Guns Bark at Air 'Enemy,'" *New York Times*, February 26, 1942; Lawrence E. Davies, "Hails Los Angeles for Air Defense," *New York Times*, February 27, 1942; Stimson and Knox differing accounts of incident from "West Coast Raided, Stimson Concedes," *New York Times*, February 27, 1942; DeWitt praise for defenders from "Gen. DeWitt Praises Readiness of Anti-Aircraft Batteries 'to Meet Possible Enemy,'" *New York Times*, February 27, 1942.

7. Distance from Sacramento to Saint-Nazaire from latitude-longitude calculator at Indo.com; U-701 activities during February 23–26, 1942, from U-701 *Kriegstagebüch* (daily war diary), comprising its in-port stay and second war patrol from February 2 through March 31, 1942 (hereafter "U-701 KTB 2").

8. Weak US coastal defenses from BdU KTB for January 24, 1942; Hardegen report details from BdU KTB for February 8, 1942; torpedo failures from BdU KTB for January 29, 1942.

9. The surface warships to Norway were the battleship *Tirpitz*, battle cruisers *Scharnhorst* and *Gneisenau*, pocket battleship *Admiral Scheer*, and heavy cruisers *Prinz Eugen* and *Hipper*, from Blair, *Hitler's U-boat War*, 1:442; "unconditional obedience" from "Fuehrer Conferences on Naval Affairs—1939–1945," in *Brassey's Naval Annual*, ed. H. G. Thursfield, Rear Adm. RN (New York: Macmillan Company, 1948), conference dates January 22, 1942; twenty U-boats to northern waters from Blair, *Hitler's U-boat War*, 486; a major complicating factor was the historic ice buildup in the Baltic Sea, which during the winter of 1941–1942 immobilized more than one hundred newly constructed U-boats for months; war effort "best served" from Dönitz, *Memoirs*, 209; details of U-701 second war patrol from U-701 KTB 2; German propaganda remark from Schwendel 2011 interview; details of Operation Chariot from Blair, *Hitler's U-boat War*, 1:559–561.

CHAPTER 8: UNPREPARED DEFENDERS

1. British aircraft sank no U-boats in World War I from "U-boat War in World War One" at http://www.uboat.net/wwi; Coastal Command struggle for resources from Blair, *Hitler's U-boat War*, 1:315–319; USAAF rivalry with navy over land-based aircraft from Blair, *Hitler's U-boat War*, 1:463–464; 396th training described in Kane Oral Interview; air corps expansion from Geoffrey Perrett, *Winged Victory: The Army Air Forces in World War II* (New York: Random

House, 1993), 13–17, 36–51; new bases from Frank Futrell, "The Development
of Base Facilities," in *The Army Air Forces in World War II*, vol. 6: *Men and
Planes*, ed. Wesley F. Craven and James L. Cate (Chicago: University of Chicago Press, 1955), http://www.ibiblio.org/hyperwar/AAF/VI/AAF-VI-4.html;
total USAAF aircraft production from engine aircraft procurement during
1940–1941 from USAAF Statistical Digest.

2. I Bomber Command status on December 8, 1941, from Arthur B. Ferguson, "The AAF in the Battle of the Atlantic," in Craven and Cate, *Army
Air Forces*, 1:522–523, at http://www.ibiblio.org/hyperwar/AAF/I/AAF-I-15
.html; units transferred included the 22nd Bomb Group (Medium), the 34th
Bomb Group (Heavy), and the 43rd Bomb Group (Heavy), leaving only the
2nd Bomb Group (Heavy) on the East Coast; USAAF attack on USS *Trippe*
described in the destroyer's deck log for Tuesday, December 18, 1941, from
NARA RG 24, Box 9159; King request for USAAF bombers from Blair, *Hitler's
U-boat War*, 1:463; poor army readiness description from Ferguson, "The AAF
in the Battle of the Atlantic," 523.

3. Coastal Command progress against U-boats cited in Blair, *Hitler's U-boat
War*, 1:316–318, and Maurice W. Kirby, *Operational Research in War and Peace:
The British Experience from the 1930s to 1970* (London: Imperial College Press,
2003), 99–103, 109; yet to sink a U-boat from Blair, *Hitler's U-boat War*, 315.

4. *Gleaves*-class destroyer specifications and armaments from Richard
Worth, *Fleets of World War II* (New York: Da Capo Press, 2001), 312; five
U-boats operating within one hundred miles of Cape Hatteras compiled from
BdU KTB entries for April 1–8, 1942: they were the Type IXB U-123, Type
IXC U-160, and Type VIIC U-552, U-754, and U-203.

5. *Hambleton* and *Emmons* patrol off Hatteras compiled from the ships' deck
logs for those dates and from ESF War Diary for April 1942; U-160 patrol and
attacks on shipping from "U-160" at Uboat.net, http://www.uboat.net/boats
/patrols/patrol_3978.html; Allied ships sunk and damaged in the ESF area during
April 1–15, 1942, from "Ships Hit by U-boats" at Uboat.net, http://www.uboat
.net/allies/merchants/losses_year.html?qdate=1942-04; nautical miles steamed
by USS *Emmons* during April 2–9 from ship's deck log for those dates; Wellborn
letter to Andrews cited in ESF War Diary for April 1942, ch. 2, 6; proposed
coastal convoy system described in ESF War Diary for March 1942; special
Atlantic Fleet escort operations in April 1943 from Blair, *Hitler's U-boat War*,
1:758–759.

6. Q-ship sinkings in World War I from V. E. Tarrant, *The U-boat Offensive:
1914–1945* (Annapolis, MD: Naval Institute Press, 1989); Project LQ and the
fate of the USS *Atik* from Kenneth M. Beyer, *Q-ships Versus U-boats: America's
Secret Project* (Annapolis, MD: Naval Institute Press, 1999); Hardegen attack
on the *Atik* from U-123 KTB entries for March 26–27, 1942.

7. "Hooligan Navy" and Civil Air Patrol contributions from ESF War Diary
for April 1942 and from Morison, *The Two-Ocean War*, 132–133.

8. "Bucket Brigade" convoys formed from ESF War Diary for April 1942, ch. 3; decline in sinkings between April 15 and 30 compiled from "Ships Hit by U-boats" for April 1942, at Uboat.net, http://www.uboat.net/allies/merchants /losses_year.html?qdate=1942-04; Morison description of April losses from ESF war diary for April 1942, 1; Churchill quote from "The Greatest Winston Churchill Quotes," University of Georgia, http://jpetrie.myweb.uga.edu /bulldog.html; Dönitz comments from BdU KTB for April 30, 1942.

CHAPTER 9: TO AMERICA, WITH MINES

1. U-701 deployment and mine-laying mission details from Degen, *Glory and Tragedy*, and ONI U-701 Interrogation Report.

2. Linder and Deecke assignment to transport Operation Pastorius teams from Michael Dobbs, *Saboteurs: The Nazi Raid on America* (New York: Vintage Books, 2005), 65, 80; Hessler denigration of saboteurs from Hessler, *The U-boat War*, 2:19.

3. Details of the Type XIV U-tanker from Hessler, *The U-boat War*, 1:118; daily tonnage figures of Allied ships attacked from January through April in a presentation by Dönitz to Hitler and senior military officials on May 14, 1942, recorded in "Fuehrer Conferences on Naval Affairs—1939–1945"; Hessler comments on scarcity of East Coast shipping from Hessler, *The U-boat War*, 1:18.

4. Description of the A-29 Hudson from "Contractor's Handbook of Service Instructions for the Model A-29 Airplane," US Army Air Corps Air Service Command, Wright Field, Dayton, Ohio, January 30, 1942 (henceforth "A-29 Contractor's Handbook"); also "Pilot's Handbook of Flight Operating Instructions—A-29 and A-29A Airplanes," Headquarters USAAF Air Service Command, Patterson Field, Ohio, December 20, 1942 (henceforth "A-29 Pilot's Handbook"); Kane comments from Kane Oral Interview.

5. 396th Medium Bombardment Squadron receives A-29 Hudsons, personnel increases, and assignment to Naval Air Station Alameda from 396th History; Kane comments on A-29 from Kane Oral Interview; USAAF personnel, aircraft numbers, casualties, and accidents from USAAF Statistical Digest, Tables 14, 34, and 213; in 1942, USAAF combat deaths totaled 3,477 compared with 2,384 in training or other stateside fatalities, but as the service went into large-scale combat operations in 1943, combat deaths increased at a higher rate. By the end of the war, 40,061 airmen had been killed in combat; yet 14,903 airmen were unable to take that risk since they had died before getting the chance to deploy overseas; Stimson concern over West Coast security was in his personal diary for April 21, 1942, and Marshall warning to Dewitt, both cited in Conn, Engleman, and Fairchild, *United States Army in World War II*, 89.

6. U-701 departure and stopover in Lorient from Degen, *Glory and Tragedy*; details of TMB mine from Uboat.net, http://www.uboat.net/technical/mines

.htm; U-boat mine-laying procedure and daily life aboard U-701 from Degen, *Glory and Tragedy.*

7. Sighting of trawler and liner *Drottningholm* from Degen, *Glory and Tragedy.*

8. Battle of Midway details from Gordon Prang with Donald M. Goldstein and Katherine V. Dillon, *Miracle at Midway* (New York: McGraw-Hill Book Company, 1982); additional Midway details, including army fear of West Coast attack and DeWitt cancellation of alert on June 8, from Conn, Engleman, and Fairchild, *United States Army in World War II*, 88–92; 396th Medium Bombardment Squadron transfer to Cherry Point from 396th History.

9. Tension as U-701 neared coast, absence of American patrols, MacArthur Day, and decision to ignore BdU operations order from Degen, *Glory and Tragedy*; ESF awareness of U-boat mining operation from ESF War Diary for June 1942, ch. 2, 1–3.

10. Intelligence warnings of U-boat mines from ESF War Diary for June 1942, ch. 2, 1–2.

11. U-701 minelaying operation from Degen, *Glory and Tragedy.*

12. Saboteur team on U-202 from Dobbs, *Saboteurs*, 48–49; U-202 departure from BdU KTB for May 27–28, 1942; U-202 runs aground from Dobbs, *Saboteurs*, 95–97. The fifth special operation U-boat, U-584, successfully landed its four Abwehr agents at Ponte Vedra Beach in northern Florida without incident on June 16.

13. Andrews's warning on U-boat mine laying from ESF War Diary for June 1942, ch. 2; shipping losses from World War I mines from Clark, *When the U-boats Came to America*, 148–150, 308. The *San Diego* sinking was remarkable in that only 6 men of the 1,189-man crew died in the incident.

CHAPTER 10: THE WAR COMES HOME

1. Batten experience at Virginia Beach from a letter to the author, July 9, 1982; Convoy KN109 arrival from ESF War Diary for June 1942, ch. 2; coastal convoy data for May 15 to June 15, 1942, compiled from ConvoyWeb.org; 312 ships sailing without loss from rosters of KN and KS convoys correlated with U-boat sinkings for that month at Uboat.net; the actual number of vessels involved was 272, but 40 of them made passages in more than one convoy.

2. Different speeds of sound in air and in water from Hypertextbook.com; reports indicate the ships were between four and five miles from shore; Martin comments from "Battle of Atlantic Pushes Virginia's Shores—Two U.S. Merchant Ships Torpedoed Before Eyes of Thousands Who Line Resort to See Grim War Drama," *Virginian-Pilot*, June 17, 1942; Blomquist actions on *Esso Augusta* from his affidavit, "Esso Augusta—Damaged as a Result of War Perils," June 16, 1942, from NARA RG 38, 10th Fleet files; *Dione* and *Bainbridge* depth charge attacks and sinking of *Kingston Ceylonite* and *Santore* from ESF War Diary for June 1942, ch. 2, 5–7, 11–12; phantom U-boat sightings from *Virginian-Pilot.*

3. Cross-country flight of the 396th Medium Bombardment Squadron and loss of two aircraft and description of Cherry Point construction from Kane Oral Interview; details of base from "History of U.S. Marine Corps Air Station Cherry Point," 4–5 (henceforth "Cherry Point History"); U-boats patroling within ESF boundaries between June 15 and July 7, 1942, compiled from their patrol reports at Uboat.net; number of ships damaged and sunk and tonnage totals from Uboat.net; description of patrols, ship sightings, and machine-gun attack on floating fuel tank from Kane Oral Interview.

4. World War II events in June 1942 from Polmar and Allen, *World War II*, 21–22; British agenda at Argonaut Conference from Blair, *Hitler's U-boat War*, 1:592.

5. Marshall memorandum to King, King reply, and FDR complaint to King from Blair, *Hitler's U-boat War*, 1:594–596; Roosevelt refusal to approve *Treasury*-class cutter or destroyer escort production from Blair, *Hitler's U-boat War*, 1:449–451.

CHAPTER 11: HUNTER AND HUNTED

1. U-701 deploys to Cape Hatteras, reloads torpedo tubes, and escapes attack from patrol bomber from Degen, *Glory and Tragedy*.

2. U-701 hunts in vain from Degen, *Glory and Tragedy*; coastal convoy records from June 1942 at ConvoyWeb.org show that northbound Convoy KN110 passed Cape Hatteras during the day on Wednesday, June 17, and southbound Convoy KS511—minus the 7,117-ton collier *Santore*, which had sunk after striking one of Degen's TMB mines—traversed the area the following day; encounter with patrol craft from Degen, *Glory and Tragedy*.

3. Background and details of USS YP-389 and its crew from "Record of Proceedings of a Court of Inquiry to Inquire into Circumstances Attending the Attack on YP-389, July 19, 1942," NARA RG 125/P2; other details from ESF War Diary for June 1942, ch. 5; U-701 attack on YP-389 from Degen, *Glory and Tragedy*; the court of inquiry into the loss of YP-389 recommended that Lieutenant Philips be tried by general court-martial for failing to seek encounter with the enemy and for being "culpably inefficient" in the performance of his duty. Vice Admiral Andrews at Eastern Sea Frontier rejected the recommendation on grounds that Philips had attempted to delay the patrol due to the solitary gun being out of commission, which rendered YP-389 unable to defend itself; BdU congratulatory message from Degen, *Glory and Tragedy*.

4. Convoys off Cape Hatteras between June 19 and 26 from ConvoyWeb .org; they were southbound convoys KS512 and KS513 and northbound convoys KN111 and KN112; details of attack on *Tamesis* from Fifth Naval District report of attack, July 4, 1942, NARA RG 38; *British Freedom* attack from "Summary of Statements by Survivors of MV *British Freedom*," OP-16-B-5, July 10, 1942, NARA RG 38; minor damage to U-701 from U-701 Interrogation Report; attack on *William Rockefeller* from Degen, *Glory and Tragedy*, and

"Summary of Statements by Survivors of SS *William Rockefeller*, Standard Oil Company of New Jersey, Enemy Attack on Merchant Ships," Office of Naval Intelligence, OP-16-B-5, July 10, 1942, NARA RG 38; Stewart description of attack from "Affidavit of William R. Stewart, Master SS *William Rockefeller*, Torpedoed and Sunk, June 28, 1942"; sinking of tanker from Degen, *Glory and Tragedy*.

5. Schwendel comment on poor air quality from Schwendel 2011 interview; Degen decision to ventilate the boat from Degen, *Glory and Tragedy*; U-701 message of July 6, 1942, from BdU reconstruction of U-701 patrol compiled from KTB war diary and message traffic.

6. A-29 engine startup procedures from A-29 Contractor's Handbook; MCAS Cherry Point described in Cherry Point History.

7. Degen decision to ventilate U-701 from Degen, *Glory and Tragedy*; Junker reprimanded from U-701 Interrogation Report.

8. Sighting of U-boat from Kane Oral Interview.

9. Attack on U-701 from Kane Oral Interview; two depth charges straddle U-boat from Kane's "Report on U-boat Attack to I Bomber Command," July 7, 1942.

CHAPTER 12: THE ORDEAL

1. Accounts of the sinking of U-701 by three former crewmen were originally in personal letters to Horst Degen (Herbert Grotheer, November 23, 1965; Gerhard Schwendel, January 16, 1966; and Werner Seldte, August 22, 1972) and were provided to the author by Degen; Vaupel encounter with Junker in the control room recounted in a letter to Degen on July 22, 1951; Degen's account of the sinking from *Glory and Tragedy* and Annex B to the U-701 Interrogation Report.

2. Kane and aircrew attempt to help U-701 survivors from Kane Oral Interview; A-29 life raft installation from A-29 Pilot's Handbook; Kane comment on "beaten" U-701 crew from Dennis Rogers, "A Duel at Sea Destined to Allow Only One Victor," *Raleigh News & Observer*, September 1, 1980.

3. Events of Degen's group for late July 7 from Degen, *Glory and Tragedy* and Annex B to the U-701 Interrogation Report.

4. Kane attempts to obtain rescuers for U-boat survivors from Kane Oral Interview and "Log of Events, Lt. Kane's Attack on U-boat," annex to "Report on U-boat Attack to I Bomber Command."

5. Events of July 8–9 for U-701 survivors from Degen, *Glory and Tragedy*, Annex B to the U-701 Interrogation Report, and Grotheer's 1965 letter to Degen.

6. Kane fury over navy officials' doubt of sinking and meeting with Degen in Norfolk from Kane Oral Interview.

EPILOGUE

1. Naval Intelligence suspicions of a third U-boat ferrying saboteurs from undated ONI Memorandum reviewing the German sabotage mission, from

NARA RG 38UD; Degen conversation with Bernard in ONI transcript of intercepted conversation, August 10, 1942, also in NARA RG 38UD.

2. U-701 survivors transferred to Massachusetts from U-701 Interrogation Report; Dasch and Berger betrayal of Operation Pastorius from Dobbs, *Saboteurs*, 123, 189–191; seven weeks after landing ashore, six of the eight men were executed after a military commission found them guilty of violating the law of war, but Dasch and Berger received lengthy prison sentences and were deported in 1948; ONI interrogation of Degen and his concealment of U-701 mining mission from U-701 Interrogation Report, 9–13.

3. U-701 War Diary reconstruction by BdU; attacks on U-402 and U-576 and loss of U-576 from Blair, *Hitler's U-boat War*, 1:626–627; background of U-402 and U-576 from Uboat.net, http://www.uboat.net/boats/listing.html, and Busch and Röll, *German U-boat Commanders*, 71, 97; Convoys KN117 and KS520 ships and tonnage from ConvoyWeb.org; roster of escorts for two convoys from same; BdU calls off coastal campaign from BdU KTB for July 19, 1942; U-boat deployments and Allied shipping losses in the western Atlantic from US littoral waters to 060:00 degrees west longitude from January through July 1942 compiled from Uboat.net, "Ship Losses by Month," http://www.uboat.net/allies/merchants/losses_year.html, and "U-boat Losses During 1942," at Uboat.net, http://www.uboat.net/fates/losses/1942.htm.

4. Squadron redeployment to West Coast from 396th History; Kane meeting with his future wife from Kane Oral Interview; additional details from 2012 interview with Marguerite Kane Jameson.

5. Camp Blanding and Camp Papago Park background and American POW camp system details from Ronald H. Bailey, *Prisoners of War* (New York: Time-Life Books, 1981); additional material from the *Papago Scout*, November 1994, newsletter of the organization by the same name; Degan praised as "trustworthy" POW in letter from Captain Wayne E. Kartchner to Elsa Marston, November 8, 1945.

6. Admiral Dönitz did not call off mine-laying operations or infiltrating Abwehr agents as a result of the June 1942 missions. On September 10, 1942, U-69 laid twelve TMB mines near the mouth of the Chesapeake Bay, and U-455 laid a minefield at the entrance to Charleston, South Carolina, without success. In the summer of 1943, three U-boats attempted to lay minefields. U-230 dropped twelve TMB mines off the Chesapeake Bay on July 5, while U-566 planted eight larger TMC mines there on July 26. U-107 dropped twelve TMB mines off Charleston on August 28. None of these attempts caused any damage or sinkings (see Blair, *Hitler's U-boat War*, 1:687, 2:387); during 1943 and 1944, U-boats also landed Abwehr agents in Ireland, Canada, Mauritania, and Maine, but all of the missions failed. The Type IXC/40 U-1230 landed two Abwehr agents in the Gulf of Maine on November 29, 1944, but as in the 1942 mission, one of them turned himself in to the FBI and led agents to the second man (see Blair, *Hitler's U-boat War*, 2:646); daily average number of U-boats at

sea from Harald Busch, *U-boats at War* (New York: Ballantine Books, 1953), 176; British end Enigma blackout from Kahn, *Seizing the Enigma*, 226–227; Battle of Atlantic shift to northern convoy routes and soaring Allied losses from Blair, *Hitler's U-boat War*, 2:820; fate of ninety-five U-boats in the North American campaign compiled from Wynn, *U-boat Operations*, vols. 1 and 2; casualties in 396th Medium Bombardment Squadron from 396th History.

7. Kane family postwar life from Marguerite Kane Jameson interview.

8. Horst Degen postwar life recounted by his son, Günther, in several letters to the author during 2011 and 2012.

9. Degen reaction to USS *Scorpion* disappearance from Eberhard J. Fuchs, "The Last Seven from U-701," *Neue Revue* (Hamburg, Germany), June 30, 1968 (translated from the German); capsized hull of a sunken freighter from Richard C. Bayer, "Divers Checking Unidentified Hull, Navy Doesn't Think It Is Scorpion," *Ledger-Star* (Norfolk, Virginia), May 31, 1968.

10. Kane search for Degen recounted to the author in an April 1982 interview and mentioned in letters Kane exchanged with Degen; Degen-Kane relationship revealed in a series of several dozen letters exchanged by the two during November 1970 and July 1980 and provided to the author by Günther Degen.

11. Kane involvement with USS *Monitor* discovery team and unsuccessful 1980 search from Kane-Degen letters.

12. Kane and Degen reunion recounted by Günther Degen, 2012; Degen wore Bellamy lifejacket recounted by his sister, Kay Bellamy Smires in a 2012 telephone interview.

13. Discovery of U-701 and 1992 wreath-laying ceremony recounted in Henry C. Keatts and George C. Farr, *Diving into History*, vol. 3: *U-boats* (Houston, TX: Pisces Books, 1994, 141–146.

BIBLIOGRAPHY

BOOKS

Abbazia, Patrick. Mr. *Roosevelt's Navy: The Private War of the U.S. Atlantic Fleet, 1939–1942*. Annapolis, MD: Naval Institute Press, 1975.

Bailey, Ronald H. *The Air War in Europe*. New York: Time-Life Books, 1981.

———. *Prisoners of War*. New York: Time-Life Books, 1981.

Barr, Niell. *Pendulum of War: The Three Battles of El Alamein*. New York: Overlook Press, 2006.

Beesly, Patrick. *Very Special Intelligence: The Story of the Admiralty's Operational Intelligence Centre, 1939–1945*. London: Hamish Hamilton Ltd., 1977.

Behrens, C. B. A. *Merchant Shipping and the Demands of War*. London: H. M. Stationery Office, 1955.

Bergström, Christer. *Barbarossa: The Air Battle, July–December 1941*. Hinckley, UK: Classic Publications, 2007.

Beyer, Kenneth M. *Q-ships Versus U-boats: America's Secret Project*. Annapolis, MD: Naval Institute Press, 1999.

Blair, Clay. *Hitler's U-boat War*. Vol. 1: *The Hunters: 1939–1942*. New York: Random House, 1996.

———. *Hitler's U-boat War*. Vol. 2: *The Hunted: 1942–1945*. New York: Random House, 1998.

Bowers, Peter M. *Boeing Aircraft Since 1916*. London: Putnam & Company Ltd., 1989.

———. *Curtiss Aircraft, 1907–1947*. London: Putnam & Company Ltd., 1979.

Brauer, Luc. *Saint-Nazaire During World War II*. Batz-sur-Mer, France: Musée de la Poche de Saint-Nazaire, 2004.

Buell, Thomas B. *Master of Sea Power: A Biography of Fleet Admiral Ernest J. King*. Boston: Little, Brown and Company, 1980.

Busch, Harald. *U-boats at War*. New York: Ballantine Books, 1953.

Busch, Rainer, and Hans-Joachim Röll. *German U-boat Commanders of World War II*. Annapolis, MD: Naval Institute Press, 1999.

Campbell, John. *Naval Weapons of World War II*. Annapolis, MD: Naval Institute Press, 1985.

Churchill, Winston S. *Memoirs of the Second World War* (abridgement of the six volumes of *The Second World War*). New York: Houghton Mifflin Company, 1959.

Clark, William Bell. *When the U-boats Came to America*. Boston: Little Brown & Company, 1929.

Conn, Stetson, Rose C. Engelman, and Byron Fairchild. *United States Army in World War II: The Western Hemisphere—Guarding the United States and Its Outposts*. Washington, DC: Office of the Chief of Military History, Department of the Army, 1964.

Conn, Stetson, and Byron Fairchild. *United States Army in World War II: The Western Hemisphere—the Framework of Hemisphere Defense*. Washington, DC: Office of the Chief of Military History, Department of the Army, 1958.

Coyle, Brendan. *War on Our Doorstep: The Unknown Campaign on North America's West Coast*. Surrey, British Columbia: Heritage House, 2002.

Craven, Wesley F., and James L. Cate, eds. *The Army Air Forces in World War II*. Chicago: University of Chicago Press, 1955. http://www.ibiblio.org/hyperwar/AAF/VI/AAF-VI-4.html.

Cremer, Peter. *U-boat Commander*. Annapolis, MD: Naval Institute Press, 1984.

Cressman, Robert J. *The Official Chronology of the U.S. Navy in World War II*. Annapolis, MD: Naval Institute Press, 1999.

Dobbs, Michael. *Saboteurs: The Nazi Raid on America*. New York: Vintage Books, 2005.

Dönitz, Karl, Grand Adm. *Memoirs: Ten Years and Twenty Days*. New York: Da Capo Press, 1997.

Eden, Paul, ed. *The Encyclopedia of Aircraft of WWII*. London: Aerospace Publishing, 2004.

"Fuehrer Conferences on Naval Affairs—1939–1945." In *Brassey's Naval Annual*, edited by H. G. Thursfield, Rear Adm. RN. I–II (1941), III (1942). New York: Macmillan Company, 1948.

Gannon, Michael. *Black May*. New York: Dell Publishing, 1998.

———. *Operation Drumbeat*. New York: Harper & Row, 1990.

Greer, Thomas H. "Individual Training of Flying Personnel." In *The Army Air Forces in World War II*. Vol. 6: *Men and Planes*, edited by Wesley F. Craven and James L. Cate. Chicago: University of Chicago Press, 1955. http://www.ibiblio.org/hyperwar/AAF/VI/AAF-VI-17.html.

Gretton, Peter, Vice Adm. RN (Ret). *Convoy Escort Commander*. London: Cassell & Company Ltd., 1964.

Hadley, Michael L. *U-boats Against Canada: German Submarines in Canadian Waters*. Montreal, Quebec: McGill Queen's University Press, 1990.

Hardegen, Reinhard. *Battle Stations! (Auf Gefechtsstationen!)*. Leipzig: Boreas-Verlag, 1943.

Hessler, Günter. *The U-boat War in the Atlantic: 1939–1945*. London: H. M. Stationery Office, 1989.

Hickham, Homer. *Torpedo Junction: U-boat War off America's East Coast, 1942*. Annapolis, MD: Naval Institute Press, 1989.

Kahn, David. *The Codebreakers*. New York: Scribner, 1996.

———. *Seizing the Enigma*. New York: Random House, 1991.

Keatts, Henry C., and George C. Farr. *Diving into History*. Vol. 3: *U-boats*. Houston, TX: Pisces Books, 1994.

King, Ernest J., Fleet Adm. *U.S. Navy at War, 1941–1945: Official Reports to the Secretary of the Navy*. Washington, DC: US Navy Department, 1946.

King, Ernest J., and Walter Muir Whitehill. *Fleet Admiral King: A Naval Record*. New York: W. W. Norton & Company, 1952.

Kirby, Maurice W. *Operational Research in War and Peace: The British Experience from the 1930s to 1970*. London: Imperial College Press, 2003.

Linder, Bruce. *Tidewater's Navy: An Illustrated History*. Annapolis, MD: Naval Institute Press, 1991.

Meacham, Jon. *Franklin and Winston: An Intimate Portrait of an Epic Friendship*. New York: Random House Trade Paperbacks, 2004.

Moffat, Alexander W. *A Navy Maverick Comes of Age: 1939–1945*. Middletown, CT: Wesleyan University Press, 1977.

Morison, Samuel Eliot. *The Two-Ocean War: A Short History of the United States Navy in the Second World War*. Boston: Little, Brown and Company, 1963.

Perrett, Geoffrey. *Eisenhower*. New York: Random House, 1999.

———. *There's a War to Be Won: The U.S. Army in World War II*. New York: Random House, 1991.

———. *Winged Victory: The Army Air Forces in World War II*. New York: Random House, 1993.

Polmar, Norman, and Thomas B. Allen. *World War II: America at War*. New York: Random House, 1991.

Prang, Gordon, with Donald M. Goldstein and Katherine V. Dillon. *Miracle at Midway*. New York: McGraw-Hill Book Company, 1982.

Roskill, Stephen W., Capt. RN (Ret.). *The War at Sea*. Vols. 1–3. East Uckfield, Sussex, UK: Naval and Military Press Ltd., 1956–1960.

Showell, Jak Mallmann. *Companion to the German Navy, 1939–1945*. Port Stroud, UK: History Press, 1999.

———. *German Naval Codebreakers*. Surrey, UK: Ian Allan Publishing Ltd., 2003.

———. *Hitler's Navy: A Reference Guide to the Kriegsmarine, 1935–1945*. London: Seaworth Publishing, 2009.

———. *Hitler's U-boat Bunkers*. Port Stroud, UK: History Press, 2002.

Spector, Ronald H. *Eagle Against the Sun: The American War with Japan*. New York: Vintage Books, 1985.

Stewart, Richard W., ed. "World War II: The Defensive Phase." In *American Military History*. Vol. 2: *The United States Army in a Global Era, 1917–2003*, gen. ed. Maurice Matloff, 77–100. Washington, DC: Center for Military History, 2005.

Sweeney, Michael S. *Secrets of Victory: The Office of Censorship and the American Press in World War II*. Chapel Hill: University of North Carolina Press, 2001.

Tarrant, V. E. *The U-boat Offensive: 1914–1945.* Annapolis, MD: Naval Institute Press, 1989.

Topp, Erich, and Eric Rust. *The Odyssey of a U-boat Commander: Recollections of Erich Topp.* English ed. Westport, CT: Praeger Publishers, 1992.

Warnock, A. Timothy. *The Battle Against the U-boat in the American Theater.* Montgomery, AL: Center for Air Force History, Maxwell Air Force Base, 1991.

Winkler, Heinrich, with Alexander Sager. *Germany: The Long Road West: 1933–1990.* New York: Oxford University Press, 2007.

Worth, Richard. *Fleets of World War II.* New York: Da Capo Press, 2001.

Wynn, Kenneth. *U-boat Operations of the Second World War.* Vol. 1: *Career Histories, U-1–U-510.* Annapolis, MD: Naval Institute Press, 1997.

———. *U-boat Operations of the Second World War.* Vol. 2: *Career Histories, U-511–UIT-25.* Annapolis, MD: Naval Institute Press, 1998.

U-BOAT WAR DIARIES

Kriegstagebücher (KTB): Daily war patrol diaries for selected U-boats, translated by U-boat Archive (www.uboatarchive.net) from the originals in storage at the German Bundesarchiv, Freiberg, Germany:

- U-123: KTB for Seventh War Patrol, December 23, 1941–February 9, 1942
- U-552: KTB for Second War Patrol, April 7–May 6, 1941
- U-701: KTB for First War Patrol, December 27, 1941–February 9, 1942
- U-701: KTB for Second War Patrol, February 26–April 1, 1942
- U-701: KTB for Third War Patrol, April 1–July 7, 1942 (reconstructed at BdU Headquarters from BdU KTB and message traffic from U-701)

MANUALS FOR THE LOCKHEED A-29 HUDSON

"Contractor's Handbook of Service Instructions for the Model A-29 Airplane," US Army Air Corps Air Service Command, Wright Field, Dayton, Ohio, January 30, 1942.

"Pilot's Handbook of Flight Operating Instructions—A-29 and A-29A Airplanes," Headquarters USAAF Air Service Command, Patterson Field, Ohio, December 20, 1942.

"Preliminary Handbook of Operation and Flight Instructions for the Models A-28 and A-29 Attack Airplanes," US Army Air Corps Air Service Command, Wright Field, Dayton, Ohio, January 30, 1942.

GOVERNMENT, MILITARY, AND INTELLIGENCE DOCUMENTS AND REPORTS

Administrative History of the U.S. Atlantic Fleet in World War II. Norfolk, VA: Commander-in-Chief, US Atlantic Fleet, 1946.

"Affidavit of William R. Stewart, Master SS *William Rockefeller*, Torpedoed and Sunk, June 28, 1942," National Archives and Records Administration, College Park, Maryland, Records Group 38, 10th Fleet.

"Army Air Forces Statistical Digest (World War II)," US Air Force, June 1947.

"B-Dienst" (radio intelligence), Spot Item Report, OP-20-G (Office of Naval Intelligence), November 12, 1943, declassified from Secret.

"Battle of the Atlantic—Allied Communications Intelligence, December 1942–May 1945," SRH-009, National Security Agency, transcribed for online posting at the HyperWar Foundation, www.ibiblio.org/hyperwar/ETO /Ultra/SRH-009/index.html.

"Battle of the Atlantic—U-boat Operations, December 1942–May 1945," SRH-008, National Security Agency, transcribed for online posting at the HyperWar Foundation, www.ibiblio.org/hyperwar/ETO/Ultra/SRH -009/index.html.

"The Conference at Washington, 1941–42 [Arcadia Conference]," in US State Department, *Foreign Relations of the United States*, posted at the University of Wisconsin Digital Collections, at http://digicoll.library.wisc.edu/cgi-bin /FRUS/FRUS-idx?id=FRUS.FRUS194143.

"Deck Logs," *USS Emmons* (DD-457), National Archives and Records Administration, College Park, Maryland, Records Group 24, Box 3111, 1942.

"Deck Logs," *USS Hambleton* (DD-455), National Archives and Records Administration, College Park, Maryland, Records Group 24, Box 4082, 1942.

"Deck Logs, *USS Trippe* (DD-403), National Archives and Records Administration, College Park, Maryland, Records Group 24, Box 9159, 1942.

"Esso Augusta—Damaged as a Result of War Perils," June 16, 1942, National Archives and Records Administration, College Park, Maryland, Records Group 38, 10th Fleet files.

"Former German Submarine Type IXC: Torpedo Handling, Loading and Storage," Report 2G-9C, Portsmouth Naval Shipyard, Portsmouth, New Hampshire, February 1946, declassified from Confidential.

"Functions of the 'Secret Room' (F-211) of COMINCH Combat Intelligence," Atlantic Section, Anti-Submarine Warfare, WWII, SRMN-038, undated.

"German Radio Intercepts and Cryptanalysts," Commander, Naval Forces Germany, September 18, 1950, declassified from Top Secret.

"German U-boat Casualties in World War II," in *United States Submarine Losses in World War II*. Washington, DC: Naval History Division, Office of the Chief of Naval Operations, 1963.

"Germany Mines: A History," updated January 2012, NavWeaps, www navweaps.com/Weapons/WAMGER_Mines.htm.

"History of the 396th Bombardment Squadron (M), Headquarters, 41st Bombardment Group (M)," Hammer Field, Fresno, California, 1942.

"History of U.S. Marine Corps Air Station Cherry Point, North Carolina—1941–1945," compiled by Florence K. Jacobs, 1st Lt. USMCWR, Air Station Historical Officer, undated.

"Monthly Anti-Submarine Warfare Reports," Vol. 6 (1945), British Admiralty, ADM 199/2062.

"Operational Intelligence Centre Special Intelligence Summary," January 12, 1942, PRO ADM 223/15, declassified from Most Secret, Public Records Office, Kew, United Kingdom.

"Record of Proceedings of a Court of Inquiry to Inquire into Circumstances Attending the Attack on *YP-389*, June 19, 1942," National Archives and Records Administration, College Park, Maryland, Records Group 125/P2.

"Report of Interrogation of Survivors of U-701 Sunk by U.S. Army Attack Bomber No. 9-29-322, Unit 396 B.S. [Bombardment Squadron] on July 7, 1942," published in "Post-mortems on Enemy Submarines," Office of Naval Intelligence, ONI 250-G, 1942, National Archives and Records Administration, College Park, Maryland, Records Group 38.

"Report on U-boat Attack to I Bomber Command," July 7, 1942, courtesy of UboatArchive.net.

"Statistical Review: World War II," Army Services Forces, published by the US War Department, Washington, DC, undated, posted at HyperWar.com, www.ibiblio.org/hyperwar/USA/StatReview-ASF.pdf.

"Summary of Statements by Survivors of MV *British Freedom*," OP-16-B-5, July 10, 1942, National Archives and Records Administration, College Park, Maryland, Records Group 38.

"Summary of Statements by Survivors of SS *William Rockefeller*, Standard Oil Company of New Jersey, Enemy Attack on Merchant Ships," Office of Naval Intelligence, OP-16-B-5, July 10, 1942, National Archives and Records Administration, College Park, Maryland, Records Group 38.

"Transcripts of Recorded Conversations Between German Prisoners," Office of Naval Intelligence, National Archives and Records Administration, College Park, Maryland, Records Group 38, Entry UD, various dates.

"U-boat Situation," Special Reports on German Navy and U-boat Force, Operational Intelligence Centre, British Admiralty, PRO ADM 223/16, London, United Kingdom.

"U-boat Situation Reports," December 15, 1941–July 27, 1942, Operational Intelligence Centre, British Admiralty, PRO ADM 223/15, London, United Kingdom.

"Unit Historical Data Sheet, 396th Bombardment Squadron (M) of 41st Bombardment Group," 1943, courtesy of the US Air Force Historical Research Agency, Maxwell Air Force Base, Alabama.

US Coast Guard, "WWII Reports Concerning Merchant Vessels Sinking, 1938–2002," National Archives and Records Administration, College Park, Maryland, Records Group 26, Box 22.

"War Diaries," Commander, Eastern Sea Frontier, December 1941–June 1942, declassified from Secret, posted online at U-boat Archive, http://www.uboatarchive.net/ESF.htm.

"War Record of the Fifth Naval District," 1942, Fifth Naval District, Norfolk, Virginia, National Archives and Records Administration, College Park, Maryland, Records Group 181.

ARTICLES AND MANUSCRIPTS

"180 Germans to Sail on Portuguese Liner," *New York Times*, June 13, 1942.

"10,000-Ton Ship Sunk by U-boat off Canada," *New York Times*, January 14, 1942.

Andrews, Lewis M., Jr., Lt. (USN). "Wild, Cold Ruthless—That's the Atlantic." *New York Times*, March 7, 1943.

Associated Press. "Knox Assails Acts That Pass 'Piracy,'" *New York Times*, November 2, 1941.

———. "Navy in Grim Hunt: The Malay, Crippled by Shells, Makes Port." *New York Times*, January 20, 1942.

———. "Sinkings Indicated: 'Some Recent Visitors Will Never Enjoy Return Trip,' Says Spokesman." *New York Times*, January 24, 1942.

Barlow, Jeffrey G. "The Navy's Atlantic War Learning Curve." *Naval History* (Annapolis, Maryland), June 2008.

"Battle of Atlantic Pushes Virginia's Shores—Two U.S. Merchant Ships Torpedoed Before Eyes of Thousands Who Line Resort to See Grim War Drama." *Virginian-Pilot*, June 17, 1942.

Bayer, Richard C. "Divers Checking Unidentified Hull, Navy Doesn't Think It Is Scorpion." *Ledger-Star* (Norfolk, Virginia), May 31, 1968.

Beesly, Patrick. "Convoy PQ17: A Study of Intelligence and Decision-Making." *Intelligence and National Security*, April 1990.

Belke, T. J., Lt. j.g. "Roll of Drums." *U.S. Naval Institute Proceedings* (Annapolis, Maryland), April 1983.

Davies, Lawrence E. "Evacuation Area Set for Japanese in Pacific States." *New York Times*, March 3, 1942.

———. "Hails Los Angeles for Air Defense." *New York Times*, February 27, 1942.

———. "West Coast Order Shifts Japanese." *New York Times*, March 2, 1942.

Decker, Hans Joachim. "404 Days! The War Patrol Life of U-505." *U.S. Naval Institute Proceedings* (Annapolis, Maryland), March 1960.

"Drottningholm at Lisbon: Exchange Liner Docks with Axis Nationals from Americas." *New York Times*, June 12, 1942.

Editorial. "The Los Angeles Mystery." *New York Times*, February 27, 1942.

———. "The Sea War." *New York Times*, April 7, 1943.

Erskine, Ralph. "The First Naval Enigma Decrypts of World War II." *Cryptologia* 21, no. 1 (January 1997).

Erskine, Ralph, and Frode Weierud. "Naval Enigma: M4 and Its Rotors." *Cryptologia* 11, no. 4 (October 1987).

Fleming, Thomas. "The Big Leak." *American Heritage* 38, no. 8 (December 1987).

Friedland, Klaus. "Raiding Merchant Shipping: U-boats on the North American Coast, 1942." *American Neptune* (Salem, MA), spring 1991.

Fuchs, Eberhard J. "The Last Seven from U-701." *Neue Revue* (Hamburg, Germany), June 30, 1968 (translated from the German).

"Gen. DeWitt Praises Readiness of Anti-Aircraft Batteries 'to Meet Possible Enemy.'" *New York Times*, February 27, 1942.

Heinrichs, Waldo. "President Franklin D. Roosevelt's Intervention in the Battle of the Atlantic, 1941." *Diplomatic History*, fall 1986.

Hulen, Bertram. "Our Stand Clear, Officials Insist." *New York Times*, November 2, 1941.

Knapp, Richard. "Liberty Ships & Airships: North Carolina and the Battle of the Atlantic." *Recall* 10 (fall 2004).

Kurzak, Karl Heinz. "German U-boat Construction." *Naval Institute Proceedings* (Annapolis, Maryland), April 1955.

"Los Angeles Guns Bark at Air 'Enemy,'" *New York Times*, February 26, 1942.

Milner, Marc. "The Battle That Had to Be Won." *Naval History* (Annapolis, Maryland), June 2008.

"Navy Has No Word—Check Fails to Confirm Report of New Victim of U-boat off Coast." *New York Times*, January 16, 1942.

"New U-boat Victim Confirmed by Navy." *New York Times*, January 17, 1942.

O'Connor, Jerome M. "FDR's Undeclared War." *Naval History* (Annapolis, Maryland), February 2004.

Offley, Ed. "Wartime Foes Reunite as Friends" (U-701). *Ledger-Star* (Norfolk, Virginia), July 7, 1982.

———. "Chesapeake Bay Mined, War Came Close to Home" (U-701). *Ledger-Star* (Norfolk, Virginia), July 8, 1982.

———. "Confrontation in the Atlantic: The Death of U-701." *Ledger-Star* (Norfolk, Virginia), July 9, 1982.

Polmar, Norman. "Ships That Were Lighter Than Air." *Naval History* (Annapolis, Maryland), June 2011.

Roach, John. "Shoring Up N. Carolina Islands: A Losing Battle?" *National Geographic News*, November 10, 2003.

Rogers, Dennis. "A Duel at Sea Destined to Allow Only One Victor." *Raleigh News & Observer*, September 1, 1980.

Rohwer, Jürgen. "Allied and Axis Radio-Intelligence in the Battle of the Atlantic—a Comparative Analysis." In *The Intelligence Revolution—a Historical Perspective*. Proceedings of the Thirteenth Military History Symposium, US Air Force Academy, Colorado Springs, Colorado, October 12–14, 1988.

———. "The Operational Use of Ultra in the Battle of the Atlantic." In *Intelligence and International Relations*, edited by Christopher Andrew and Jeremy Noales, 275–292. Exeter, UK: University of Exeter Press, 1987.

———. "The U-boat War Against the Allied Supply Lines." In *The Decisive Battles of World War II: The German View*, edited by Hans Adolf Jacobsen and J. Rohwer. New York: G. P. Putnam's Sons, 1965.

"Ship Found Awash: Rescue Craft Rushed to Tanker When Plane Reports Plight." *New York Times*, January 15, 1942.

Shirer, William. *The Rise and Fall of the Third Reich*. New York: Simon & Schuster, 1959.

"'Sighted Sub; Sank Same,' Radios a Modern Perry in Naval Plane." *New York Times*, January 30, 1942.

"Stimson Disclaims Raid Story." *New York Times*, March 6, 1942.

Taylor, Blaine. "The Onetime U-boat Commander's Career Ladder Led All the Way to the Top—as Hitler's Own Successor." *World War II Magazine*, March 1988.

Tennant, Diane. "Torpedoed." *Virginian-Pilot*, special report, August 2–9, 2009.

"Text of President Roosevelt's Addresses in Boston and Hartford." *New York Times*, October 31, 1940.

Trussell, C. P. "Navy Called Slow in Submarine War." *New York Times*, April 21, 1943.

Walling, Michael G. "Dangerous Duty in the North Atlantic." *Naval History* (Annapolis, Maryland), June 2008.

"West Coast Raided, Stimson Concedes." *New York Times*, February 27, 1942.

UNPUBLISHED OR PRIVATE MANUSCRIPTS

Degen, Horst. *U-701: Glory and Tragedy*. Unpublished manuscript, November 1965.

Low, Francis S., Adm. USN (Ret.). "A Personal Narrative of Association with Fleet Admiral Ernest J. King, U.S. Navy." Unpublished essay, 1961.

Poyer, David C. "Death of a U-Boat." Manuscript provided by the author, April 1982.

ORAL HISTORY INTERVIEWS

Kane, Harry J. "Oral History Interview, Harry J. Kane." East Carolina University Manuscript Collection, Oral History Interview No. 71, September 29, 1978.

McRea, John L. "Reminiscences of Vice Admiral John L. McRea USN (Ret.)." Oral History Collection, US Naval Institute, Annapolis, Maryland, 1990.

ONLINE SOURCES

American Merchant Marine at War: www.usmm.org

HyperWar: Hypertext History of World War II: www.ibiblio.org/hyperwar

Individual Allied convoy reports, posted at ConvoyWeb:
www.convoyweb.org.uk

Naval-History.net: www.naval-history.net

NavSource.org: www.navsource.org
U-boat Archive: www.uboatarchive.net
Uboat.net: www.uboat.net
Ubootwaffe.net: www.ubootwaffe.net
Warsailors.com: www.warsailors.com
Wreck Site: www.wrecksite.eu

INDEX